The Bedside 'Guardian' 27

THE BEDSIDE 'GUARDIAN'

27

A selection from
The 'Guardian' 1977-78

Edited by
W. L. Webb

With an Introduction by
Dennis Potter

Cartoons by
Gibbard and Bryan McAllister

COLLINS
St James's Place, London
1978

William Collins Sons & Co Ltd
London · Glasgow · Sydney · Auckland
Toronto · Johannesburg

First published 1978
© Guardian Newspapers Ltd, 1978

ISBN 0 00 216093 5

Set in Monotype Imprint
Made and Printed in Great Britain by
William Collins Sons & Co Ltd Glasgow

Introduction

I have no idea what the *Guardian* offices in London look like, and the ominously pale man from the financial pages of the paper who has a week-end cottage near to my home is unforthcoming about his working conditions. In moments of not entirely malicious speculation, however, I am diverted by the thought of a haphazard ramble of corridors with punning graffiti on the walls which, in the chance wit of longer perspective, settles down into something reminiscent of a suitably enlarged tin of salmon – middle-cut, of course, but totally free of the unreasonable botulism which comes from somewhere outside in the poisonous filth of the world. Such a building would have the architectural merit of reflecting the tone and style of the product it regularly misprints, for the reader who opens the pages of the *Guardian* cannot altogether avoid the taste of soft pink politics tempered by occasional tooth-like bones which much too often turn out to be as easy to chew and swallow as the surrounding flesh.

Culinary metaphors are usually dyspeptic rather than flattering, but this one does at least hint at an edibility, or even a savour, that certainly eludes most of the junk meals served up in the grubby fast-food eateries of Fleet Street. Daily journalism is designed for instant consumption, which frequently means that at the tabloid counters the rotting meat of prejudice, timidity and reaction is heavily seasoned with the monosodium glutamate of sensation, shock, scandal and trivia. *The Times*, by contrast, is too much like lumpy cold porridge with neither sugar nor salt, and the *Daily Telegraph* leaves one uncomfortably aware of the taste of congealed blood on one's thin and stretching lips. In such circumstances, the pale pink tang of the *Guardian* is not to be too easily scorned.

Nations often confuse their history with their orthodoxy, but Great Britain must be almost alone in seeing its future through a murk of headlines. Any genuinely representative

5

collection of articles, cartoons and editorials from any other British newspaper than the *Guardian* would surely display the sour rancour and pessimism and bloody-minded ill-will which, in the accompanying cant jargon, make us 'perceive our situation' in terms of doom and gloom and doubt and despair. The wry tones in which James Cameron ends his contemplation of the Lebanon are seldom imported to describe our own interior landscapes: '. . . below the Israeli-Lebanon border is a plain, known as Armageddon. Fortunately it is a very long word for a headline.'

Perhaps the most remarkable thing about this particular collection is the essential good-humour which it conveys. This is not at all the same as complacency, of course, although there are sufficient signs in these pages of the smugness that is probably inseparable from the paper's distinctive brand of liberalism. One of the regular feature writers in the paper, and the collection, also spoils her good eye with tacky blobs of condescension about other people's means of enjoying themselves. The *Bedside Guardian* could hardly be honest if it did not include at least some lengthy examples of the newspaper's most obvious vice. Similarly, it is a relief to find at least one specimen of excruciating and tasteless punning in the pieces which follow.

The good-humour and the wit do not shut out the feelings of anxiety or even crisis which may make one mildly surprised to see Union Jacks stretching and cracking in a Whitehall breeze instead of hanging in limp exhaustion against their splintered flagpoles. A wider apprehension of Western stagnation or malaise also gets through – sometimes in a manner where the reader can almost see the simper freeze into an uneasy grimace. And yet, mercifully, there remains the sense that even dread itself can be spaced out into ordered prose in which consecutive subordinate clauses appear, for a while, to imitate the sequence of rational thought strong enough and clear enough to hold back the ignorant armies of the night. If that is indeed an illusion, then it still needs to be the last illusion we have. It is possible to live for a very long time on tinned pink salmon.

6

The *Guardian*, in short, has a style and a composure that is more valuable now than it has ever been. It is undoubtedly irritating, often smug, sometimes condescending, and too often filtered through a mesh of gleefully childish jokes and appalling puns. The *Bedside Guardian*, in culling what is best in the paper, reminds us less of these palpable defects than of the good writing which makes the daily easily the most stimulating and enjoyable newspaper in Britain. And it will be a bad moment when we can get through the *Guardian* without several snorts of derision to balance the pleasure gained by so many of the pieces collected together in these pages.

I cannot imagine any other daily newspaper that could begin a review of the previous night's television with, 'Seeing American footballers makes one realize that Othello was not pulling Desdemona's leg', or a political column that generates so much pleasurable malice in inventing the necessary new verb 'to heseltine'. Whether it is Keating on a football manager or Clancy Sigal on a folk singer, or slightly pained features on dogs, psychobabble, dancing or the Special Branch, the air of would-be combative enjoyment and actual, snide relish invariably lifts the piece well clear of the grey slabs of newsprint within which it might be forever entombed.

'All we need is plain English and good jokes.' The sentence comes at the end of one of the pieces in this book. The position is perilous, but characteristic. You have to be unbearably sure that you have written a good article to end in such a manner, and even then the contortion to be witnessed as the writer pats himself on the back with both feet helps to explain why so many of us find the *Guardian* indispensable. The 27th selection from the paper, carrying what might almost be called the good news from the news-stand to the bedside and thence to the shelves is a proper celebration of this fact. You do not really need a tin-opener to savour what follows, but a little insomnia would be entirely appropriate.

Dennis Potter

Mr Justan Larstinpeece

Whenever President Sadat approached a poignant phrase in his speech to the Knesset, ITV flashed on the screen the message: 'The Big Match will be at 3.15'. It was not deliberately rude, as it would have been in Damascus. It was intended to reassure those who have not been following events in the Middle East and were aggrieved, to put it no more strongly, that their Sunday routine of booze-up, Yorkshire pudding and maiming on the Kop had been disturbed for what seemed like the Open University in Arabic. This was bound to be one of ITV's restless occasions. For almost an hour they could not show a commercial, and when the hour was up they went for a jingle like a chain-smoker leaving a funeral.

Both channels had interpretation problems, so that apart from just-and-lasting-peace, which occurred not only *passim* but *frequenter*, the two accounts of what the President said had little in common beyond the general impression that he was not declaring war (which would not have been appropriate since a state of war exists already). There is every sympathy for the interpreter, having to match Mr Sadat's speed and store up one sentence for retrieval while still translating the sentence before, but on one channel there were intervals when nothing was being translated at all. Perhaps the President was going over old ground.

It is not common for parliaments to have simultaneous translation systems. Israel does, and Belgium, and Canada, but surprisingly the Welsh MPs have not insisted on headphones at Westminster to help them to follow the proceedings. (Welsh motorway drivers, after all, are not expected to understand 'Heavy lorries take left-hand lane for dock gate' unless it is made to read like an Eisteddfod entry for the bardic crown.) On the whole it is better to manage without, lest the translation fall to the inexpert. Even between French and English, demanding means only requesting and encore does not mean again. It may

9

upset Monsieur Edouard Eat to be called the ancien premier ministre but at his age a literal translation might upset him even more.

22 November, 1977   **Leader**

Mood indigo

As the train was drawing out of one of the Hamptons, a striking black woman, cool and expensive, entered the carriage. She dusted the seat opposite me with a grey leather glove, unwrapped a soft, grey scarf and took off a houndstooth cape. Opening a leather briefcase, she took out *Newsweek*, *The Times*, *Vogue* and a cluster of other fat magazines.

I mentioned how much nicer the Hamptons are in winter without the summer people. She looked surprised, considered me for a moment and responded. During the two-hour journey into New York, we discussed books (she read widely) and the theatre (she went often). She was going to Tiffany's to leave a watch for repair and then out to dinner alone at a restaurant I recalled was expensive. Judging by appearances, as is the New York way, I assumed that Norel Baillie was well off, college-educated, with a good job.

We met on the train again. Then I ran into her unexpectedly. We went round to see John Smithson, a friend of ours – and found Norel his live-in housekeeper (she prefers 'major domo'). For 60 dollars a week, she cleans, cooks, organizes his papers and his life. The house is exquisite: plump chintz sofas, plants, flowers, beautifully garnished soufflés for lunch. John Smithson's sense of style she has made her own.

One day last week she came into the city and we talked. With her permission, I should like you to know about her life:

'I was born Eleonor Baily on October 14, 1942, in Portsmouth, Virginia. My father was 18, my mother was 17. I'm an illegitimate child, need I say. From the hospital I went to my father's mother. My mother didn't show any partiality for me. She didn't keep any of her children – she had nine. My father was killed a year later.

'My grandmother was a bootlegger; for almost thirty years she sold whisky by the shot in her apartment over my grandfather's barber shop. She was rich and we lived well. When I was five, my mother gave me to some of her friends. They asked for one of her children and she gave me because I was the darkest.

'This lady had to be 68, because her husband was 72. They had an outhouse out back, next to the pigs' pen. I don't know till today why they wanted me. From the day I arrived until I ran away in 1954, I had a beating every day, including Christmas. No child could have been that bad.

'The South was still segregated, and there was a development of white people near us. Three times a week on garbage collection days, I had to wheel a baby carriage up there to collect all the thrown-out food that didn't have glass, spit or coffee grounds on them. That's what we ate. I went to a two-roomed school; the first three grades in the room on the left, the others in the one on the right.

'When I ran away, my grandmother took out a juvenile warrant for me. I was had up before the judge and since my grandmother wouldn't have me back, I had to be sent to a training school. She gave me a $20 bill and said, "You'll be a better person when you come out."

'I'd been in the school for two weeks when my grandmother came to see me. She said someone had told her male friend, Captain Charlie, that I liked girls. I was 12 and so green that I hadn't had any kind of sexual encounter but I said, "I tell you I don't know, but by the time you come back I will." So then I had to find someone to teach me and I found I liked it.

'They let me out after three years and seven months. I pleaded with them not to release me to my grandmother but they did. I felt that all that hell and damnation I went through was unnecessary and I'd never forgive her as long as I live. I didn't go back to school: I took jobs as a waitress and went to New York for a while as a maid. But I couldn't stand that.

'When I was 17 and back in Virginia, I took up with Addie May. A year later, her mother had me arrested. Addie May was

15. I was found guilty on two charges "contributing to the delinquency of a minor" and "crime against nature" (that's homosexuality). I did my time in this prison farm and when I came out I was so confused, in such a mess, that I needed to get away.

'I couldn't go to Bermuda, could I? So I broke this window of a jewellery store and went down to the precinct and told them. When the judge sent me to the state penitentiary for two years, I said, "thank you."

'I'm not big or aggressive and when I went in I reckoned that I'd better hook up with someone strong. I hooked up with Ruth who was 36 and in for selling drugs. When we came out she went to New York and sent me $500 to join her. I lived with Ruth and then I got married to a drug pusher from Portsmouth for a few months and after that I was just going between Virginia and New York. No matter who I was with, I always took a job.

'I've done it all; I served in a shop, did bookkeeping, did computer programming (they said I had an IQ of 200), worked as a waitress. Few jobs check on your record and the right part of me says I should be self-supporting, earn my way, not live on my sexuality, my looks or my wits.

'In 1973 I went into a drug hospital in Kentucky for 11 months and when I moved back to New York I ran into Addie May again and she lived with me till last year. I used to go back to Virginia until I realized that most of the people I used to know are either dead or in jail and I thought Why did I keep running back there?

'I met my present employer through Addie May. She was cleaning people's apartments and I deemed she didn't have to work so I did them for her. When Smithson built this house in the country he asked me to come out and run it for him. I live in self-imposed isolation. I don't see anyone but the two women next door. I don't have any relationship, sexual that is, with anyone now and sometimes I think if I don't soon I never will. I'm old, really old. I don't feel so chancey now; I get up every morning and say "Keep cool, fool."

'I think that had I not been black my childhood couldn't possibly have been that bad. Had I been white (since I've always had people browbeating me about how high my IQ is), someone would have invested time and money in me and seen that I got an education. Being gay hasn't been a problem. If I walk into Tiffany's, my gayness doesn't hurt me if I have the money. They wouldn't say "Hey, here comes a gay person!" They might say "Here comes a black person. Let's hope she isn't a thief."

'Smithson always says that I have a millionaire's taste and a pauper's pocket. If I had money, I'd want clothes, jewellery and good food in that order. I'd also like to be able to buy any book or magazine that I wanted.

'Happy? No. Underline that, emphasize it, write it in capitals. I suppose I've had moments of happiness but there's never been any on the inside. When I start thinking my mind goes wild and I get a headache. I just have to cut it off, the pain is unbearable. Oh God, if I thought about my life for a moment I could find it really depressing.'

That is one person's experience of being black and a woman in America. Tomorrow, there's an International Woman's Day rally in New York. I've heard all the speeches; they make it sound simple. 'No, I'm not going,' said Norel Baillie. 'They haven't got anything for me.'

10 March, 1978   **Linda Blandford**

One was not amused

It was snowing outside the White Swan in Halifax. At exactly five to nine the four-car procession was drawn up outside and drivers and detectives were blowing their knuckles and stamping their feet. Mrs Thatcher emerged into an icy wind, which almost miraculously didn't ruffle a single golden hair. She was most unsuitably dressed in a thin navy coat and tiny elegant black shoes that disappeared into the snow.

The local evening paper had blazoned the news that when she called on the Mayor for coffee this morning there would be a large demonstration of Asians waiting outside the town hall. We could hear shouting already from up the street. Mrs Thatcher, surveying the scene, decided on the spur of the moment to walk to the town hall and not go by car. She walked right through the demonstrators, the TV cameras and microphones pointing at her. But the demonstration was very small, entirely white, and the shouters were holding Socialist Worker banners. There were so few of them that as she passed they were abashed and lost their nerve. It was only when she had turned up the steps and out of sight that someone dared shout, 'Fascist bitch!'

Coffee was served in a ceremonial room full of trophies and plaques of civic interest. The Mayor and Mayoress were there to greet her. They discussed the demo outside. Mrs Thatcher said, 'I didn't see any immigrants. I was looking for some to stop and have a word with, but there only seemed to be some Socialist Worker people with whom I have absolutely nothing in common.' Everyone laughed. She and her aides would be looking for the rest of the day for immigrants to have a word with.

Her entourage for the day was large, with public relations men, detectives, her Parliamentary Private Secretary and the Tory Party baron of Yorkshire, Sir Frank Marshall. The next visit on the itinerary was to John Crossley and Sons, the biggest carpet manufacturer in Europe. 'She loves factories,' said her PR man, and I believed him. Out there on the factory floor she wandered around the huge carpet weaving machines which clanked and banged as the shuttles whisked up and down, and she looked, for her, quite excited. She chatted to anyone she came across, calling out a jovial 'Morning!' One woman was quite overcome after talking to her, 'Oh she's lovely, isn't she lovely? Just lovely!' She said she'd vote for her, though she wouldn't dare tell her husband.

Mrs Thatcher found a woman mending a fault in an enormous carpet with a needle and wool. In a moment she had taken up the needle and was much photographed at sewing. A notice on the wall read 'A stitch in time saves nine customers;' or maybe voters.

One man stopped his machine to show her how it worked. Would he vote for her? I asked afterwards. 'No!' he said but then added, 'Her voice didn't sound so bad as when she makes speeches.' Another man standing by a panel of buttons chatted to her but when I asked what they'd talked about he said, 'Well, it wasn't politics. I'd like to have asked her a thing or two, but she didn't seem to expect it. She just asked how long I'd worked here, and what the machine was.' What would he like to have asked? 'How's she going to give us all this money, no pay freezes, and not have it turn back into rubbish money through inflation, for instance.' But no one mentioned politics to her, nor did she ever raise an issue with them. This was a state visit, or something like it.

Most of the carpets we saw were bright patterns, garish and frightful. I notched up a few points in her favour when we came to the design department. Watching the designers etching out some of those modernistic horrors not even she could bring herself to say she liked them.

In one department photographers pounced upon an elderly Asian tucked away in a corner. They hustled him along towards the group round Mrs Thatcher but she didn't see him. They had to bring him along for a while before they managed to squeeze him in front of her. He looked shy and deeply reluctant, but she was extremely glad to see him, and posed with him lengthily for the photographers. Press men scrambled to get his name. No one knew, but finally a company PR went off to discover and spelt it out slowly to us: Jamal Kidwal.

Mrs Thatcher glimpsed a tea room behind a glass partition

where groups of women were standing around a slot machine that dispensed fish cakes and mushy peas, and liver and onions. She said to one woman what lovely carpets they were all making. The woman answered sharpish: 'But they're very expensive for us working people.' Mrs Thatcher patted the woman's hand and said, 'We're *all* working people, and it's very expensive for *all* of us!'

Her next task was to preach to the assembled converted of five local marginal seats. Two hundred Conservative Party workers were gathered together for an especially unappetizing lunch at the Mytholmroyd community centre hall, thin soup, the thinnest slices of beef, floppy lettuce with salad cream in sachets, and shaving cream gâteau. But if she'd got up on that stage and read from the Halifax telephone directory they'd still have thumped the tables and shouted for more. She bustled through the Tory catechism – in praise of the getting of the wealth rather than the spending or redistributing of it, and a little joke or two. 'A year ago last September we published *The Right Approach*, and my goodness, what would Labour have done without it?' She touched on every subject in the Tory prayer book and a few slogans: 'We had lower taxes without North Sea Oil than they have with it!' And she ended with a rousing call for the use of 'North Sea oil to build free enterprise and not to grease the slide to socialism!' Her PR man stood at the elbow of the AP reporter prompting him. 'That's new. That's old. That's old said in a new way.'

After one or two tepid questions she came down from the platform in her orchid corsage and mingled for a while. A woman grabbed her arm and said, 'My daughter's only nine but she thinks you're the most beautiful lady in the land!' Another shook her hand and said, without a trace of Yorkshire in her voice, 'as we say around here, Thou'll Do!' Elbows started to jostle corseted posteriors in the push for autographs until she had to be rescued and she was borne away to the cars.

At Todmorden market came her first walkabout. The place was so small and the crowd packed around her so tight that the detectives had trouble keeping up. Like all politicians, she is said to like walkabouts best of all, meeting the people, finding out what they really feel and all that. She shook a lot of hands, and chucked many a young chin, but I wouldn't have called it meeting people.

Mostly people were pleased to see her and crowded to get closer, but some shoppers were angry. 'All this for one stupid woman!' puffed a stout old lady, who had been sandwiched in a mob. I saw one mother who'd temporarily lost her small daughter give her a fair clout and shout at her, 'What did you want to go shaking her hand for?' and the girl answered indignantly, 'Well, she just gave it to me!'

Sir Frank Marshall was scurrying around looking for immigrants. He found a couple of Asians in woolly hats by a wall. 'You want to meet her then? Want to say how do?' But they shrank back in fear. I don't know if they understood.

Several women workers from a local mill belonging to Wilson's friend, Lord Kagan, managed to get through to her to tell her the mill was being closed. She got the candidate who was behind her to take their names. Then a man from the same mill pushed through to her. 'I'm 48. I'm too old a dog to learn new tricks. What am I to do when they make me redundant?' It was a cry of pain. She held his arm firmly and said, 'You can be retrained. Of course you can. Don't lose faith in yourself!'

But otherwise very few issues emerged. For Mrs Thatcher, meeting people meant physical proximity and platitudes. She touched the people, clasped hands and didn't let go until she'd finished speaking to them. She touched people whenever she could, patting arms, standing as close as she could, giving sincere looks with her head on one side. But all most people got was a couple of stiff phrases about shopping, or the children's half term.

The Keighley walkabout was much the same, except that a few people came to congratulate her about race. 'You did right to say IT!' and 'It's time IT was said!' and 'Don't let them stop you saying IT!' No one actually said what IT was, because IT is a dirty word, but their meaning was clear enough, as was Mrs Thatcher's satisfaction.

A drunken Irishman lurched up and grabbed her. 'You're a lovely lady,' he kept saying until detectives prised him away.

'Will you give back our grammar schools?' a man asked. An old woman said: 'You look cold, dear,' as indeed she did. Everyone was muffled and wrapped up, but she in her thin coat and shoes was a curious apparition in the street, a shop window dummy whose plaster toes and nose wouldn't redden and freeze in the snow.

She spied a refreshment stall in the covered market and hurried over to buy herself a tea. She sat down abruptly at a table with two embarrassed-looking women, and a young girl. Photographers' cameras flashed. She smiled at them and sipped her tea but conversation flagged painfully and petered out. It had looked like a good spontaneous gesture. It would be fine in the photographs, but where was the natural warmth and jollity to carry it through? She had a whole steaming cupful to get through before she could go. The crowd pressed around to watch. But once she and the lady next to her had agreed that the day had started snowing but 'turned out nice', there was no conversation left. Now she had a real chance to meet some people, and she dried up. I'd been told that out here among the people she came to life: this was where she found her popular strength. But sitting there in that tea stall, she was one stranded Chelsea Conservative lady unable for the life of her to strike up an even passable conversation with three working-class Yorkshire women.

It was nine in the evening when she arrived at the Yorkshire Television studios. She'd been going for 12 hours, but she still looked like she'd only just been taken out of the box she came in, tissue paper and cellophane wrappings left in the dressing room. The studio had brown curtains for a backdrop. Her PR man had checked days in advance and had chosen her a dress that would go well, the navy blue with green silk collar and cuffs that she had worn all day. In the studio she wasn't happy about the aspidistra in a jardinière standing behind her. She called for the flowers that had stood in her dressing room and asked for them to be placed on the table in front of her. 'People forget that there are women watching who like flowers,' she said. But when the pink carnations arrived they obscured her and her two interviewers.

18

She was asked questions about herself, not politics. If the questions became too bold, she would suddenly switch on the royal One. Asked why she had kept her husband's first marriage secret for over 20 years she said, 'One didn't keep it secret he'd been married before. One wasn't asked. One doesn't just talk about a thing like that.'

She was asked what women she admired. She said Marie Curie, Anna of *The King and I*, Elizabeth Garrett Anderson, Elizabeth Fry. 'All of these One has admired.' How does she get on with the Queen? 'She's absolutely marvellous. She's the most gracious person, so of course we get on.'

Does she ever cry? She said she had often gone home and cried. 'Silently, alone, when I feel I have not done something well enough.' Recently? 'No, not recently. I've got used to criticism.'

It was the end of a gruelling day. This Yorkshire tour was leading up to her speech yesterday at the Young Conservatives conference in Harrogate. What purpose do these walkabouts serve? What purpose do they serve for those who managed to catch a glimpse of Mrs Thatcher in the flesh, or even to exchange some inane commonplace with her? They learned far less from the experience than they would learn from seeing her interviewed on television in the comfort of their own homes. She was shaking hands as if each shake sealed a vote, though I doubt whether politicians seriously believe that people are so frivolous and gullible to be much influenced by a squeeze of a palm one snowy February day out shopping.

What purpose did it serve for her, then? It seems that all politicians in the age of electronic politics feel the need to seek communion with the people. They feel the need to touch and smell and rub up to them, to persuade themselves that there is a two-way relationship, despite appearances to the contrary. Was it, as I've been told, the real Mrs Thatcher that I saw out there in the streets? Or did I see Mrs Thatcher in the process of convincing herself that she is real after all?

13 February, 1978   **Polly Toynbee**

Still glad to see an Englishman

A couple of weeks ago I chanced to be in Rawalpindi, up in the hilly north of Pakistan, gripped with what seemed at the time a frantic need to be in Lahore, 200 miles south in the dustbowl of the Punjab. Time was of the essence – it was something to do with Jim Callaghan's visit – and it seemed fairly essential that I take one of the three little planes that PIA sends between the cities early each morning. But, of course, there were no seats. The Punjab milk run was crammed solid with businessmen, off to Lahore. There seemed no chance at all that I could squeeze in beside them.

'But kindly be waiting one minute,' said the clerk. 'You are from England, are you not?' I allowed as how, indeed, I was. 'Well, I have a brother who lives in Wolverhampton, you know, and I am always most glad to see an Englishman. Perhaps you would kindly be signing this form?'

And he pushed over a yellowing slip of paper, headed 'Request for journey – VIP.' It seemed that I was to make a formal declaration that I was one of the five most important people in Pakistan. Not being a man given to false modesty, I made my mark with enthusiasm, and the clerk took the paper back 'For countersignature – it is the regulation.' Any wanderer, to a man with a brother in Wolverhampton, must be at least the fifth most important being in the immediate vicinity, and no perjury was involved in the filling of the form, he assured both himself and me.

I got on the plane, blessing Mr Azeem and every Pakistani I met that day, and landed in Lahore 50 minutes later. The fate of the man whose seat I took, I regret to say, I do not know.

They are such a kind people, these South Asians. Not a day goes past, here in Delhi, over in Lahore, back east in Dacca, or in any city or village I know, where that small singularity does not make itself felt time and again. The very act of, in India, making Namaste, the palms pressed together and the fingers almost touching the nose, seems a greeting that means so much more – it takes so much more effort – than the cold formality of a handshake.

The politeness of the language, the eternal offerings of cups of tea while you wait in the office of some bureaucrat, the genuine pleasure people extract from seeing that you are pleased with what they have done – one could go on and on. The demography of kindness and courtesy and charm has ignored partition, and it cannot be said that Pakistanis are in any way more or less kindly than their Hindu neighbours or their Nepali cousin-brothers.

Kindness to the stranger is as peculiar to the sub-continent as is black hair. There can be no region of the world where a foreigner is made to feel more welcome, where there is real pleasure expressed at your being there, taking part in the experience that is India. And yet, how very unkindly the British seem to treat them. Our officials, at least. The tales one hears, day after day, of the indignities suffered by ordinary Indian men and women – Punjabis, mainly, or Gujeratis – who come to beat feebly at the gates of our United Kingdom. You see them waiting in the sun on the verandah outside the British High Commission's Immigration Section, not allowed in until their appointment is announced (and they may wait a day only to find there has not been enough time to see them that day). If they encountered in one of their villages one of the officials with whom they will shortly be dealing, they would be courtly and kind and proud and quite astonished at the suggestion that human beings should deal with each other in any other way.

'My brother will learn English when he gets over to Birmingham,' a Punjabi woman told the immigration official who was assessing the brother's case for entry. 'He'll never learn it – none of your sort ever do,' the official returned. 'If I had my way I'd keep all of you out, but the rule says this one can go in.' And he stamped the passport with, as the woman recalled, something approaching venom.

'You don't really want to go to England for a holiday,' said another British immigration clerk, when a Harvard-educated wealthy young woman friend from Bombay came to have her passport validated. 'Why don't you go to America or somewhere? They'd much rather have you, you know.'

You hear stories like this all the time. 'The smell in that immigration room,' was a typical comment of a High Commission secretary, who has to visit the section with the clerk's tea, or something. What she doesn't care to realize is that that smell, far from being offensive, is part of the smell of India, and that what is so terribly important here is that she takes the time to catch what Robin White in Paul Scott's *The Jewel in the Crown* caught, when his hatred of India finally turned into love.

'I remember standing in the open doorway,' White wrote, 'and breathing in deeply and getting it: the scent behind the smell.' No one in the vast British High Commission here – or virtually no one, for there are perhaps a pair of honourable exceptions – will ever take the time or trouble to find that scent, and regretably it's not just their loss.

It is a dreadful place, the mission in Delhi. Most of the staff live and work behind the six-foot stone walls of the compound. Inside, there is tennis and swimming, a bar and a café, flats as ugly as any you see in Harlow new town, green lawns and an almost total lack of either litter or, save for the servants, Indians. The men and women who work there regard it, for the most part, as a hardship post. They detest Indians. They see only those parts of India – the Taj Mahal and Fatepuhr Sikri – that are conveniently close and spectacular. They eat resolutely British food. They wear shirts and ties, not kurtas and baggy trousers.

They still worry about having shiny shoes, and rarely take the sensible way out of the Indian dust by adopting open-toed chappals. They live in a transplanted few acres of London suburbia, their suburban attitudes reinforced every time they see a ragged Sikh on the street outside, or smell the smell of the Immigration Office, and they spend their lives – or the poorer of immigration people do – turning away applicants for entry to Heathrow with, to judge from the tales one hears, a brusque rudeness that is so astonishing to the Indian that he reels away from the contact quite bewildered that these British – these people about whom he has heard so much that is good – can be so very unpleasant.

Perhaps it would not be a very bad idea if the staff at the High Commission were forced, every once in a while, to take up bed-rolls and travel second class down into the further regions of the Punjab or Gujerat, where their victims have their homes. A few days among the kindness and courtesy of village India might bring about a sea-change that would do much for the fading reputation of Britons. It might also do the Britons themselves good, even if they only tried to detect the scent that lingers behind the acrid odour that pervades India and her Asian neighbours.

28 January, 1978   **Simon Winchester**

Across the fairway and into the booth

It is always hot inside an American telephone booth in summer, and the caller often pumps the split-hinged door like a concertina in the hope of wafting in gusts of bearable air.

That's what the man was doing. But it wasn't summer. It was spring in Georgia, which can be as intolerable as any Northern summer. And he wasn't making a social call, he was dictating copy to some cool girl at the Manchester end. He was pumping the door all right, but not just for relief. On the outside, close at hand, was a henchman or legman, clutching a bit of paper that bore hasty hieroglyphics, up-to-the-minute notes on what was going on outside.

What was going on outside was the annual Masters Tournament in Augusta, and the legman – name of Cooke – was trying to feed the latest birdies and bogeys, especially if they were being performed by an English golfer, to the desperate man inside the booth: a hawk-like figure with the exact profile of Goya's Duke of Wellington. This distinguished image was a little roughed up at the time, because the man's steel-grey hair had recently been subjected to a trim by a one-armed barber with blunt scissors, and from the poky strands of it rivulets of sweat were coursing through the clefts and canyons of a face that just then looked more like that of an impoverished Mexican farmer who was calling his landlord in a failing attempt to prolong the mortgage.

No wonder. It was ninety-eight degrees outside, out along the rolling fairways and under the towering Georgia pines of the most beautiful inland course on earth. Inside the press building, it must have been a hundred and ten. And inside the man's booth, you could name any figure that might suggest a sauna on the blink or the inner rim of the crater of Vesuvius.

Imprisoned in this inferno the man was shouting, against the clatter of a 100 typewriters, the squawking amplification of the relayed television commentary, and the hullabaloo of other maniacs in other booths. He would shout out a phrase, glance at a paper, drop it, curse, bend over and crash his head, curse again, swing the door open and pant – 'Was Jacklin's birdie on the twelfth or – blast it! – the eleventh?' He'd get the legman's word, swing the door shut again, sweat some more and shout out the cadence of the sentence he was writhing through.

I say cadence deliberately, because even in the bowels of hell this is not a man to toss out unkempt sentences of sloppy subsidiary clauses. When the stuff was in print, you would always assume it had been written by some imperturbable oldster brought up on Hazlitt and Bernard Darwin: always the loving delineation of the landscape, the knowing adjective, the touch of Edwardian grace, and the meditative close.

He was coming to the close now. He was hunched against the door and I could see him mouthing the words with exaggerated articulation, like a goldfish waiting for the water to be renewed. I saw him chew on a word, wring his free hand, and glare at the mouthpiece with Max Wall's Bela Lugosi face. I opened the door to give him a breath. He was screaming: 'In the serenity of the Georgia twilight . . . Ser-en-ity! SER-ENN-IT-TEE!!' He covered the mouthpiece and hissed at me: 'Bloody idiot! She can't get it.' Then back again and saying to the girl: 'That's it, yes, serenity, thnksvermuch. Goodbye.'

He emerges, the rivulets having now formed spreading lakes beneath his armpits. 'This goddam time-zone business!' he says. For the further exasperation of the British correspondents, the Masters is always played during that brief interval between British and American (Eastern seaboard) summer time, so that the time difference is not the usual five but six hours. Since the climax of any day's play tends to happen around 6 p.m., the impossible assignment is that of describing the finest hour to that cool girl transcribing it at Manchester's midnight.

The reader may be puzzled to recognize in this raw slice of life the lineaments of his favourite golf writer. The alert *Guardian* subscriber might be expected to guess that there has to be some agile hole-hopping, some frantic checking of the leader board, behind the smooth account of a tournament and the planted hints of why it was inevitable that the victory should go to Watson's iron discipline or Nicklaus's competitive stamina.

But the reader of Ward-Thomas's weekly musings in *Country Life* must believe that he is reading the oldest member, a gentle sifter of hot memories cooled by tolerance.

Well, the man in the booth is nobody but Pat Ward-Thomas on active service, from which he is now retiring, full of honour, fond memories and troops of friends. He is one and the same with the *Guardian*'s austere reporter and *Country Life*'s weaver of stately prose in the twilight. I must say that if there is a regret which obtrudes about his talent, it must be that in print he always distilled his disgust at some idiotic rule, some passing vulgarity, into a mannerly sigh, leaving only those who know him well the relish of having seen the splendour of his original indignation.

That, in its raging pristine form, was reserved for nobody but himself. I see him now, the top of his spiky head rather, banging away in a bunker at Maidstone, with the sand flying and the seagulls wheeling away in dismay from the obscenities that were rocketing out at them. Any true account of a round of golf with him would require, before publication, more 'expletives deleted' than all the Nixon tapes.

This year, the Masters at Augusta seemed more serene than usual because – the crack circulated – Pat was not there, for the first time in 14 years. Augusta was also considerably less fun than usual. In the press building, there were lots of the familiar cronies. But way down there, on the eighth row, there was an empty chair and a silent typewriter. No more the blacksmith's back bent over, the elbow leaning a millimetre away from a smouldering cigarette, the index finger poised for just the right verb. No more the smothered curses, but no more the quick smile, the bottle-blue eyes greeting chums and bores with equal good nature.

There were two things about his golf reports that set him apart from all the others. He tramped the courses, when most were settled in the press building scanning the big scoreboard and – on the basis of a figure change – tapping out 'he fired a birdie on the ninth.'

And he loved the landscape, all the landscapes of golf, from the ocean beauties of California's Pebble Beach to the Siberian wastes of Rye, from the pine and sand undulations of Swinley Forest to the yawning bunkers of Pine Valley and the cathedral aisles of Augusta. He knew the terrain, and made you know it, and how it shaped its peculiar form of golf, of every county of England and Scotland.

When others settled for 'this magnificent course', he pictured the beeches and copses, distinguished an upland from a weald, weighed the comparative hazards of a cypress tree or a swale. Nobody has ever conveyed so easily the sense of being in Wiltshire or County Down or Fife or Arizona.

He will be greatly missed, but not by everybody. Only by those who care about the good earth and its cunning conversion into golf strategy, about the unsleeping conflict between character and talent, about the courtesies as well as the joys of the game, about many small favours, and about unfailing geniality to man, woman, and beast.

27 May, 1978   **Alistair Cooke**

Home from sea

One most valid reason for moving to Norfolk some years ago was that the strange old links at Brancaster would become a home club. I had long been enchanted by the slender stretch of unspoiled linksland between a wild salt marsh and the North Sea. The charm of the course is that it has not been modernized. Holes have only been altered or created because nature destroyed others.

A paramount concern of the Royal West Norfolk Club has been to preserve great natural, albeit in some places old-fashioned, quality. The course is one of few where bunkers still are shored with old black railway sleepers, and if the bunkers are not as formidable as once they were, they can pose fierce problems.

Another virtue is that every hole is entirely different in character. There is no danger of boredom because the course can change from day to day. It is open to the elements and the winds can be savage and cold.

Always the views are restful and often surpassingly beautiful, particularly when playing the noble holes across the marsh towards the turn. Then at a glance, there is Scolt Head, the inlets stealing into the harbour at Brancaster Staithe, with bright sails cutting back and forth on summer days; and far beyond the quiet, wooded hills rising to the broad Norfolk skies. A golfer could ask for little more.

29 May, 1978   **Pat Ward-Thomas**

Public enemy no. 1

'Don't weep for me now, don't weep for me never.
I'm going to do nothing for ever and ever.'

An epitaph on a Victorian skivvy's gravestone and, perhaps, on our children. In one of those surveys, as gloomy as they are glossy, which at least keep economists off the streets, the Institute of Manpower Studies at Sussex University calculated that 'assuming a cautiously realistic growth rate of 2 per cent', unemployment in Britain will be pushing seven million in the year 2001. One in four if my sums serve me, and the unemployed are likely to be the young, some of whom may never work as long as they live. It is, said a union official, a question of retirement at 16, and Barbara Ward, like some Sibyl sulphurously inspired, talked about the children of affluence who feel 'This society is unjust. My God, I'll blow it up.'

It reminded me of a remark I overheard at the start of the recession – that those who were not panicking just didn't understand the situation. Unemployment: Public Enemy No. 1 (BBC-1) produced by Christopher Brasher and Colin Riach, was rather too clear for comfort. It did not, for instance, get its teeth stuck in such fudge as Verdoorn's law, which stumps the reader of the Manpower Report.

Industry, even the most successful, is shedding men like leaves. Autumn is on us. The service sector is overtaking industry as industry once overtook agriculture. A service job is the Prime Minister, for instance. You should, therefore, aim to be Prime Minister.

A somewhat Arcadian solution – though you never can tell – was advanced by Professor Stonier, whose name was so painfully appropriate that Mr Brasher (pronounced Braysher) disguised it with a French accent. A shorter working week, a flexible ability to change jobs, to develop several talents, to undertake community service. 'We should let industrial robots create the wealth and we should spend our time taking care of

28

each other. Service jobs, people caring for people, are the kind of jobs which make people the happiest.'

One of the things which made me happiest was the sight of Mr Brasher playing with his Viewdater, television-telephone-computer, which courteously greeted him with 'Welcome' and 'has all the information available in the world.' Though not, apparently, the information that Blake did not mean cotton when he wrote Dark Satanic Mills. There, there, I am simply striving not to feel superfluous.

It was a pretty irony and a typical one that 'A man-made fibre does not need as many men.'

13 January, 1978   **Nancy Banks-Smith**

A dog's life

Parliament is full of creeps. They sit on both sides, but they are most obvious when their party is in power. What they do is to stand up at Question Time, make some fulsome, laudatory and wildly optimistic remarks about the astonishing success of the Government, toss in a phoney question to meet the rules of order, and sit down. Then the Prime Minister, or whoever it is, can stand up and agree wholeheartedly, adding a few more dubious facts and opinions to make it sound as if his honourable and creepy friend had stumbled on some important political insight.

Mr William Molloy, the Labour member for North Ealing, is one of this group, ready to do his duty at any time without hope of reward. Mr Molloy has become rather popular on the Tory benches where they have come to look forward to his inter-ventions. Unfortunately, he does not seem to understand their baying and jeering, choosing to see it as evidence that he has scored a damaging political point. Yesterday, for example, he had tabled a question asking Mr Callaghan when he last met the TUC and the CBI. Usually these innocent-sounding questions hide a cutting barb, to be brought out in the supplementary. In Mr Molloy's case the question usually conceals a scented bouquet for the Prime Minister, and the Tories stirred with obvious pleasure as he rose.

'When my right honourable friend does meet the TUC and the CBI will he discuss with them the remarkable improvement of the British economy . . .' At this point the Tories collapsed with laughter and delight. Mr Molloy plunged on, '. . . which is bound to cause irritation to the Conservative Party in their anti-British campaign overseas and in this country . . .' A few Tories, slow to enjoy a joke, protested. The rest dissolved in happy mirth, as Mr Molloy made some point about inflation.

The Tories are less kind to Mr David Steel, whom they regard as a king-size creep, and for whom they keep the same contempt that a class has for the boy who sneaked and got everybody kept in on Sports Day. When he rose to demand that the Prime Minister kept the firemen to the 10 per cent rule, the Conservatives all began talking at once, not actually shouting at him, but holding their own, very loud, conversations. Mr Steel kept trying, and the Tories kept talking. The Speaker rose, and demanded 'the right honourable gentleman must be heard' though quite why, since we had heard it all many times before, the Speaker didn't say. The Labour MPs, whose view of Mr Steel is that he is a nice chap, though a bit wet to sell his party out, cheered. The Tories then all waved their order papers at the cheering Labour members which is parliamentary sign language for 'what did we tell you!'

At the end of Question Time, there was a short ceremony to introduce Mr David Atkinson, who is the new Tory MP for Bournemouth East. A lifetime – well, four years – of observing Parliament has taught me that the MPs who first arrive looking cocky, confident, and generally at home in the place are the ones who disappear fastest without trace. Mr Atkinson looked exceedingly at ease and full of confidence, so I expect we shan't be hearing very much from him.

Then the chamber suddenly emptied as if some inaudible dog whistle had summoned away hundreds of MPs. The reason was, of course, the beginning of yesterday's devolution debate which is, in fact, much more interesting than people think. Some of yesterday's debate was about what has now been called the West

'I've just had this dream. The firemen went on strike, there was a fire at the House of Commons and it spread halfway down White-hall, the firemen reckoned they'd made their point and were about to return to work – but public opinion forced them to stay out.'

Lothian Question, framed originally by the Labour MP for that constituency, Tam Dalyell. His question is: 'How is it that after devolution I shall be allowed to talk and vote on all issues affecting West Bromwich, but on very few issues affecting West Lothian?'

So far this little teaser has not been seriously answered and most attempts by the Government to do so seem to boil down to 'Yes, it is unfortunate, isn't it!'

30 November, 1977   **Simon Hoggart**

The battle of Warwick Castle

Every year around this time the peacocks at Warwick Castle strut in the formal garden before the orangery, parading their plumage to impress uninterested females and drawing the eye of the visitor from the magnificent white marble Warwick Vase. This spring there is nothing to see but the peacocks. The orangery, built to house the fourth-century BC vase, is filled with plastic tables and chairs, and is renamed the 'conservatory cafeteria'.

The new guidebook to the castle does not mention the vase, one of Warwick's choicest treasures since it was raised, 200 years ago, from a lake at Hadrian's villa near Rome.

The guidebook does not mention either the 26 paintings that have vanished from the castle over the last four years. Where the six Van Dycks, the four Canalettos, the Holbein, the Teniers, the four Rubenses and the rest hung, there are mirrors or chunks of armour. The women guides have learned to talk about the furniture instead of pointing to the paintings that earned Warwick the distinction of housing the best private art collection in the country.

The family motto of the Earls of Warwick is: 'Vix ea nostra voco' – I scarcely call these things our own – a sentiment firmly rejected by the current Earl, tax-exiled in Rome, and his son, Lord Brooke, ditto in France. While Lord Brooke has kept silent about the systematic sale of treasures from the castle, his father has argued hotly that he has as much right to sell them as a council-house dweller has to dispose of his property.

The Earl, who is 67, left Britain 20 years ago, handing over the castle to his son to escape death duties. There was just the castle and contents to change hands: over the years the family has sold off all its land, its farms and other properties. For a time it seemed that Lord Brooke was going to make the most of what was left. He brought in an estate manager with proven skill in the stately home world, and started the turnstiles clicking.

So far the dwindling number of treasures has not hurt attendance figures. Even on a cold April day the tourists thronged the great hall for the recorded message that gave them the castle's history and welcomed them to 'this splendid home of treasures'. Some of the visitors are regulars, heritage-watchers mingling with the tourists, jotting details of missing or moved items.

Dennis Farr, director of Birmingham Museum and Art Gallery, is one of the regulars. From an old list of contents, he checked off the paintings as we moved from room to room, doubling back to make sure of this, clarify that. At the end he was as satisfied as a man could be who knew the situation was bad but had made sure it was no worse. No paintings had gone since November; the most recent victim was the Warwick Vase.

The vase, apparently in a London warehouse and speculatively destined for the Paul Getty museum, is the subject of a legal battle in the town. Warwick District Council is urging the Department of the Environment to issue a listed building enforcement order on Lord Brooke to force him to return the vase to the orangery. In the council's view the vase is part of the orangery as the orangery was designed to house it, and, as the orangery is a listed building, then the vase must be put back.

Even the keenest member of the Heritage in Danger pressure group admits that Lord Brooke, and owners like him, face a heavy burden of taxation. Works of art produce no income and although Warwick Castle boasts 480,000 visitors (at £1 adult entrance fee plus extras) the expense of running, staffing and maintaining the castle is enormous. Lord Brooke is not being blamed for selling the treasures; what angers the pressure groups is that he is making no effort to keep them in Britain.

As director at Birmingham, Dennis Farr is anxiously watching the fate of two of the four Canaletto views of Warwick Castle. In mid-November it was announced that export licences had been withheld for two of them and British galleries had six months to raise £275,000 for each. Birmingham and the Ashmolean at Oxford began to look for funds.

They were not clear whether they would have to find all the money or whether there would be a grant aid in which case they might have to find only half of it. And no one knew how or when the extra £1 million Mrs Shirley Williams had promised in October to help purchase heritage items would be available. Eventually, the announcement was that it would be spread thinly. Birmingham and the Ashmolean are unlikely to get their Canalettos.

In other countries, like France, central government can buy works of art and allocate them to museums. Here it doesn't, but Dennis Farr sees no reason why it should not be possible, given the political will, to set aside a fund for the purpose. The only hope, he says, lies with the imminent select committee report on the Land Fund and what should be done with the £18 million in it. 'I know we can't buy everything and turn everything into a showpiece, but we should draw up a shortlist, say what our priorities are and when they come on to the market acquire them,' says Farr.

2 May, 1978   **Lesley Grant Adamson**

Demo diary

What a weekend for protest. A field day for amateur sociologists and takers of the pulse of contemporary Britain. On Saturday it was the ecological country mouse, with anorak and rucksack and a return ticket to Bath and Wells, healthy old ladies and children in prams saying 'No' to a nuclear Britain. On Sunday it was the turn of the town mouse, stepping out confidently in its urban habitat, aggressively punk, tens of thousands of pairs of jeans, rocking against racism. After two days of such exotica, the annual May Day outing on Monday organized by the orthodox Labour movement, was more like the Lord Mayor's show.

Saturday's anti-Windscale march, from Marble Arch to Trafalgar Square, looked like an action replay of the CND demonstrations of yesteryear. Only the environment has changed. It was not the honest British Saturday afternoon shopper that got the message, but the Arabs and the European tourists, staggering out of the shops of Oxford Street. Abject sinners, they were told to reject the consumer society and the plutonium economy. Laden with perishable purchases, they were warned that 'radioactive waste lasts for ever'.

Polytechnic students, the demonstrators looked like for the most part, the product of mass higher education, on the verge of rejecting their inheritance. Generalizations are absurd, but Saturday's gentle advocates of the alternative society, led by a corps of dismounted bicyclists, looked very different from the serried ranks of the comprehensives that shouted their way from Trafalgar Square to Victoria Park on Sunday.

Both in their way were important events, but one was a victory march, a resounding re-affirmation of the power and strength of the urban industrialized working class, the other was more like a wake, a celebration of a pre-nuclear age of innocence, long since gone. William Blake and William Morris would have been at home on Saturday's march, and one group of country mice could be heard singing 'Jerusalem', as though they had escaped from a Women's Institute outing.

I mock not, for I too would like to say 'No' to Denver power station, to join hands with the 'Scottish campaign to resist the atomic menace', and I sympathize with the woman who urged us 'to engage in civil disobedience for a non-nuclear, non-sexist Europe'. I accept that British Nuclear Fuels are 'the real nuclear terrorists', and I share the conviction that there will be 'no justice from Parker'. But I hold out little hope that the intelligent, *Guardian*-reading middle class of rural Britain – represented massively on Saturday – will succeed in converting the town mice to their way of thinking. Whereas Sunday's march – the most impressive political demonstration seen in London for years – seemed more like a victory parade. After the extraordinary defeatism registered by the political parties on the race issue, it was reassuring to observe a vast wave of humanity affirming the positive value of a multi-racial Britain. Students and schoolchildren, punk rockers, young Liberals and Gays against Fascism, the myriad sects of the revolutionary Left, all proclaiming a belief that there will be 'no fun, no freedom, no future' with the National Front.

Huge demonstrations, of course, prove nothing. Hundreds of thousands of protesters can still produce a derisory result at the polls. Many people on Sunday were merely walking to a rock concert. For them, the call to 'drown the Nazis in music' may have been an optional extra. But before cynicism sets in, it is worth recalling that it was a very remarkable occasion, marking the first explicit amalgamation of political protest with the dominant popular culture of the day.

Idiosyncratic and non-conformist, the rockers against racism and their much-bebadged cohorts of town mice may change the face of contemporary Britain in a way that their country cousins from the anti-nuclear movement will never achieve.

2 May, 1978   **Richard Gott**

Queen's messenger

Just because the Queen has received a large pay increase outside the pay guidelines, I wouldn't want you to think that she is not practising any economies. Her rise comes in spite of the fact that she is enlisting the aid of MPs as unpaid messengers.

Liberal MP Jo Grimond was busy buying a particulary nice brand of honey in a Shetland shop just before coming to London, when the shopkeeper asked whether he would mind taking the Queen's consignment of honey down to London. Freight charges, the shopkeeper explained, were rather an expensive burden to impose on Buckingham Palace.

A surprised but loyal Mr Grimond agreed, and as a temporary Queen's Messenger took delivery of a large number of sticky jars. Arriving in London he rang Buckingham Palace and said sweetly: 'You had better come and collect the honey before the monarchy collapses.' An unsurprised messenger arrived to collect the jars. Isn't is funny how a Queen likes hunny?

10 November, 1977   **Peter Hillmore**

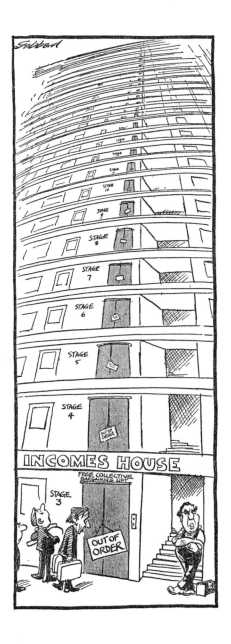

37

The blue Elizabethans

Britain's first film to reflect the punk era – *Jubilee* (X, of course) – arrives this week at the Gate Two. Which, in case you don't recognize the cinema, is the former EMI International, Blooms-bury, now leased and one hopes given a new lease of life, by David and Barbara Stone of the Gate, Notting Hill. And what have we in the foyer but a splendid collection of historic film posters from the collection of David Robinson, film critic of *The Times*. The *Guardian* is represented by claw-marks on the wall.

Jubilee, directed and part-written with James Whaley, by Derek Jarman who made the successful *Sebastiane*, is not exactly a punk movie. But it does contain music from Adam and the Ants, Siouxsie and the Banshees and Electric Chairs, and characters with such names as Crabs, Amyl Nitrate, Mad and Chaos. The scent of anarchy is near at hand and the current fad for believing that there is nothing left to believe in is everywhere apparent ('Love snuffed it with the Hippies. Sex is for geriatrics,' says someone. Myra Hindley is described as a childhood heroine).

Jarman's story looks promising enough, Queen Elizabeth (Jenny Runacre), that historic precursor of modern capitalism, arrives back in a future London (courtesy of John Dee, al-chemist, and the Angel Ariel) to find her perfumed garden in total rout. Law and order no longer exist, the old and cherished institutions have finally crumbled and extremists of both left and right are out on the blitz. Royalty is now best repre-sented by Borgia Ginz (Orlando, of the Lindsay Kemp Troupe), a giggling media mogul who gives the people what they want and thus controls them. He uses Buck Palace as a giant recording studio.

The past and future meet on a waste tip in Deptford where Bod (Ms Runacre again) crowns herself Queen as the leader of a band of harpies that include a pop singer, a pyromaniac and a nymphomaniac. Amyl Nitrate (Jordan) has been chosen by Borgia to represent England in the Eurovision with a bump-and-grind version of Rule Britannia. But first an ageing punk star has to be eliminated, and meanwhile Crabs (Little Nell) falls for the Kid (Adam Ant) who gets snuffed by the Special Branch. And the gang seeks bloody revenge.

Thus, or so the synopsis informs us, the film progresses from black comedy into real terror. Actually it tends to go from somewhere to nowhere very much. This has a lot to do with the thinness of the political and social comment, the disjointed nature of the narrative and some overbearing and/or underskilled playing. Shock tactics alone won't suffice in the cinema, though they may well pay dividends in box-office returns.

But one thing the film does possess is a fevered and restless imagination, and the images and music to go with it. Brian Eno's score is first-class, and the general feel of a world hideously out of joint (vide the Goddardian burning pram sequence) is well maintained. *Jubilee* may not be a very good film. But the fact that it exists at all is a kind of justification in the present circumstances. Besides, I'm inclined to think that the humour behind its pretension ('Piss, I've broke me Winston Churchill mug') might just be the saving of it. That and Mr Jarman's genuine talent for confounding expectations.

23 February, 1978   **Derek Malcolm**

Greek bearing gifts

Electra, Helen and Clytemnestra, all together in one woman, in the topless tower of the Intercontinental: Irene Papas! Furthermore, she overflows them all. She can speak fine rhetoric without the help of Euripides, and she carries the burden of beauty as if it were an empty suitcase, luggage politely acquired to reassure the hotel management. The beauty of Helen was merely local, she says. Ask Africa for beauties and they will show you filed teeth and big bottoms.

Africa notwithstanding, this Greek actress looks beautiful. May the Furies overtake me if ever I recant on that. In a rustling, panelled black and purple gown, but her shoes off, sitting at my feet in thick pile, talking about tragedy, coaxed into reading from her own unpublished poems, awestruck by the range of miniatures in the fridge, overwhelmed by laughter, she casts the same glamour.

She says that as a man I'm lucky, that I can walk with my face in the wind, with no other task but to be interesting. Whereas women, etcetera . . . Look, she says, the hair – and she runs her hands up through it and her bosom surges forward like a spinnaker breaking forth from a yacht – she wears it like this because she wants to be loved. (She is loved).

She is a big woman, and does not remember even as a girl being little. She went to drama school at 12 and they kept her for a year before they found out and sent her home to grow up. She found on rejoining that her maturity was costing her many parts. People are narrow minded, they think all young girls should be small, blonde and delicate. Literature mistakenly gives strong people black eyebrows. Not true! Some tiny blondes are so strong they can shake the world, some big girls haven't the strength to remove the skin from a rice pudding.

They gave her madames to play, and grandmothers. She made her film début at 17 as a bad woman in *Lost Angels*, with wicked veils and a nasty attitude to the heroine. She only got to play her own age in summer revues, political satires. She has a fond memory of these, and while in Athens rep – 14 shows a week – of lunching with an English lawyer who taught her through dandy writers like Wilde and Maugham and Poe. Ah, what a relish Poe's vocabulary was – his 'evanescent dreams'! Then a year in New York visiting the Actors' Studio gave another shock to her classical background.

In that background her father was a strange and compelling figure. True Illyrians, the family vaunted its pure lineage, but she was born in the south 50 years ago, between Corinth and Mycenae, home of the Atridae. Her mother, father, and aunt were teachers. Her uncle collected scandalous tales of the heroes. Her father was like Julian of Byzantium and wanted to live like the ancient Greeks. He allowed her to read nothing after Goethe. Everything since, he said, has been repetition. She rebelled against his teaching, but somehow it distilled in her.

But she still has no use for pride in the parish pump. Why be only Greek? All people are brothers. Everywhere people are urged to be heroes for their country, and she sees why politicians want it, but it is a confidence trick. She declares that she has been deeply upset and confused by the problem of her own cowardice. She feels she has only two per cent heroism to offer. How can she wear a sweater to keep out pneumonia, and bare her breasts to bullets?

Heroism, I say, is usually forced upon people, as it was upon Iphigenia. Exactly, she cries. It's in order to leave something behind her that Iphigenia makes that marvellous speech to justify her sacrifice, when she goes to her death for the dirty Trojan war. And so today we compensate our young people by parading them in white gym slips before sending them to their deaths.

She's not, however, scared to tackle the great classical roles in exotic tongues. She roundly affirms that she wasn't born to serve them, they were born to serve her. No matter that she doesn't speak English, French or whatever too well, she'll not be inhibited. In Vicenza she did the Medea in Alvaro's *La Lunga Notte*, and if she were not ashamed to use superlatives, she'd say it was smashing. Well, 18 minutes of curtain calls! Too much, of course, but all the same fantastic.

Yet fantastic gets tiring. After five months as Clytemnestra in New York she had to retire with a swollen gall bladder. You cannot play tragedy and be good every night. And anyway, she says, she never has any technique. What technique can you have for these plays, or for Shakespeare? Technique is for other plays. You just stand in the middle of the stage with no coffee to drink and kill yourself, that's all. And when you've played Electra, the longest part in the canon, you're purged of ambition to play any other big part, you're content to die.

Nevertheless, she wants to play Cleopatra. She's been reading around the scene of that amazing intellectual, who spoke all 15 tongues of the peoples she ruled. But will the English mind, she wonders, if she mangles their beautiful language? Perhaps they might forgive it, seeing Cleopatra was a Macedonian?

The room is lapped in her laughter, but she says she can never relax, above all when happy. In Greece when they laugh they immediately cross themselves, for fear something will happen and break it. After occupations, assassinations, cruelties of all kinds, there's always a drama, fiercer than Euripides, burning by that Aegean Sea. So happiness is connected with guilt. She believes in devouring love, and prodigies of fidelity – as much as five years at a time! Her acting, a tenth of her life, relies on peaks of life already scaled, what she calls 'memories of terror'. The rest is an apartment in Athens, a cash income of a thousand dollars a month, private marriage, love, reading, poems and travel, and a heroic struggle to sever the connection with guilt.

5 May, 1978   **Alex Hamilton**

Diva takes dive, brings house down

Florence, and visitors to that city's *Maggio musicale* festival, are hoping that Montserrat Caballe, the Spanish soprano, will grant them her now famous 'settimo bis' (seventh encore) as part of her song recital there on Saturday night.

On Monday, Madame Caballe gave a similar recital at La Scala Opera House, Milan, accompanied only by her pianist, Miguel Zanetti. After opening with some liturgical arias from Vivaldi, followed by romantic songs from Pergolesi, Marcello, and Paisiello, she closed her programme with some Spanish songs by Granados and Obradors. The audience demanded more and Madame Caballe, being nothing if not a generous woman, sang an encore, and then another and another. By the time she had got to number seven, also a Spanish song, she quite probably could not resist adding a little footwork. She may even have longed for a pair of castanets.

She essayed a few flamenco steps and collapsed, gracefully and silently as a tent, on the floor of the stage.

Those who know Madame Caballe's incredibly beautiful and velvety voice only from recordings may not know that she is also beautiful in her person, in a monumental and robust way. In plain words, the soprano is large, and she can joke about her needing an especially strong bed to die upon when she plays Puccini's consumptive heroine, Mimi.

Madame Caballe did not rise from the floor. Maestro Zanetti did not miss a note. The singer went on singing, finishing her fiery fandango from floor level, and remained there until the curtain was brought down.

The 'settimo' had also brought down the house. The singer was later brought to her feet, unharmed, with her fans more devoted to her than ever.

Small wonder, then, that her Florence fans are hoping that Madame Caballe will honour them also with a seventh encore; and, being obviously as good a sport as she is a great singer, she just might.

18 May, 1978   **George Armstrong**

At the aerodrome

For the nostalgic generation of the nineteen-sixties there was a difficult choice this weekend: Eric Hobsbawn on 'Intellectuals, the Labour Movement and Class Struggle' at the opening session of the Communist University of London, or Bob Dylan at Blackbushe aerodrome. No prizes for guessing that a quarter of a million chose Bob Dylan.

All day the radio had been warning of traffic jams, but no one takes much notice on a carefree Saturday in July. Like thousands of others, we sped down the M3 without a thought. 'Dylan concert, take exit 5' said the road-side signs – a certain invitation to follow the proverbial sandbarge on to the sandbank. Sure enough, by the Fleet service station the road had gummed up completely.

Like Amazon explorers in adverse circumstances, there was no alternative but to abandon the faithful bearer and to struggle across country on foot and alone. A few like-minded and long-haired trailbreakers were in similar straits – without maps or compass in the hostile short-back-and-sides territory of Camberley, Aldershot, and Sandhurst – on the frontiers of darkest Surrey.

But in the distance the deep tribal boom of an electronic muezzin could be heard across several miles of field and forest, calling the faithful to prayer. 'Are we allowed through here?' I belatedly asked a friendly forester, as we picked our way through a sandy glade. 'Yes,' he replied surprisingly, 'this land belongs to the people. I'm just here to see that you don't set it alight.' The campfires of the Magi had become a headache for the Forestry Commission.

Beyond the forest lies the aerodrome, dominated by four monolithic constructions pumping out sound. The usual kind of end-of-civilization feeling that prevails at pop concerts is accentuated on this occasion by the fact that it's being held on an airfield. The tarmac shows up between the sleeping bags to remind one of the use to which the land was once put. But for the weekend it has been reclaimed by ardent ecologists for the benefit of what look like refugees from some fearful disaster.

The prevailing age is between twenty-five and thirty-five, young marrieds with their children. Teenagers and the over-forties are strikingly absent. So too are punk rockers and blacks. The prevailing colour is pale indigo – bringing a warm glow to the bank accounts of jeans manufacturers.

After several hours of somnolence, the vast crowd stirs appreciatively. Eric Clapton gives way to Joan Armatrading. The family alongside brings out the Martini and the nuts, and a well-bred voice across the way asks brightly if there are 'any candidates for the sponge fingers'. A helicopter circles lazily overhead, avoiding the clusters of pink balloons that hang over the airfield, its rhythmic roar providing backing for the band, competing on equal terms with the loudspeakers.

44

Late at night, with dusk and the temperature falling, Bob Dylan appears. The crowd is too huge for any but the privileged in front to be able to catch more than a vague picture of a right hand striking a guitar a full half-second before the chord crashes across the amplifiers. The binoculars come out as though we were at Ascot. Reclining couples stiffen to attention as 'Like A Rolling Stone' and 'It's All Over Now, Baby Blue' come rasping out, huskier than ever before.

Like all such events, it is anti-climactic. Dylan, like his audience, is growing old. 'The times they are a'changing' he used to sing. Now they have changed – not altogether in the way that was hoped, nor necessarily for the better. The crowd prepares silently to hive off into the night with tired children.

It is bleakly cold, the ground is damp, the amplification indifferent – but the magic of a mystical occasion is not wholly absent. Bob Dylan is a folk-hero who encapsulated the ambitions and emotions of an entire generation. He was rarely overtly political, but the words of some of his poems seemed to touch on many public as well as personal predicaments. The weekend crowd was there not just to do homage to the singer, but also to bear witness to the message of the song.

17 July, 1978   **Richard Gott**

Transcendental reconstruction

Of all the solutions offered to the problems of the inner city, few can have received so little attention as the wheeze of inducing a state of restful alertness in the population. Indeed, it is often alleged by off-duty politicians that too many of the populace are restful – if not alert – enough as it is.

But the Maharishi Mahesh Yogi – of Beatles fame – has now turned his attention to inner city decay, and yesterday the chosen people of the London borough of Hackney learned that they had been selected to become restfully alert guinea pigs. In other words, to prove that inner city problems begin to melt away if only 1 per cent of the population takes up TM – transcendental meditation – for 20 minutes a day. TM is defined as a state of restful alertness, which is 'deeper than sleep but which, unlike sleep, is characterized by increasing orderliness and synchrony of functioning'.

Two of the Maharishi's disciples in Britain announced yesterday that they are starting the programme of 'bringing invincibility to the people of Hackney'. Mr Bill Hite, a 29-year-old computer programmer, and Mr John Windsor, a former Fleet Street journalist, said that Hackney had been chosen because it had the poorest population and worst social problems in the country. But everyone who thought that poverty was the prime cause of decay in Hackney was wrong, Mr Windsor declared cheerfully. The prime cause was lack of creativity – and creativity can be tapped by TM.

At this point the press conference gently left its moorings and floated into the ether. Borough councillors were to be approached, said Mr Windsor, and asked to learn meditation. There would be courses in how to do it – £15 for the unemployed and full-time students, £7 for OAPs. The aim was that in a year 2,000 people, or one per cent of Hackney's population, were to be taught meditation at the rate of 40 a week. And the results – in greater employment, falling crime rates, and general bonhomie all round – would be almost instantly apparent.

A local businessman, Mr Fred Bates, said that he employs 24 people in his display unit factories and two years ago took up meditation himself. Since then he had had the best two business years ever and had induced his works manager to meditate as well. He thought that TM would help workers to concentrate better, be less tense and hence more employable. If 1 per cent of Hackney's workforce took it up, employers would be more prepared to move back into the borough.

However, it looks as if the scheme – which might well appeal to the Minister in charge of inner city policy, Mr Peter Shore, on the grounds that restful alertness does not cost anything – will meet formidable obstacles among the cynical citizens of Hackney. 'Twenty minutes doing nothing?' asked one man. 'I do that for eight hours a day. No, I won't tell you where I work.'

Back at the North-East London Centre for the Age of Enlightenment, Mr Windsor said amiably that he was used to being pooh-poohed by people who had not actually found a solution to all their problems. Meditation was easy, quick and wonderful and the search for recruits was on.

4 January, 1978   **Lindsay Mackie**

A hospital made for two

The long, low, arcaded building is modestly called a 'medical pavilion'. It is rising now on some spare ground near the palace of His Highness Sheikh Zayed bin Sultan al-Nahyan, President of the United Arab Emirates and Ruler of Abu Dhabi. It has full air conditioning, an operating theatre, X-ray unit, physiotherapy department, dental and eye clinics, laboratory and pharmacy. It will cost £2½ million, and the total number of in-patients it will house at any one time is two.

Bernard Sunley and Sons, the British building firm which won the contract for the Sheikh's pavilion, is rather reticent about who will be using it. A spokesman for the company said yesterday that it was for the Sheikh 'and his household'. The household is reputed to include 12 wives and 30 sons, but Sunley's declined to be drawn on the total size of the extended family which will be using the hospital. It took a certain amount of checking and counting up of rooms on the plans to provide the information that the sleeping and recovery rooms and the lounge (complete with closed circuit television, so that doctors can observe their patients) were all part of a hospital made for two plus, of course, the no doubt numerous people who will use the out-patient facilities. Sunley's were equally reticent about precisely where the pavilion is being built, and would not go beyond saying that it was 'close to the palace'.

The Sheikh had set a deadline for completion in eight months' time, and by the standards of his country it looks as though he is getting a bargain. It was announced last week that a new five-bedroom house for Britain's ambassador to Abu Dhabi would cost £550,000 and a Foreign Office spokesman said it 'would not be lavish'.

29 March, 1977   **Hugh Hebert**

Healing comedy

The Baron, so we read, travelled seventeen stops on the Metro, descended at the Place de l'Opéra and, without using his little finger which had been sent on in advance, dialled his wife from a drug store, as Americans called the shop, chemists' or pharmacy to you and me, where they have breakfast. Drugs: what a curious subject! It must have been the Dumas-like adventures of the baron which suddenly sent a frightening image from some long-ago silent film into my mind: Catherine de Medici mixing a poison, or possibly what Bernard Miles's peasant called a love lotion, as used by Isolde in Wagner's opera.

What an important part medicines have played in our lives. 'Take your medicine like a man,' almost the first words we can recall. Victorians among the grey heads proffering this advice would talk of 'nasty physic' and nasty it often was. Castor oil and plasters of table mustard baked on to brown paper, powders so bitter you had to follow them up with a spoonful of raspberry jam. There was even a phrase, now never heard, 'It must be something chemical between them,' which in the days before dabbling in psychology, might crop up in a conversation between friends of friends who were inexplicably in love. 'I can't see what he sees in her, or she, him. It must be something chemical between them': it seemed quite a rational thing to say.

I like freedom to take medicines if I want, but seldom in fact do so, merely window shopping for them, gloating over stale and long-ineffective bottles, yeast, tincture, pill boxes, steel illustrations of bisected Edwardian beauties displaying the effects of the healing fluid posing by arrow-indications to the affected spot. I must have taken lots of simple medicines in my time: quinine for a cold in doses so large it filled your ears with the sound of Niagara, aspirins in hundreds (spaced), liver salts, so euphemistically named.

But I did small damage. Once, longing to attend a costume ball for which I had rigged up a fancy dress, I was so laid out with cough and cold that I thought I must renounce. Then a friend brought a 'mixture' which I quaffed, went to the ball after all like Cinderella and came home elated; leaned my elbows on the chimneypiece and saw in the mirror that my eyes were as wide and deep and lustrous as those of Mrs Patrick Campbell. Focusing these orbs on the bottle, I reread the label. 'Take three drops in a wine glass of water.' I had drunk two-thirds of the whole flask. We live and learn, or learn at any rate.

I began wondering just how about LSD, which also meant something else when I was young and caused much anxiety: and those long sentences passed on the pushers. Quite right, I decided, it is the pushing and fraud which were being punished: as one should have punished those barmen who, in the postwar days of gin scarcity, used ethyl in their expensive cocktails. But is the drug itself criminal? I have an open mind (just what the doctor ordered). I once smoked a whiff of opium when a student in France and felt so unutterably ill and slowed-up that merely crossing the street was like crossing the Gobi desert.

But LSD and so on – well, like Rosa Dartle I only ask . . . I recall a conversation with a high powered lady at a television conference (which dates it for me in memory). Aldous Huxley had come out with a book called *The Doors of Perception*, and there was talk about mescalin from the South American fungus. This lady told me she had taken it, then revealed that many advanced thinkers had done so and that I could subject myself, if I had never had jaundice, to an experiment in South Kensington where an intellectual woman novelist would control a safe supply and record your observations on tape. I did not take the stuff once I had listened to the tapes by men I admired: stony silence, sighing streams of smut (from a great astronomer).

The other day I was in such pain in the kneecaps, from a stupid accident (no wonder the IRA pick this target area) that I accepted painkillers and grew composed and happy but more than somewhat hallucinated, stumbling out of bed to telephone cousin G, who one presently realized had been cremated in 1951. Better stick to reality, really. Going about London very slowly on a stick brings its own crop of new experiences. The escalator is out of service. The news vendor waits till you have staggered slowly to his side before calling out, 'No papers, guv.'

Perhaps happiness is just a chemical thing after all. A fawn coloured sleek Labrador dog slowly overtakes me. He is the picture of contentment, well nourished, smiling, unhurried and proudly carrying in his soft mouth, lucky dog, an *Evening News* and a copy of *Private Eye*, happy chemically and spiritually, though he won't be able to understand the message or the jokes he so lovingly bears.

1 April, 1978   **Philip Hope-Wallace**

That's torn it

If your gerbil gets at one of the new shrunken pound notes, you will, alas, find it no easier than before to exchange it for a crisp new one. The Bank has disclosed its new rules for getting replacements at either Post Offices or commercial banks. With the old notes, where the serial number was printed twice you had to have part of both sets of numbers. Now that it is only printed once, you do not need to have it at all.

Instead, you must present not more than four fragments of the note, the whole of the clause 'I promise to pay the bearer on demand' and at least one-third of the Chief Cashier's signature.

If you cannot manage to salvage that, then you have to go to the Bank of England itself (or one of its branches) and try your luck there . . . if, with inflation, you can still end up ahead after you have paid for the tube.

17 February, 1978   **Hamish McRae**

The Series 3 Nativity

The Church of England is revising the language of its services. A version of the Nativity in modern English, taken from St Luke and St Matthew, may be ready in time for the Festival of Nine Lessons and Carols next year.

The position was that the colonial administration, headed in Syria by Cyrenius although overall control rested with Caesar Augustus, had recently established a system whereby the provisions for personal taxation were to be progressively extended to make them universally applicable, and everyone was advised to contact his or her relevant local authority, in this particular instance Bethlehem, Judea. Consequently Joseph and Mary – she was pregnant at the time - were in transit from their Nazareth, Galilee home to Bethlehem when Mary began to have labour pains. The child - it was her first - turned out to be male. She dressed him in a romper suit but in the event she had to improvise an ad hoc cot in the form of an animal feed container due to the accommodation at the hotel all having been previously allocated to other clients.

As it happened some workers in the agricultural sector were in the neighbourhood supervising sheep on an overnight basis. It was to their considerable surprise, not to say alarm, that an angel suddenly materialized out of nowhere accompanied by startling lighting effects. 'Not to worry,' he told the workers. 'First, the good news, not just for you, but for all concerned – you know?' And he briefed them with the latest information about the child being born and then about the interim structure for child welfare arrangements involving the animal feed container. The child would, he added, become a nationalist leader. So the workers took time out to see what was happening.

Coincidentally with this, three intellectuals – they had been intrigued by the appearance of a super-nova – arrived in Bethlehem via an eastern route which meant a stopover in Jerusalem. They had been following the super-nova for some time but, as it transpired, it eventually stopped over the precise location of the child, which came as a relief. They went into the hotel service quarters, met up with the child and his mother, and knelt down as a gesture of respect. When they had had their baggage sent in they made him a donation of gold, spruce resin, and a substance known as myrrh, which is derived from shrubs of the genus Commiphora. But their anxieties were by no means over, and following an uneasy feeling in the night about their route for the return journey – the story is slightly complicated, but basically the local chief, Herod, had devised a plot to intercept them so that he could have the child killed as a threat to his own supremacy – the trio decided that in the general interest it would be prudent to make alternative arrangements.

24 December, 1977   **Leader**

Cutting the cloth

In the parish of Stock with Lydlinch in Dorset they shared the patronage out like this. Colonel L. L. Yeatman had the second and fifth turns, G. Pitt Rivers Esquire had the first, fourth and sixth, and the Vicar of Iwerne Minster had the third. It was a recipe to avoid Trollopian squabblings. In future there will (probably) be no need either for the gentler manoeuvrings of Austen characters in pursuit of patronage, nor the real life sorrows of a Kilvert deprived of it.

Private patronage, a fifteen-hundred-year-old tradition, has been doomed by the Synod at York and its fate is, more or less, sealed. The reign of squires, declared observers, has come to an end. In many parishes it already had, and the private patronage is now in the hands of a motley crew. After the bishops, who hold a high proportion of the one in five livings whose incumbents are appointed in this way, come University colleges, old clerical families, the Crown, public schools and companies.

Tarrant Hinton in Dorset has both Pembroke College, Cambridge, and University College, Oxford, taking it in turn to appoint the vicar. Lord-lieutenants of counties tend to have the privilege, men like Sir John Wills of the tobacco firm, who holds a living near Bristol where his company made its fortune. The Society of Merchant Venturers of Bristol, Leeds Corporation, an iron works and the Mercers Company are all private patrons. The Goldsmiths Company is the patron of St Dunstan's in East Acton in London, and Eton College holds the living of Stogursey in Somerset.

The *Guardian* film critic Derek Malcolm, an Old Etonian, once found himself with the livings of two Devon parishes to dispose of when they fell vacant. Under the terms of his father's will he had succeeded to the privilege, but as the parishes didn't trouble him and he didn't trouble them he assumes that the incumbents are either very long-lived or the Church can manage very well without him.

Abolitionists say that patronage had become a shambles and that until a new appointments system had been introduced little could be done to reshape the Church's reduced manpower. Certainly patronage threw up anomalies. Atheists, children, and Roman Catholics can own livings, for instance. Atheists can appoint but children and Roman Catholics must have someone else do that for them. In practice the new breed of patron tended to work closely with the bishop of the diocese.

Sometimes the new-style patrons take great interest in their unusual privilege. For thirty-nine years Tom's Foods Ltd, a subsidiary of Smiths the potato crisps people, owned the living of All Saints at Nocton in Lincolnshire. The Americans in the parent company were, apparently, particularly fascinated by the concept of big business having the say-so about who entered the pulpit of Nocton Church. When the living fell vacant on the death of the long-lived vicar, the company took a keen interest in the affair. The chairman of Smiths Foods invited an old friend, a vicar in London, to visit the parish and advise the Tom's Foods people.

The new man was with them for about five years and then the vacancy cropped up again. This time applicants were interviewed by the churchwardens of Nocton and Dunstan (the two parishes have been linked) and the estate manager, Jim Smart, was in close touch with the bishop of the diocese.

When the choice was made it was Mr Smart who did the patron's job of presenting the new incumbent, the Rev Raymond Rodger, to the church.

In 1975 the estate changed hands and it is now owned by British Field Products, the Norfolk-based agricultural company. So far they have not had occasion to perform any of the patron's few but special functions. And unless there is a sudden change of heart at York they probably never will.

11 July, 1978   **Lesley Adamson**

Calcutta Christmas

The marble tip of the monument to the 123 men who died in the Black Hole can just be seen rising from behind a brick wall at the back of an old petrol station in the crowded heart of Calcutta. Standing there in the haze of last Sunday evening, immersed in hawkers' cries, rickshaw bells, and blaring horns, a visitor could just hear, from behind the same wall, the faint breath of a homely and familiar sound.

Drifting through the din was the thin and reedy singing, by a choir of less than a dozen small boys, of East India's version of the Festival of Lessons and Carols: Christmas in Calcutta, courtesy of the dwindled and now rather sad congregation of Bengal's oldest church, St John the Baptist, in Court House Street, hard by what once used to be the Viceregal palace and the centrepiece of empire.

St John's parish was 300 years old a couple of weeks ago. It was founded in late 1677 by the East India Company to provide spiritual sustenance 'for those employed in our factories in Bengal', and £50 a year was voted for pay to one John Evans, of Oxford, who, selected by the Bishop of London, arrived as 'chaplain to the Bay Settlements' in early 1678. It was 110 years before Evans and his successors – who included at least one chaplain who died in the Black Hole, and others with splendidly ecclesiastical names like John Chippindale, Montesquieu Bellew, and Desmond Bickersteth Ottley – were given a handsome church from which they could minister to their rapidly growing flock.

The St John's that stands today, hemmed in by petrol pumps, Bazaar Street, and a crumbling office block, is, give or take a few architectural changes and the unceasing processes of monsoon decay, the same structure crafted by master masons in 1787. There is a stone spire – the only one in Calcutta – and a clock that does not work, there are marble pillars and monuments to long-dead soldiers who fell with Sir David Ochterlony and Sir Henry Havelock and Admiral Watson and other giants of imperial might. The whole pile was modelled on St Stephen's, Walbrook, and Zoffany painted a gigantic 'Last Supper' to hang in the transept to celebrate its consecration: there it still hangs, fading in the steamy air, but worth, the London valuers say, at least £200,000.

The chaplain today is a young Bengali bachelor pianist, Noel Sen, who lives in the adjoining vicarage with a bull terrier called Flash who, in the space of the last few weeks, has somehow, and to everyone's great distress, managed to kill the cats belonging to the church milkman and the head verger. Mr Sen, who studied music at Yale and took his religious instruction in Calcutta's Bishop's College, presides over a community much dwindled from the days of Montesquieu Bellew and Bickersteth Ottley: at an average evensong he will get no more than five or six of the faithful, and even at Sunday's Carol Festival there were only fifty or so.

'There is only one Englishman left in the congregation now,' he says, a little ruefully. 'He is one of the real old boxwallahs, a man who made ink, I believe. He's retired, and makes my life hell because he is such a conservative. He keeps telling me how things were during the Raj, and it's difficult to explain that times have changed, even at St John's. The others are all Indian Christians – mainly middle class, because St John's and St Andrew's really were the fashionable places to worship on a Sunday. St Thomas's gets the Anglo-Indians: we don't see them here, which is perhaps just as well, since they are all so very poor, and seem to spend half their time trying to get money out of the vicar. We have virtually nothing to give them here, and we'd just have to turn them away.'

Next Saturday night, Mr Sen will hold the traditional Christmas Watchnight Service at St Andrew's, the Calcutta church that, like so many others in British India, is a precise copy of St Martin-in-the-Fields. 'We always get the bigger congregations there. Somehow St John's, even though it is the senior church of Bengal, is running down, and there's not much I can do about it. It's just like a little meeting of Christians, rather than a service. There aren't many of us in Calcutta, so times like these are rather special for us, if a little sad as well.'

22 December, 1977   **Simon Winchester**

Aches en Provence

One Christmas in Provence, not long ago, it snowed so heavily, so unexpectedly, that many people were marooned on the auto-route, unable to reach their families shivering away in a country-side that rarely sees a snowflake. I was lucky. I managed to beat the snow. But we couldn't get the car up the last hill to the house; and when we finally slithered up to the door, we found the water-pipes frozen. The only way to get water was to collect snow in buckets and melt it by the blazing fires.

But in spite of the hardships, it didn't take long to settle down to the serious business of a French Christmas holiday: that is to say to eat even more than is customarily eaten in Britain, or for that matter anywhere else. In my native Austria, the big feast is on Christmas Eve. In Provence, it turns into a string of big meals washed down by rather larger amounts of wine and champagne.

The Christmas Eve feast more often than not turns into a Christmas dawn affair. The village, Seguret, has a traditional midnight mass and it is a wondrous affair. We, the visitors, always go before the 'reveillon'. Afterwards, a whole tribe of friends and family congregate at a neighbour's house. Sometimes there is a debate whether to start off with oysters, or foie gras. Both have to be worked through before we reach a turkey, made infinitely more succulent by roasting it with crushed garlic – a French secret that should be adopted here.

After the turkey, there is salad; and since we are in France, there is no way of leaving out the cheese-tray. By then it may be 3 or 4 a.m., and most stalwarts are beginning to wilt. But one friend, who is usually with us at Christmas, has a sweet tooth, and could not survive a reveillon without a 'buche' – France's answer to a Christmas pudding, which is a rolled sponge cake shaped like a log, the longer the more impressive, layered with cream, and to my taste one of the most insipid desserts ever devised in France.

After such heavy labour, Christmas lunch tends to get served rather late. But it is only a little less elaborate. After that, there is a routine of visiting neighbours, who all assume that they are receiving the starving masses. This goes on, all the way to New Year's Eve with more oysters, hams, smoked salmon, buches, and so on and on. Occasionally, I manage to persuade everyone to have a poor man's dish, which nevertheless tastes good on a cold evening, when a great many people have to be fed. It's a Viennese version – aberration some might say – of the French choucroute. It's a LENTIL soup, with plenty of Frankfurters cut into it.

LENTIL SOUP
½lb lentils
bacon lard
salt and pepper
lemon juice
rosemary
sliced Frankfurters

Soak the lentils (approx ½lb for five people) for at least 24 hours. Fry small squares of bacon lard, add the liquid in which the lentils have been soaked, season with pepper, lemon juice, and rosemary (fresh if available). Taste carefully, before adding salt.

Bring to boiling-point; add the lentils, and simmer very gently for two-three hours, or longer, until they are tender. The consistency should be fairly thick. Add Frankfurters, cut in one-inch slices, and continue simmering for another 20 minutes or so. Serve in warmed soup plates. The soup is just as good, if not better, re-heated.

Christmases in Provence are very much a communal affair, so everyone always arrives with goodies ready to be consumed. My standard contributions usually include two Viennese confections.

The first is Vienna's answer to the English Christmas cake, and is called Bischofsbrot.

BISCHOFSBROT
6oz castor sugar
2oz butter
3 eggs
3oz almonds, sliced thinly
3oz sultanas
4oz mixed peel
grated lemon
4oz plain chocolate, cut into chips
6oz flour
rum

Mix sugar, butter and beat in the egg yolks. Beat the egg whites, and fold in gently. Add all the other ingredients, again very gently, with the flour put in last.

Put in a well-buttered cake-tin (preferably rectangular) and bake in a medium hot oven (350 deg. F) for about one hour – until thoroughly brown.

Unless eaten fresh, wrap in foil, after it has cooled.

The next concoction takes a bit of patience.

CHOCOLATE BALLS
8oz Bourneville plain chocolate, grated
8oz ground hazelnuts
1 egg white
a little sugar
FILLING
2oz butter
rum sugar
hard-boiled egg

Mix ingredients for chocolate mixture well, and leave in a bowl, while you prepare the filling consisting of the butter creamed together with rum sugar and the hard-boiled egg, that has been passed through a sieve. Let this mixture stand for about 30 minutes.

Form the chocolate mixture into small balls, around a little of the filling. Roll in confectioner's chocolate. Put into paper cases, and keep in a tin.

To go with the chocolate balls, I sometimes shape marzipan into small mushrooms. But it's easy enough, instead, to make *vanille kipferl* (vanilla crescents).

VANILLE KIPFERL
7oz butter
4oz ground almonds (ground out of unskinned almonds)
3oz sugar
8oz flour

Work all the ingredients into a dough. Shape into small crescents. Bake in a medium hot oven (about 300 deg. F) for 15-20 minutes.

Roll in vanilla sugar while still hot (you can make vanilla sugar by keeping a jar full of icing sugar with a stick of vanilla pod inside).

15 December, 1977   **Hella Pick**

On the 'now' switchback

Mr Kingman Brewster, American Ambassador to the Court of St James, thinks 'the British eat like crazy'. Well, cheeseburgers, french fries, malted shakes, T-bone steaks and mom's apple pie to that. Not to mention blueberry muffins, hominy grits, pastrami on rye and three large martinis before breaking sweat. But, more seriously, Mr Brewster is also quoted in the *New Yorker* as finding the British in 'manic depressive' mood. 'There was a kind of all-is-lost, woe-is-me attitude in June and

July, and now . . . there is great euphoric optimism, neither of which, probably, is justified.' Pause for media uproar. 'Jimmy's man sees Britain as psychiatric basket case' and the rest. Of course, though, Mr Brewster said much the same three weeks ago in an interview with Hella Pick. And there his ideas were set in context: the context of an obsession with what he calls 'now-ism' infecting major democracies, the context of observing that America too was in 'manic depressive' shape.

'Now-ism' is a nasty coinage. But it means something. Six months ago Helmut Schmidt was (variously) 'tired', 'discouraged', 'grey', and 'ready to quit'. Now, after Mogadishu, he is steely, confident, dynamic and irreplaceable again. Six months ago Giscard d'Estaing was irrelevant, discredited, doomed and impotent. Now, after the Mitterrand-Marchais split, he is refreshing, farsighted, incisive and 'a master politician'. Six months ago a weary Mr Callaghan had lost heart and control. Now he is Moses. Six months ago Jimmy Carter was the greatest thing since Roosevelt (possibly Teddy Roosevelt). Now he is floundering, ageing, raddled by doubt and prey to the *Newsweek* cover question: 'Can Carter cope?'.

In fact students of the American press may already detect signs that that last question – a good four weeks old – is even now being answered affirmatively by precisely those pundits who posed it, largely because Carter has taken their advice on relations with their contacts on the Hill. But this is only the most ludicrous example of the 'now' cycle. It operates across Western Democracy with increasing ferocity and increasing mindlessness. Of course, events and people do change history. Mogadishu may historically have been the saving of Helmut Schmidt. But the usual and inevitable reality is one of the checks and bureaucratic balances, not pop-star lurches. Moods change but not (often) essential situations. A thought to sustain Mr Brewster as, suffering from an acute case of now-ism, he faces a grisly but totally insignificant three months as 'Carter's controversial envoy'.

10 December, 1977   **Leader**

A welcome for the Shah

Tear gas wafted across the south lawn of the White House yesterday and reduced President Carter's state welcome for the Shah of Iran to an astonishing affair of coughing and weeping. Mr Carter wiped his eyes and passed a handkerchief to his wife. The Shah's wife cried and put on dark glasses, while the Shah, who was just due to thank Mr Carter for his official greeting, proceeded to ramble through his notes and was barely audible behind the wail of police sirens.

Hundreds of Iranian students had broken through a thin police line at the back of the White House just as the cannons fired the official welcoming salute. They moved towards two makeshift stands where scores of the Shah's supporters were waving the Iranian flag and pictures of the royal couple.

Watchers on the lawn could see people running to and fro about 100 yards away. Suddenly, the large banner saying, 'Welcome Shah', which was being held up outside the railings, disappeared. Minutes later, as Mr Carter finished praising what he called the remarkable progress made by Iran under the Shah's leadership, the Iranian ruler began to feel his first acrid whiff of Western democracy, as the tear gas rolled in.

At first Mr Carter looked angry, but he managed to remain more composed than the others on the podium. The Shah spoke very briefly, ending with the inappropriate comments: 'We've never had the slightest shadow over our relations, and I pray God that it remains so.' The gas dispersed quickly, and by the time the two leaders had moved up to the balcony on the south side of the mansion they managed to smile again. Most of the assembled guests were still wiping their eyes and coughing.

President Carter tried to make light of the incident, when reporters saw the two men shortly afterwards at a ceremony in which the Shah gave a tapestry to the President. He said he had apologized to the Shah for 'the temporary air pollution' in Washington.

Even before the tear gas incident the shouts and jeers of hostile demonstrators were audible at the welcoming ceremony. There were shouts of 'Down with the Shah,' and 'Shah – US puppet'. In scenes unknown since the height of the protest against the Vietnam War, a dozen members of the Executive Protection Service stood in a line along the front of the White House just inside the railings. They wore tear gas masks and carried riot shields, and had their truncheons at the ready. Outside, scores of mounted US Park Police were drawn up along Pennsylvania Avenue as thousands of demonstrators, almost all masked and hooded, marched in Lafayette Park. The Shah was burnt in effigy several times. Many of the slogans called for armed revolution against the Shah, and scoffed at Mr Carter's human rights policy. 'Carter gives the arms. The Shah kills the people. The people take up arms', one banner read.

16 November, 1977   **Jonathan Steele**

The flip-flop President

President Carter is a weak president. Pinned on to the wall of the office of one of his advisers is a graphic illustration of his weakness, a chart on which his standing in the opinion polls is plotted against that of other presidents over an equivalent period of office. Sixteen months in the White House and he had established a new record, below Harry Truman and Gerry Ford.

Few in Washington dispute the President's weakness. His cabinet officers and his aides know it to be a fact. On Capitol Hill party friend and foe alike take account of it. The pollsters measure it; the press, for the most part, revels in it; and the Russians, or so it is feared, take advantage of it. The interesting question for the visitor to Washington is not whether the President is weak, but why?

The conventional answer, born of disdain for the 'outsider' president, is that the weakness derives from an incompetence, is a technical failure. A hicksville president came to town unversed in its mysteries, ill-equipped with 'Hill people' for managing the Congress and lacking the eloquence to move the country. He was a moralist and not a politician, but also an engineer and not a politician, simultaneously effusive and coldly calculating; a man with an aura but no real vision, uncertain as to where to go and how to get there; hence – as they say in Washington – the 'flip-flop president'.

Another explanation, and a more serious one, takes account of the circumstances in which Mr Carter came to power, indeed the very reasons for his advent. He is the legatee of after-Vietnam and after-Watergate and he was also the executor of those legacies, appointed by the American people. Inexperienced he may be in some regards, limited in others, but the failure – if failure there is – is neither personal nor technical in its essence but rather an amalgam of systemic factors of which the nomination and election of Jimmy Carter was itself a symptom.

Even people who are ready to attach a more simple and direct blame to the President himself pay some deference to this other analysis when they wonder, for example, whether any president could have got any kind of effective energy measure through the Congress. The Speaker, Mr Tip O'Neill, who is the Democratic Party leader in the House, says it's 'the darnedest issue' he has seen in 25 years. But energy isn't the only one on which the President is trying to move forward in the absence not only of any kind of national consensus but also of a working consensus even within the ranks of his own majority party.

Europeans are getting Carter wrong because their memories are too short. They have forgotten what American democracy is like in normal times, and there have been no normal times since the war, with the possible exception of the benign interregnum of General Eisenhower.

In Truman's time the Cold War forged a steely bipartisanship in the Congress and thrust a greatness upon the little haberdasher who inherited the White House. The grand-scale presidency of John Kennedy, who ended the Eisenhower peace, caught the imagination of the world but existed only in the text-book dreams of Professor Richard Neustadt when its exponent was cut down. After that it was assassination, war and scandal – a nightmare decade ending in the bad waking dream of the Ford presidency, a kind of American parody.

Europeans have forgotten, but so have many Americans, how beset is an American president in normal times, how politically charged are the acts of statesmanship expected of him, and how difficult it is – as Tocqueville first noted – for a federal state to pursue in times of peace a strong foreign policy.

President Carter presides over a fast-changing society at home and a fast-changing world abroad. The two interact: the conservative mood which is enveloping the country is in part a case of recessional blues, a sense of lost hegemony and waning superiority; the probings of the Russians – if that is what they are – derive from their perception of the weakness.

Americans articulate these concerns in ways which ring familiar bells in English ears. One Senator talks about 'our post-Algiers, our post-Suez state of mind'. Another speaks of 'our retreat from empire mentality'. The problems of inflation are discussed with reference to Weimar, a classic symptom of the English sickness. A senior cabinet officer worries about declining productivity, falling exports and lost technological superiority.

The notion of a global equivalence with the Soviet Union is psychologically troublesome and is the emotional force which drives the opposition to a second agreement on the limitation of strategic arms. Adjustment to the ending of the age of limitless plenty is proving difficult too, although, five years after the advent of OPEC, it is beginning to happen – Americans are beginning to discard the throwaway society.

Painful changes produce their reactions. Panama was a great presidential victory up on the Hill but it was more significant as the harbinger of the latent chauvinism in the land. 'No one expected the Panama issue to take on such life,' said the first Senator. Protectionism, perhaps even isolationism, lurk not far beneath the surface.

It would be wrong to suggest an ominous atmosphere in the nation's capital and still less – by all accounts – in the nation itself. The economy has been booming. For most Americans not only the quantities of their well-being but also the quality of their lives has been improving as they jog farther and live longer, eat and breathe better, their children learning more in better schools. And in Washington, a city given to globalist gloom and unhealthy political preoccupation, the atmosphere is open and relaxed, even gay: the administration is at least engaging in its ineptitude and the city as cheerful at least as, say, Vienna pre-1914, where the situation was hopeless but not serious.

Up on the Hill, Mr O'Neill, smoking a cigar of truly congressional dimensions, said: 'I don't hear much talk of Africa up here; I don't hear much mention of Cubans.' Out campaigning in what he called 'the back streets', he had met few, he said, who knew, for example, that Africa contained a country called Nigeria where they spoke a different language to other countries. 'Africans,' he said, 'are blacks like blacks from the South.'

So much for foreign policy, so much for the front pages of the *Washington Post* and the lunchtime preoccupations at the Sans Souci. Zbig who? 'We don't pay much attention to presidential politics up here,' explained one of the Speaker's aides.

Downtown they complain that the President doesn't know how to manage the Congress. The real trouble is that the Congressional leadership can no longer manage the Congress, not even the partisan Mr O'Neill and still less the more ambiguous majority leader of the Senate, Mr Robert Byrd. The weakness of American government begins not with the presidency, neither the office nor its present incumbent, but with the disintegration of party.

Reform, the sire of the Carter candidacy, has caused some strange mutations to the political process. For example, primaries and open caucuses have released candidates from the embrace of party into the arms of lobbyists and professional media manipulators, special interest groups and big money, chiefly corporate. 'We have a bought Congress,' said a White House aide. 'There has been a sharp increase in the influence of business over the House,' said one of its leaders.

Reforms on the Hill have contributed to this new regime of the interests. The abolition of pluralism in the chairmanship of House-committees, for instance, has resulted in 147 sub-committee chairmen, each a baron with an independent staff, each more susceptible to the pressures of the interests than to the disciplines of party. The political action committee, the mailing list, the media consultant – these are the tools of a new style of politics practised by a new kind of man, not a party man but a professional at the art of re-election – parochial, pork-barrel. What is more, 70 per cent of them ran ahead of the President in 1976.

This new technology of American politics is connected with the phenomenon of the 'new conservativism'. Conservative-inspired and bankrolled political action committees showed what they could do on Panama. Conservative candidates did well in the Congressional primaries in which liberal Republican Senator Clifford Case of New Jersey, a prime target, was toppled. The political action committees grew up as a counter-vailing force against the left-wing movements of the war and Watergate periods: now they are better organized, better financed, more adept.

But there is more to the conservative revival than technique. The mood which brought Carter to power, at the same time intensely ideological about issues and weakly attached to party, is the mood behind the tax revolt, the indignation at inflation and the mounting hostility towards the Russians. And so we see a president under intense political pressure in an election year, a president weak because he lacks foundation in the power of party or in anything much more substantial than that persuasive mood. An amalgam of liberal and conservative instincts, a product of the 'New South' and of no firm ideological mould, President Carter seems able to swim only with the tide. That tide is flowing towards a rigorous fiscal conservatism at home and a tougher foreign policy.

14 June, 1978   **Peter Jenkins**

A country diary: Kent

The first starling arrived just an hour before sunset, flying low
and fast from the darkening horizon. It was followed after an
interval by a group of eight, then 20, then two. For the next
hour starlings streamed in from the south-east in equally varied
groups. They became progressively more difficult to pick out
even against the barren trees on the skyline. All had the flight
of birds with a destination and a purpose, so direct that they
seemed to clear the roof of the house on the hill at the last moment
to reach the avenue of trees that was their mustering point.
Within a quarter of an hour of sunset there were upwards of 500
birds settled there in four of the trees, whistling, chuckling,
chattering with gregarious good humour as if exchanging the
news of the day. As other flights arrived and swooped down,
there was a general turnaround and the flock spilled over to
adjacent trees until the whole avenue was alive with their babble.
A murmuration seemed the least appropriate group name
imaginable. One or two small groups ignored the hubbub and
sped straight across the pale sky. Suddenly at sunset almost to
the minute, there was complete silence. It lasted a mere second
or two, yet it was as dramatic as an orchestra stopping in the
grand finale. Then the birds were gone, the only sound the rush
of a thousand wings. In dark clouds they winged their way due
north-west to complete their daily journey to the heart of
London and a warm roost. Two minutes later three more birds
arrived, wheeled uncertainly above the trees and then continued
on the flight line. The ritual was over for another day.

2 December, 1977   **John T. White**

Difficulties in getting the bird

Sir – I noticed in the popular press last week that villagers near Exeter are being driven mad from dawn to dusk by exceptionally noisy cuckoos.

Have any of your readers noticed marked changes in the behaviour of all wild birds this summer? Unless I am imagining things not only are they much bolder and noisier this year, but also more *articulate*, so that I am frequently distracted from work in order to make out what they are talking about. There is a thrush in my garden who keeps announcing that he wants a sabbatical, and another who seems to believe that Chomsky is a metal kettle.

Most interestingly, however, for the first time ever I've seen birds wasting their time. Could this phenomenon be associated with language acquisition? –

Yours faithfully,

28 June, 1978   **Alan Harris,** *Bedfordshire.*

Broken fences

A couple of weeks ago I was up on that border between the Lebanon and Israel, between the fogs of the Mediterranean and the snows of Mount Hermon: a pretty region. I was up at that place past Metullah that they called the 'Good Fence', because it was – maybe is? – the one open frontier point between Israel and the Arab world: every day hundreds of Lebanese swarmed over it to do jobs in Israel, to get medical attention, often just to do their shopping. At evening they went back; it was a paradoxical sight.

It was also a first-class public-relations deal; they brought busloads of tourists up to the Good Fence to see fraternity at work and to buy preposterous little hats carrying both the

Israeli and Lebanese emblems. Sometimes they were also printed with the dove of peace. Everybody was very uplifted by this, and sent back picture-postcards to Cincinnati and New York, and felt the better for it, as did I. I knew the neighbourhood well, but I had never seen the Good Fence. I would suppose that I never shall again.

What now? The Israeli invasion of Lebanon was inevitable, sooner or later. The Palestinian outrage on the Haifa road was, I am sure, conceived as a provocation, and the Israelis were duly provoked, as the PLO intended, and over-reacted as the PLO intended, and presented themselves as bullies rather than avengers, exactly as the PLO intended all along. I think it was a terrible mistake, but then I do not live in Israel and I have no right to judge the behaviour of a people whose nerves have been stretched too far, and for too long.

I spent the last night in the Upper Galilee at the settlement town of Qiryat Shemona, which achieved a brief morbid fame not long ago when PLO infiltrators crossed the border and took hostages in a block of flats, killing 20 of them. Even up to last week the Israelis in the north were getting the odd Katyusha, the rocket-driven missile which makes a dauntingly horrible howling sound on its way across the border and an even nastier bang at the end.

The Galileans at least will applaud the Israeli occupation of the buffer zone in Lebanon, even though it adds another 300 or so square miles of invaded territory to be wrangled over for who knows how long to come. Almost in spite of itself, it seems, Israel gets bigger every year.

It is ironic that it has been Lebanon – the one neighbour-state that stayed out of all the Israel wars – that physically suffered within its own borders more than any other. The Lebanese army is the one that in 30 years has not fought one battle against the Israelis.

The Lebanese believe that foreign affairs belong on the *bourse*, not the battlefield. All the Lebanese have ever wanted is to get on with their job as entrepreneurs and stock-jobbers of the Middle East; they are glad enough to profit by wars but not to join in.

And yet of all the Arab capitals (using the word loosely; the Lebanese are fanatical about nothing except business) it is Beirut that has been smashed to smithereens by civil war, bombed in reprisal raids, and has now had its rump cut off in retaliation for outrages committed by other people. One has to admit that it seems like hard luck.

At the same time the Lebanese administration has been singularly futile, even for a region not noted for its diplomatic finesse. Its Government's writ runs hardly anywhere now; effectively it has been usurped by the Syrian peace-keeping forces in the centre, and the PLO in the south. Along the 60 miles of frontier with Israel you can stare for days over the barrier and never see a Lebanese soldier, nor indeed anyone except the day-return refugees who stream through the Good Fence. Or used to; I suppose even that small sign of grace has stopped now.

The Lebanon is an oddity even for the Middle East. Ever since the French Mandate was withdrawn in 1943, the Syrians have only grudgingly accepted its independence. The Arab League wrote it off as an active factor long ago. The national motto is 'Vive La Commerce'. It is non-militant to the point of being almost lamb-like, yet for years it has harboured the strongholds of the PLO.

I grieve for Lebanon, but only faintly. I used to stay in a fine hotel in Beirut called the St Georges, now untimely ruined in the civil war. It had a famous head concierge, whose name was Jesus Christ. For years, long ago, I used to send him a Christmas card saying 'Happy birthday to you', hoping that one day I would get one back, which I would frame.

It never came, and now it never will. This is the story of the Levant, of Lebanon, of the Middle East. People do things, no one ever responds. I keep remembering that just a few miles below the Israeli-Lebanon border is a plain, known as Armageddon. Fortunately it is a very long word for a headline.

20 March, 1978   **James Cameron**

Warm welcome in Hadatha

'We thought for sure we had killed you,' said the Israeli officer. We had been well aware, as our ordeal lasted, that we were lucky to be still alive. But not until we met our 'enemy' did we realize just how lucky. To be mistaken for Palestinian guerillas in the biggest, hardest campaign Israel has ever launched against them, and to survive the mistake is an achievement we owed much more to providence than to our own evasive ingenuity.

It happened to three correspondents – Ned Temko of UPI, Douglas Roberts of *Voice of America*, and myself – who had set out from Beirut at 5 o'clock in the morning for a visit to the Palestinian side of the front. It happened in the village of Hadatha, 12 kilometres north of the Israeli frontier.

Hadatha is a Shiite Moslem community which once numbered 2,000 souls. Its tragedy – to be caught in the classic dilemma of neutrals in other people's wars – is shared by scores of other towns and villages set in the rolling, open hills of South Lebanon. When we entered the village at 12.30 it was an eerie no-man's land between the opposing forces.

We had left the last Palestinian position – if a handful of men armed with Kalyshnikovs qualified as that – five miles back on the road from Tyre. An Israeli armoured column, which had entered the village the previous day, had withdrawn earlier in the morning. At first we thought Hadatha was empty of its inhabitants too. But a lonely figure approached and he was eventually joined by a train of followers – grave, saddened men like himself, tearful women, excited children – who almost dragged us round the village, insisting that we see all the evidence of their misfortune.

As we made this tour of shattered masonry and mangled livestock – the humans were already buried – people peered out of doorways. If they took us for Israelis, they raised their arms in instant terror. If they took us for Americans, they pointed skywards and, in their naïve belief that Americans are masters of the world, they implored us to 'save us from them'. 'Them' were the Israeli war planes which had visited them the day before.

Our guides insisted, before we left, that we inspect the wreckage of what was once the village's special pride: its new school. It had been built at a cost of £100,000 and, with uncanny foresight, someone had insisted on a basement which could also serve as a shelter. 'Come and see it,' they said, and in the first of our lifesaving flukes we were all going down there when the first tank shells landed.

About 20 came in all. The whole structure shuddered sickeningly. We and our companions huddled into the deepest subterranean recesses – the latrines. In the one next door a woman clasped her terrified child and intoned prayers to Ali, Hassan, and Hussein, the martyrs of the Shiite sect.

The villagers began to murmur about an expected airstrike. They scattered to their homes. We stayed. Hardly had they left before the tank-fire resumed. Then after a prolonged silence we crept out in the hope of discovering what was going on. Spotted, and having come under intense mortar-fire, we took refuge in a concrete crevice which – providence again taking a hand – seemed likely to withstand anything but a very near hit.

The mortars kept on coming at intervals. Planes continuously screamed overhead but the airstrikes we feared were destined for Tabnine, just across the valley, and targets farther north. However, no sooner had our fear of one sort of dying ended than another took its place. Suddenly small arms fire erupted from all directions. The chatter of machine-guns and the crack of rifle fire moved closer and closer. We could only assume – very much to our astonishment – that Palestinians had somehow infiltrated the village, and that before long we would be in the thick of it, with one side or the other taking up positions in the house behind which we sheltered. But it all died away as mysteriously as it had begun.

At nightfall we decided that the best course was to consult the villagers who, we knew, must be experiencing much the same emotions as ourselves. We walked half a kilometre in the knowledge that if we were passing through anyone's line – whether

'*See for yourself – I am leaning backwards to accommodate the wind of change!*'

Palestinian or Israeli – they would be liable to shoot first and ask questions later. But finally we made it to the only inhabited part of the village and knocked on the door of a house through whose blackout windows we perceived the dim glow of a turned-down oil lamp. ('The Israelis are liable to fire at the lighting of a match,' a villager subsequently explained.) We were given what was perhaps the warmest welcome of our lives – the kind of welcome which only the very poor can give – and all the warmer in that here were strangers who, at least for a night, were sharing in their affliction.

In the semi-darkness, we made out the shapes of cows and goats on one side of the room and humans lying or sitting on the other side. An old man, wounded in the afternoon's sniper fire, lay silent in a corner. The family had ventured out that morning to scrape a shallow grave for his 17-year-old son, killed in the previous day's bombardment.

'You are our children,' said an old woman, 'as dear to us as our eyes. If we die, we die together.' She embraced us. What food they had they served on two large platters. Then Mohammed Fadil took us to his own house where we tried to sleep – aircraft and an occasional shell still passing overhead – amid the bales of his unsold tobacco crop.

At dawn we heard the sound of approaching engines. As the mist rose it unveiled a cluster of tanks and armoured personnel carriers on a nearby hill. Israeli soldiers, clearly relaxed, were standing around taking their ease. And what the villagers told us could be a hazardous operation – identifying ourselves to them – proved very easy.

It was then that we learned just how lucky we had been. Captain Uzi Dayan, paratrooper and relative of the Foreign Minister, is a transparently decent and humane man. When he heard our tale he replied: 'I don't like to tell you this. It was I who ordered the shelling of the school. This tank' – and he pointed to a nearby Centurion – 'did it from a distance of 1,200 metres.'

Another, British-educated, officer filled in some details: 'We were sure we had killed you with two simultaneous hits on the top and bottom floors. We were so sure that we did not bother to come and flush you out. I don't like to say it, but we assumed that it was just three more terrorists done for.'

Why had Dayan ordered the firing? 'They told me that 12 uniformed terrorists had entered the building.' That misapprehension – obvious foreigners in motley attire and a handful of men, women, and children from the village taken for uniformed terrorists – just about sums up the war the Israelis are waging in South Lebanon. It reflects not just the quality of the information available to them, but, at a deeper level, a whole attitude of mind. The despair which drove the Palestinians to massacre civilians on the Haifa-Tel Aviv highway is matched – as a contribution to the mutual hatred of Arab and Israeli – by a total commitment to the iron fist.

In our six hours' wait for transport back from the front we had a unique opportunity to talk to ordinary Israelis in action. Two questions kept coming to their lips. One – 'Are there any terrorists in the village?' – amounted to a subconscious admission that we, who had just strayed here by accident, were better placed to tell them than their own much-vaunted intelligence services.

It was obvious to us, after an hour of ordinary dealings with the villagers, that there were no terrorists left – or that, if there had been, it would not have taken very long to find out in which houses, if any, they had installed themselves. 'We do not deny they have been here over the years,' said a villager, 'but they imposed themselves on us. They had all gone before the bombardment. We only wish that just one guerrilla had honoured us by sharing our fate.'

Some Israelis are, it seems, incapable of such ordinary dealings with the Arabs. We had intervened in an effort to arrange safe conduct for 100 villagers who wanted to go north. Mohammed Fadil kept saying, as we took him to the Israelis, that they would beat him up. We said: 'Don't be silly'. But although they did not beat him up, he was more right than we were.

The transformation in some Israeli soldiers was almost pathological. Men who had talked to us in an easy, friendly way, turned mean and hostile when confronted with one trembling villager. For the Israelis, it seems, everyone is a terrorist in disguise.

The second insistent question was: 'Were any civilians killed in the bombing?' We pointed to a house under which an old woman still lay entombed. We told them that not merely had civilians died, but that they were the only ones who had; it was doubtful, we said, if so many as one of the 20-odd houses their air force had destroyed had harboured guerrillas. Yet the soldiers obviously placed more confidence in what we told them about the matter than the official propaganda. One might shrug it off, saying 'That's war'. Another might fall into embarrassed silence. But none demurred.

In the six hours that we sat and watched the bombardment of Tibnine and beyond – with aircraft and everything from mortars to massive field guns deep inside Israeli territory – only half a dozen projectiles, mere firecrackers in comparison, came in from the other side. In 'cleansing' South Lebanon the Israelis are using the opposite of their usual military techniques of high mobility.

There was, we were told, an overriding consideration: to minimize Israeli casualties. And that, we gathered, stemmed from another: the morale of the ordinary Israeli soldier was not as high as it used to be. Only after the massive bombardment would the infantry go in. It clearly troubled some professional consciences. One sharpshooter confided: 'I have killed three terrorists so far, but this artillery is a dirty business.'

Reliance on long-range firepower, I suspect, is the real reason why they did not come and get us in the school. And they even used small arms like artillery. What we, crouched in our bunker, had taken to be close-range combat was actually general spraying of the village, or as one officer put it, 'a precaution against pockets of resistance'. In the course of it all, one wrinkled old villager told the Israelis, snipers had picked off his 15 sheep one by one for amusement.

There is little doubt that, with such techniques, the Israeli army is effectively 'cleansing' the border region of the guerrillas, who, abandoned by the Arab world, stand no chance against overwhelming odds. How far will the Israelis go? 'We are ready to go all the way to Turkey,' said one officer, 'to protect our citizens.' That is the ultimate logic of security built on force alone. The Israelis will have achieved a short-term relief, but added another layer to the enduring hatred which encircles them.

To leave Hadatha, we hitched a lift on the back of Captain Dayan's tank. A goat was munching placidly at the narrow roadside. It refused to get out of the way, so he ordered his tank to defer to the goat. If that were the spirit which informed all the Israeli army, there might be some prospect of peaceful coexistence, but it certainly does not: it is more like one spared goat to 15 slaughtered sheep.

21 March, 1978 **David Hirst**

On not being terrorized

For the last six weeks the world has watched a giant tremble. The Schleyer kidnapping, now ended in murder, and the hijacking of the Lufthansa 737 have during that time totally preoccupied the government of one of the strongest democracies in the world. The government of the Federal Republic under Herr Helmut Schmidt did not flinch in the face of the terrorists' demands, but the effect of the incident has been to advertise, and – I shall argue – vastly exaggerate the vulnerability of Western democratic society to revolutionary violence.

The danger that this brings is not that the terrorists themselves will overthrow the systems they so hate but that liberal society will destroy itself through regression into a state of Hobbesian pessimism, or a kind of social Calvinism. Hobbes thought that man was innately violent but he is not; he is born merely with a capacity for violence. In one part of New Guinea, so anthropologists tell us, the natives continuously eat and rape one another while in another part of that same land they lead a life of laughter, drink and pleasant fornication. But if Hobbes was wrong the twentieth century is believed by many living through it to have engaged man's capacity for violence to an unprecedented degree. That belief is understandable in a century which has produced both a Hitler and a Stalin.

Western society rediscovered violence in the year 1968 and has remained in a state of shock ever since. It is perhaps true that sharing the century with Hitler and Stalin has had some brutalizing effect upon us all but it is unhistorical to see collective violence as a new phenomenon or as having returned on a vast scale. Those who may doubt should consult the studies done for President Johnson's Commission on the Causes and Prevention of Violence.

An erroneous belief that we live in an age of unprecedented violence, when combined with the correct belief that the cause is to be found not in human nature but in society, can lead easily to the conclusion that the society in which we live is corrupt and damned, which is what I mean by 'social Calvinism'. But there is little basis for this belief either. Political violence may appear to be a common phenomenon afflicting Western democratic society, but that appearance results chiefly from the similarity of its techniques.

Political violence in Northern Ireland, which has sectarian roots, has little, if any, connection with those conditions of 'capitalist' society which are common to Britain, Germany, Italy, and France. Even as between Germany and Italy, where a tiny section of the young middle class has espoused revolutionary violence, the differences are more important than the similarities – among them the status and the power of the State, traditional social attitudes to violence, and traditions of criminal activity and its organization.

This is not to say that political violence does not have political causes: it is to argue that its causes are importantly different in each case and therefore do not support the generalization that violence is endemic in Western democratic society – except, of course, in so far as some violence is endemic in all society.

In this regard some comfort may be found in Gillian Becker's recently published *Hitler's Children*. Miss Becker's fascinating account shows the reverse of what her title implies, that the Baader-Meinhof phenomenon is to be explained not in terms of genealogical descent from Nazi Germany, but rather in terms of specific incidents, decisions, accidents and misjudgements.

The progression from harmless utopianism to fanatical terrorism follows the pattern observed in earlier millennialists, for example, the Anabaptists. Andreas Baader, ideologically illiterate, and Gudrun Ensslin, his dominating girl friend, set fire to a department store at no risk to human life. Ulrike Meinhof, successful journalist and radical chic celebrity, in an astonishing Quixotic and destructive impulse, helps to spring Baader. As fugitives they travel the road of armed robbery and murder to prison and suicide.

They were not Hitler's children so much as the class of '68. The German authorities over-reacted to the student disturbances of that time, especially in Berlin. Many of the leaders of those disturbances subsequently were denied employment and hence the chance to grow out of their infantile political disorders. These errors were committed in the context of a more general neglect and maltreatment of students. The student upheavals were more intense in Germany than almost anywhere.

Ideology is relatively unimportant for either explaining or understanding the Baader-Meinhof phenomenon. The student milieu from which they sprang was enthused with Marcusian ideas of its own importance. How was there ever to be a revolution in the absence of a revolutionary proletariat? Herbert Marcuse, in a famous passage, had conferred the vanguard role upon 'the substratum of outcasts and outsiders, the exploited and persecuted of other races and colours, the unemployed and unemployables'. The students believed themselves to be a part of it or the vicarious embodiment of it.

In so far as the Baader-Meinhof Faction developed its own distinctive ideology it was post facto. However much the students might prate about 'praxis' they continued to imagine themselves to be playing some kind of vanguard role with regard to the proletariat: terrorist outlaws were obliged to find a different justification for their actions. They were unable to construct any kind of plausible ideology concerning their ends; the chief justification of their means lay in the delusion that in the Federal Republic of Germany they were living under 'fascism'.

Their recourse to violence took place against the background of the war in Vietnam. In America Abbie Hoffman was shouting 'Boom!' and his audiences replying 'Boom boom!' Their original act of arson was described by Baader and Ensslin as 'lighting a torch for Vietnam'. They found some encouragement in the then fashionable intellectual apologies for violence. Fanon, Sartre, and Genet provided intellectual justifications for violence based on false analogies between social struggle in industrialized democracies and wars of colonial liberation. Revolutionary terror was given justification in the notions of 'bourgeois terror' or 'consumer terror' – abuses of language in which Genet still persists, for example, in a disgraceful article in *Le Monde* on September 2.

What is novel about contemporary political violence is not its prevalence but its techniques. The technology of the twentieth century has both facilitated and concentrated terror: its tools are easier to obtain, fabricate or transport, and technological society is more vulnerable to the bomb – the aeroplane is a good example. Late twentieth-century terrorism is also more indiscriminate. Hostages are taken at random; bombs in public places kill at random.

It is, I think, these terrorist techniques and the often in-comprehensible motives of its exponents which are chiefly responsible for exaggeration of the threat which it poses to democratic societies. The fear behind that fear is the ultimate horror of the nuclear terrorist. He indeed could destroy a whole society. But such outrages as we have seen perpetrated in the last few weeks cannot do so unless a society also wills its own destruction. I believe Professor Golo Mann, the son of Thomas Mann, to be profoundly wrong in his conclusion that 'measures within the framework of traditional law' are no longer sufficient to meet the threat. In that conclusion lies the terrorist's only hope of success.

Dr Conor Cruise O'Brien, as a student of political violence in Northern Ireland, has warned eloquently of the 'pre-fascist phenomenon' of an escalating spiral of terrorism and vigilantism. To suppose that a socialist utopia might be achieved through first provoking fascistic responses from the state was the horren-dous delusion of the Baader-Meinhof gang. For there is no way of overthrowing a modern totalitarian state from within and in the era of nuclear weapons no way of destroying it from without.

The argument is not for appeasing the terrorist. The Federal Republic has not appeased the Baader-Meinhof gang nor should it have done so. What is now important for Western society as a whole is to keep the problem within proportion. The death toll from political violence is minute compared with deaths from other modern causes – air crashes or road accidents. Non-political crime is a far more serious risk to the citizen. The murder or destruction which the terrorist can inflict upon society remains well below its threshold of tolerance. Political violence is neither a novel phenomenon nor is it occurring on an unprecedented scale. There is no reason to believe that it is endemic in Western democracy or that it is bound to succeed in destroying democracy. To be resolutely specific about its causes and to refrain from exaggerating its consequences is the best insurance against abdicating to an unnecessary authoritarianism.

21 October, 1977   **Peter Jenkins**

The watch on Germany

The Federal Bureau for the Defence of the Constitution is the domestic intelligence service from which the West German authorities obtain information about prospective employees. It is known as the *Verfassungsschutz* for short – or what passes as short in Germany – and it has something of a chequered history. It was set up after the war as a means of countering Nazism. Its first chief disappeared to East Germany, where he broadcast against the West. Subsequently, he returned, claiming that he had been kidnapped and brainwashed. The bureau, in the meantime, had become what it still is, an instrument of anti-communism.

It plays a central role in the practice of *Berufsverbot*, the denial of public service posts to 'enemies of the Constitution'. If a teacher applies for a new job, he may find himself called to a hearing at which his political past is laid before him. The education authority will have gathered this information from the bureau, and it may include all kinds of circumstantial evidence: attendance at demonstrations, past associations, whatever smacks of radicalism.

A recent ruling by a Berlin court has cast doubt on the legality of many of the hearings. A professor had been barred from a job in Hanover on the basis of information apparently provided by the Berlin bureau. The judge ruled that, while the *Verfassungsschutz* was at liberty to gather whatever information it wanted, it could not give out information on the legal activities of individuals. It could only inform the authorities of such facts as might be used in a court of law. So, if the job applicant is a member of a terrorist organization, the bureau can inform the education authority. If he is a member of the Communist Party, which is now legal, it cannot. If the applicant attended a Vietnam demonstration in the 1960s, that is a secret between him and the bureau: if he tore up paving stones and threw them at the police, that is something the education authority has a right to know.

This reasonable-sounding judgement has been welcomed by Willy Brandt, the man who introduced *Berufsverbot*, and by those who campaign against secret service malpractices. If it was repeated throughout West Germany – and that is a rather big if – it would reduce the practice of *Berufsverbot* to a minimum. The suspicions of the intelligence service, which are often enough to bar a qualified applicant from earning the living for which he has trained, would no longer be available to official agencies.

Many politicians think that *Berufsverbot* is a perfectly reasonable practice. What they do not like, however, is the notoriety of the word in the rest of the world. They do not like the rest of the world pointing a finger at Germany yet again. So the growth of anti-*Berufsverbot* committees in America and Europe may prove effective. The official practice could be curtailed or dropped.

Which would make the unofficial sources of information all the more valuable to those who are keen to keep the public services pure. In Berlin, for instance, there is a fortnightly news sheet called *Tropf – Drip*, or *Drop* – which is dedicated to this purpose. Its slogan: 'Against stupidity, against laziness, against cowardice.' *Tropf* has no official publisher or editor, only an anonymous box number to which information may be sent. It is not sold. It merely appears on the desks of public officials. It has been going for four years without hindrance from any authority, and its back numbers provide a comprehensive, if wildly inaccurate, guide to radical groups and individuals in Berlin.

In the copies I have read, the formula has been simple: the name of a supposed 'enemy of the Constitution' is given, plus, whenever possible, his address and telephone number. What follows is an account of his life, activities, and associations, plus perhaps an appeal to readers for more information.

The style is paranoid. The technique involved is guilt by association: a man is a member of a committee, another member of the committee is the notorious Leftist so-and-so; a liberal went on a demonstration, Communists also took part in the demonstration, ergo the liberal is a Communist.

A man whose name has appeared in *Tropf* finds it impossible to shake off whatever slur the paper has decided to make against him. The more he struggles, the more embroiled in suspicion he becomes. And, in the nature of things, there are many accusations which it is impossible to rebut. There are many people who once met Ulrike Meinhof: that is enough to get your name, address, and telephone number in *Tropf*.

Nobody knows who produces the news sheet. Its political stance appears to be neo-Nazi. The authorities claim that, since it is not a political paper but a collection of 'facts' informally distributed, nothing can be done about it. In the meantime, it acts as a kind of freelance *Verfassungsschutz*, apparently unanswerable to law.

19 June, 1978   **James Fenton**

Solzhenitsyn's Testament

'All you freedom-loving "left-wing" thinkers in the West! You left laborites! You progressive American, German, and French students! As far as you are concerned, none of this amounts to much. As far as you are concerned, this whole book of mine is a waste of effort. You may suddenly understand it all some day – but only when you yourselves hear "hands behind your backs there!" and step ashore on our Archipelago.'

This shout of rage – this threat – is the rawest moment in the final volume* of Solzhenitsyn's vast history of the Dantean Soviet underworld of the prison camp 'archipelago', one of his last thoughts in a work that runs to nearly 2000 pages. Like the second volume, Gulag 3 ends in exhaustion and something not far from despair, for the author as well as the reader: in a flagging, fragmented sketch of the essentially unregenerate state of 'Our obtuse, our blinkered, our hulking brute of a judicial system' as he saw it in the late sixties. More than once, and scarcely half-ironically, he speaks of the boredom of telling his terrible stories to blank faces and untouchable minds.

A couple of brief postscripts remind us of the immediate reasons for both the exhaustion and the fragmentariness. In September, 1965, when this one-man research institute was most feverishly at work on its impossible project, Solzhenitsyn's flat was raided and the typescript of his novel *The First Circle* confiscated. It was necessary to disperse the sections of Gulag that had already been written, and much of the research material, and thereafter he never had the whole book together under his hands even when he finished writing it in 1967, on the eve of the fiftieth anniversary of 'the revolution which created Gulag,' and the hundredth of the year that saw the invention of barbed wire.

* *THE GULAG ARCHIPELAGO 1918–1956: An experiment in literary investigation, Vol. 3: books V-VII, by Alexander Solzhenitsyn, translated by H. T. Willetts (Collins).*

But it's the foreword (written ten years later in Vermont) to this English edition that suggests the deeper reason for the anger and darkness of its final pages.

After all the horror and suffering of the earlier books, says Solzhenitsyn, this third volume 'will disclose a space of freedom and struggle', and he goes on to speak of the Soviet regime's fear of revelations 'of the fight which is conducted against it with a spiritual force unheard of and unknown to many countries in many periods of their history'. The words are carefully chosen, but he shows the zeks beginning to straighten their backs before Stalin had gone, and provides accounts of two major and several minor local challenges to the apparently unchallengeable might of Soviet totalitarianism.

Much of the struggle Solzhenitsyn makes peculiarly his own, no doubt feeling that to be the right of a historian who had so much of his country's history taken out on his own hide. He embraces wholeheartedly two of the most taboo causes from that history – of the 'kulaks' and of the Vlasovites and others who collaborated with the Germans; and then rounds on politically sympathetic Western critics with an awkward defence of literary realism (a characteristic parenthesis worth quoting: 'If words are not about real things and do not cause things to happen, what is the good of them? . . . This is how our people usually think of literature. They will not soon lose the habit. Should they, do you think?').

Something of the difficulty he has in producing sufficiently heartening evidence of a will to 'freedom and struggle' against Communist rule shows, however, in the lengths to which the proud ex-artillery Captain Solzhenitsyn goes to defend those who collaborated or fought with the Germans. Like other Russians who fought bravely *against* them and were rewarded with brutal imprisonment by their own leaders, he has the best right to anger at the Soviet regime's subsequent political exploitation of the 'Great Patriotic War'. But in his argument here he comes dangerously close to presenting Hitler's arrival on the scene primarily as a lost opportunity for getting rid of Communism.

Wartime defections apart, the accounts he gives of the two

major revolts he was able to document – the riots over food prices in Novocherkassk in 1962 and the 40-day siege at the Kengir camp in Kazakhstan ('Ka-zek-stan') in 1954 – do stir the heart and the imagination, the latter episode especially, with the prisoners producing their own government, hydro-electricity and radio, and Ukrainian girl rebels frisking MVD generals admitted to the stockade. There are also some grimly picaresque, Gogolesque escape stories, though few of even the most determined and ingenious escapers got clear away, faced with 'such an absence of support from outside, such a hostile attitude on the part of the surrounding population'. None of these things, nor the stoicism and steadfastness of individual Russians, offers grounds enough for hope to assuage his bitterness, however.

This extends to the generation of post-war camp guards who shot to kill so readily, and indeed to 'The majority of young people who could not care less whether we have been re-habilitated or not . . . so long as they themselves are at liberty, with their tape recorders and their dishevelled girl friends'; also to all those, including ex-prisoners, who want to forget. Perhaps the most depressed and depressing chapter is a sort of Gallup poll of the rehabilitated. Concerning one, a friend deep once more in academic careerism, Solzhenitsyn muses: 'Yet the tribunal had thought him worth ten years in the camps. Perhaps one good flogging was all he deserved?').

And of course there are the 'progressive thinkers in the West', not only unable to help restore Russia to her ancient paths of righteousness (though not modern capitalism, please), but unable to begin to understand how it was and is.

'A waste of effort', then? For all his bitterness, neither we, nor he (nor, clearly, They) believe *that*, unless history is a waste of effort, for if there are times when he polemicizes almost as coarsely as his neo-Stalinist opponents there are others when he sounds like the voice of History itself.

He is everywhere present in this last volume, and not just as that uniquely unrelenting voice, cataloguing the sins of the Soviet fathers in harsh words that conjure the reality of the camps in all their squalor and valour out of the mists of history and the great silent spaces of the Soviet present. Solzhenitsyn appears here too in his own person, demonstrating that history: as a foreman in the camp at Ekibastuz, sweating out a hunger strike with a rapidly growing tumour; as a hopeless interlocutor in the security ministries during his brief hour of favour under Khrushchev; and teaching and writing, almost to his heart's content, in a curious idyll of exile in an Asian village after his 'release' from the camps.

'I seemed', he writes of that time, 'to have lost all desire to go elsewhere (although my heart stood still when I looked at a map of Central Russia). I was aware of the whole world not as something beckoning to me from outside, but as something experienced and assimilated, entirely within myself, so that nothing remained for me to do but write about it.'

Mrs Mandelstam quotes somewhere the opinion of a nineteenth-century liberal sage that 'Russia exists to teach the rest of the world a lesson'. In *The Gulag Archipelago*, Solzhenitsyn has rough-hewn - single-handed, with 'imperfections' that are partly 'the true mark of our persecuted literature' and partly his own - a whole Old Testament of lessons and parables for the Soviet peoples.

The lessons it holds for the rest of us are perhaps not all so simple as those that will eagerly be drawn by, say, Mrs Thatcher and the leader-writers of the *Daily Telegraph*. But the first of them might be to teach us to use those freedoms - beyond 'the freedom to dine at the Ritz' - which the apparatchiks of our own system would prefer to remain largely rhetorical. He might even acknowledge this as a kind of comprehending.

29 June, 1978   **W. L. Webb**

Trying for Millwall

Jim was one of the 40 football fans arrested at the Millwall-Ipswich cup tie, and in court last week, he was fined £50 for threatening behaviour.

He is no kid. He is 25, married with two children, has a good job, and takes home about £80 a week. He has been an obsessive and devoted fan of Millwall since he was a small child, and never misses a match, home or away. He is a senior officer in a crack brigade of Millwall's army of supporters. One of the players gives him his shirt at the end of every football season. He is not, he says, a hooligan. According to him, hooligans are the young kids who run wild, smash up trains and cars, and throw bricks through windows.

That doesn't mean he doesn't fight. He does, but he and his friends regard themselves as the knights who take on battles with the knights and the leading champions among the opposing side's fans. He says, they never get involved in fights except at football matches. The rest of the week he lives, breathes and talks about little but Millwall, building up for the great event each Saturday. He says he spends an average of £20 a week on football, with the cost of drinking and travelling to away games.

Two of his friends, Alan and Tom, came to give him support at court, though they themselves had not been arrested. These two said they were members of Millwall's notorious F-Troop, the hard-core fighting force of the Millwall fans, mostly the older ones. Jim didn't want me to use his real name as he had managed to hide his arrest and fine from his wife, who would be angry – especially his wife's family.

Jim and his friends described the events at the cup tie, as they saw it. 'I reckon the police were busting for a ruck as much as we were,' Alan said. Usually the fans are segregated. But for some reason the police appeared to usher in a group of 80 Ipswich supporters to the back of the Millwall stand. After 10 minutes Ipswich scored. According to the three, the 80 supporters at the back began shouting. A friend of Jim's leaped on to the rails in the front and shouted up at them. A policeman in the front took out his truncheon, and smashed this man across the throat. People nearby pulled the policeman over the railings, ripped off his trousers and beat him up. At which all the rest of the police weighed in with their truncheons.

'Everyone went mad,' said Jim. 'People were so angry at the police that middle-aged men were joining in. I've never seen anything like it. You'd have to see the way the police provoked the crowd to understand. They shout up at us, "You come down here, just you try and I'll give it to you! You come on down and try."'

Jim was arrested running around the stands and shouting. He wasn't, he says, hitting anyone, and he was charged with 'threatening behaviour' which meant shouting. He didn't make any attempt to get away. He hadn't, he says, been in any trouble at all in the last eight years, since he left Borstal, at 17. Alan and Tom had been doing some fighting, though, but they weren't arrested. Alan, who was in Dover Borstal with Jim, has been arrested four times for football offences. He has served three three-month sentences for fighting, and one nine-months sentence for hitting a policeman. He has also had his nose broken once. These experiences don't seem to have deterred him.

What if the punishments were more severe and he risked a four- or five-year sentence? 'To tell you the truth, it wouldn't affect me. I'd still support the reputation of Millwall just as much, but it would mean that if I was arrested I'd punch the copper and get away. It would be worth trying it if you stood to go down for that long.'

Tom was once stabbed at a match, and another time he was hit on the head with a brick, and has served two sentences. 'If I get hurt I just decide that next time we meet that team I'll give it to them back three times worse,' he said.

There was, of course, a lot of bravado in what they said. They like being interviewed and were proud of having appeared on Panorama last year. 'The TV blokes took us out for a lot of drinks one Wednesday, they had a great wad of money. They said they'd be at the Charlton match on Saturday. They filmed it from some high flats near the ground, and we had a ruck.' The programme was a high point in their careers, though I doubt if their behaviour is much modified by publicity.

Alan said: 'We see loyalty as being the most important thing. We're the most loyal fans there are. We're not glory hunters, just supporting a team because they're going to win.'

Curiously, their attitude to Millwall F.C. was extremely hostile. Though they supported the team so ferociously, they hated the board of the club. 'They do nothing for the supporters, nothing. There's no social club to go to in the week. They could make a lot of money out of that. We provide all the money and support, and they give us nothing in return. The grounds are a shithouse, a right khazi, and they spend no money on it. They sell the best players, and get dead beat new ones on free transfers. If it was a nice place the fans would treat it with more respect. Until last year they only had a few toilets and people used to go just anywhere.' Last year a manager had promised a £3 million recreation centre for the fans and their families, but that manager had left after only a year, for a fatter fee elsewhere, and nothing more had been heard about the recreation centre.

They were all pleased to be interviewed. At the same time they made it clear that they didn't expect a middle-class reporter to understand them. They were polite and friendly but they could see that there was no way I could cross the chasm between us and sympathize with their attitudes towards violence.

Tom said, 'If a gang of them are coming towards you yelling "Lousy Cockney bastards!" what are you supposed to do?' Why not run away, I said. They laughed. Jim said, 'If any one of us was seen running the rest would get him next week, and probably do him more damage than what the opposition would have. Millwall supporters don't run.'

Then Jim said, 'You wouldn't understand, Kensington. We all belong together and we belong to this manor. We've been in the same schools and the same Borstals. We're all mates, and we have to stand by each other. We take a pride in where we come from. We're proud of being who we are down here.'

We were all sitting in a plastic pub in the desolation of the Elephant and Castle shopping centre, a bleak area scarred by arterial roads which run through mile after mile of grassless housing estates – at first glance, not a lot to be proud of.

Did he want anything different for his two kids? 'There isn't anything different to want for them. You've got to see that. If you're born here this is where you stay, so I hope they grow up just like us. I don't want anything different for them.' Is it a tough place to grow up? 'You've got to learn to look after yourself, but that's just natural.'

Between the three of them they could only remember one person they had been at school with who had made it in a big way. 'He has a business in Australia now, but he was never one of us. He was a loner even then.'

For these Millwall supporters, fighting was a way of life, and it was organized. Getting arrested was one of the risks, but not a great risk.

But there were other people arrested at the match who claimed they were innocent. Michael, an 18-year-old apprentice, a quiet boy who plays the guitar and whose main interest is music, says that he was wrongly convicted. He arrived alone just as the game was about to start. He had been at work all morning. He found himself confronted by a lot of Ipswich supporters who set on him and beat him up. He was arrested and charged with threatening behaviour. He had never been in trouble before, and pleaded not guilty at the court.

However he was leaned on heavily by the police who said they'd put in a word about his previous good character, so he went back to the magistrate and pleaded guilty. He was given a £75 fine, more than the others for having pleaded not guilty in the first place. 'I didn't have any witnesses. It was just my word against the policeman's, and he lied. I never get involved in any fights. I was alone and I was attacked.' I only have Michael's version, but I believe him.

Two brothers were fined £50 each that day. They were arrested before they got as far as the ground. They claimed that they were not involved in any fighting. They were walking along a street where a fight had just been dispersed when their friend tripped over. A passing mounted policeman hit this boy in the face with a stick and broke his nose. The brothers shouted at the policeman and demanded his number. He shouted back at them. They went over to get help from a St John's Ambulance man on the other side of the road, and as they were talking to him, the same policeman summoned them over to where he was standing, and then, to their amazement, arrested them for threatening behaviour. They also had never been in any trouble before. They said there had been some kind of disturbance in the street before they arrived there, but they weren't part of it.

It is exceedingly difficult for the police to deal with football violence. It is not surprising that they grab whoever they can when they are so outnumbered by violent and drunken thugs. Were these people telling the truth? Or were they just covering up for acts they were now ashamed of? It must always be difficult for anyone to be sure of the facts of who did what to whom in the middle of a riot.

20 March, 1978   **Polly Toynbee**

The English religion

Class, the one surviving English religion, is so fascinating in its life patterns that you'd think the novelists would use it far more purposefully than they do. None of them would be likely to invent anything as brilliantly barmy as Enoch Powell in his hunting pink, travelling to a meet on the Underground at the end of the war.

Short of real life inspiration at that level, that dedicated folk watcher Mervyn Jones covers the field with greater range and closer attention than most, finding his own London hunting ground and devotedly recording the widely contrasting species as they glare across the tracks at each other in the rich, strange territory north of King's Cross.

*Today the Struggle** – an ironical title, since unlike Auden's use of the word in his Spain poem 'today' evidently has no term to it – is an ambitious novel, a social and political panorama across four decades in which an uncommonly wide range of classes play their part and make their more or less human point.

I can't help feeling, for all the alert observation and data collecting, that Mr Jones is more comfortable with his youth-clubbers and bohemians than with his home bred fascists; though he doesn't flinch from handling high born Fiona ('My God, you're beautiful!'), six foot in her handmade brogues and spending her honeymoon on skis with a visit to Hitler in his Berchtesgaden eyrie as its climax.

* *Published by Quartet Books*

The name is not introduced lightly. The Unspeakable Thirties (Mr Jones, I take it, would have no truck with current attempts to jolly up the image of that atrocious decade) are the novel's seeding ground, and its structural achievement is to have located, defined and bred such vast flocks of characters without mushing them into the sort of pie the family chronicle novel usually ends up as.

16 February, 1978   **Norman Shrapnel**

Gentlemanly waste of the iron manner

There is a line from the famous Monty Python sketch about the Kray twins in which one of their purported victims remarks: 'He was a cruel man, but fair.' It is much quoted by irreverent young lawyers who have had dealings with Mr Edmond MacDermott, a stipendiary magistrate who sits at Horseferry Road Magistrates' Court.

Whether Mr MacDermott is 'fair' or not in all the senses of the word is a matter of opinion. He is certainly a severe man, personally reticent (his entry in *Who's Who* does not even give his date of birth – which was 1913). He was Assistant Director of Public Prosecutions at the time of the Oz trial, in 1971: it is hardly surprising, perhaps, that he is so very harsh with the young people who appear before him.

A typical case: 'football hooliganism'. They get a lot of these cases at Horseferry Road, as that is where the boys from the Chelsea ground are sent. This particular 19-year-old boy looked pleasant and ordinary (the police, in fact, had difficulty identifying him): he is even a corporal in the Boys' Brigade. His story was that he had just happened to get innocently involved in a punch-up between Chelsea and West Ham fans: and he added that his father had told him not to wear his West Ham scarf, so as to avoid trouble. I was totally convinced, but Mr MacDermott felt differently, fined the boy £50, and said: 'The next time you appear before me I shall send you to prison.' The young man was convinced he would lose his hard-won apprenticeship as a Post Office engineer.

MacDermott is also known by solicitors as being in the top bracket of London stipendiaries for severe sentencing – a gay boy tried recently for 'cottaging' (soliciting in public lavatories) was told by his lawyer to expect a fine of £25 and had to pay £100. Off duty, Mr MacDermott (who looks rather like Selwyn Lloyd) will behave like the perfect gent and has considerable charm and courtesy; on the bench, his manner is surly if not downright unpleasant.

His professionalism is not in question: and politically he is nobody's fool. Recently he had a case before him quite different from the usual drunk-and-disorderly, driving and taking away and so forth. Eight young anarchists from a group called Black Aid, aged between 22 and 28, had been on a tiny – 200-odd strong – demo to the West German Embassy, in protest against the mysterious deaths in Stammheim gaol of the leaders of the Baader-Meinhof group. (The anarchists, needless to say, believed they had been murdered by the German political police.)

Seven of them were up for only very minor offences – obstructing the highway, or obstructing the police. But, of course, they decided to defend themselves and say that the police had been deliberately blocking their way for sinister political reasons: which meant that the trial went on for three days instead of three hours, and one felt Mr MacDermott was not best pleased. But he was immensely careful; he explained their legal rights to them regularly and clearly; he was polite and patient – until the end.

The eighth member of the group, one Gerhard Sollinger, is 24 and Austrian. He says he works as a translator, though his English is less than perfect; he was convinced that the police had been following him throughout the demonstration. He is a burly young man, and was accused, during the general mêlée which took place as the demonstrators were leaving the Embassy, of kicking a policeman in the groin (or lower abdomen, as the police officer referred to it). The evidence was muddled; the doctor who examined the policeman afterwards 'could not be

)roduced', n or could any medical notes.

Sollinger was found guilty, is now remanded in Pentonville waiting for a qualified legal adviser (without which Mr Mac-Dermott cannot pass a prison sentence). However, the magistrate said he would be 'extremely surprised' if any lawyer could persuade him not to send the young Austrian to gaol, which would almost certainly lead to his being deported.

The two youngest, most middle-class-sounding, men were found not guilty. One, a Balliol student, asked if he might have his costs for travelling up and down from Oxford. No. 'You deserve this. You have brought it on yourself,' said Mr Mac-Dermott.

Ironically enough, the Black Aid Anarchist Group proclaims itself as strictly pacifist. Its chief activity consists of trying to organize passive resistance to prison regulations.

Although it is not just with young people whom Mr Mac-Dermott is strict, I did see him remand two young blacks with Rastafarian hairstyles to gaol on a possession of drugs charge: the strictness, and Mr MacDermott's – some say – exaggerated respect for the police and their methods, were manifested here by the fact that the supposed drugs found on the young men had not even been analysed.

And on one occasion, when I sat through a whole series of cases of travelling without a ticket (an offence in which 'intent to avoid payment' is of the essence), he only believed one young woman, a very ladylike secretary, when she said that she had had 'a blind spot'. After a few remarks like 'What is "having a blind spot"?', and his regular, irritable instructions to speak up, he let her go with the avuncular warning not to be such a careless girl again. In the cases of the young men, whatever their explanation – lost ticket, forgetfulness, not realizing their season ticket was out of date – he believed the railway officials almost every time.

There is a school of thought, perhaps a little snobbish, but widely held among lawyers, that stipendiary magistrates are failed barristers. But Mr Edmond MacDermott's career has certainly been, at the very least, a consistent one if not particularly successful in the way he might have wished.

He was only a practising barrister for four years, from 1935 until the beginning of the war. He then worked for the Department of Public Prosecutions for 26 years, until 1972, when he became a stipendiary although he is said to have been disappointed not to have succeeded Thomas Hetherington, the former Legal Secretary at the Law Officers Department.

It is fashionable to believe that lay magistrates should ideally be replaced by stipendiaries. It is a view even held by Professor R. M. Jackson, author of the classic textbook, *The Machinery of Justice in England*. He is a well-known liberal; law journals described his book, when it was reissued last year as 'outspoken', and praised its 'stimulating criticisms of the status quo'. Strong language, for lawyers. After several days in Mr Edmond MacDermott's court, to use lawyer-like language, 'I beg to question the learned gentleman's view'.

15 May, 1978   **Corinna Adam**

How we run them in

If they want to draw their stand to, the flatties, dog drivers, bald tyre bandits and any other members of the Weakheart or the Babylon, including the umbrella Brigade, the Home and Colonial or the Old Bill, could do worse than clock this book.*

To translate: If they want to draw their pension, uniformed policemen, members of the traffic patrol and any other members of the police, including those in the Special Branch, the Regional Squad office or the Metropolitan Police, might take a good look at this book.

The book in question, published today, is a field manual for young constables, handing down to them the thousand and one ways of spotting criminals going about their business compiled during the 31 years' service of Mr David Powis, senior Deputy Assistant Commissioner in the London CID. It also contains a lengthy glossary of thieves' slang, among some grimmer

* *The Signs of Crime – A Field Manual for Police, by David Powis, published by McGraw-Hill.*

appendices detailing how far guns shoot and what constitutes the best protection against rifle fire.

The more traditional skills of the 'wally', or uniformed policeman – drawing deductions of criminal intent from apparently quite ordinary actions – form the basis of the book. People who have wet sleeves or cuffs, on leaving lavatories, for example, may have secreted contraband, stolen property or a weapon in the cistern. Men in cars wearing new boiler suits

should be looked out for: 'The chance of three or four men in a saloon car, all wearing new overalls, being engaged in lawful pursuits is sufficiently unlikely to justify the vehicle being stopped there and then.' The CID chief also says that those with extreme political views are 'usually scruffy and occasionally personally dirty' – and in this are very different from ordinary thieves, most of whom are 'reasonably conservative' in their dress.

Young policemen are told to watch out for loiterers possessing

'These are your rights' cards. 'Obviously they will be carried by people who consider it at least possible they will break the law. . . . Thus they will be carried by male homosexuals, by industrial and other agitators, by Angry Brigade inadequates . . . Anyway, possession of such written matter often means subsequent false complaints against you. Be circumspect with intellectual malcontents. They can be bitchy and small-minded in these complaints.'

As for loiterers, suspicious types include the jogger, running about residential streets either at dusk or in the early morning. 'There seems to be a correlation between such persons and homosexual nuisances.'

In confirming loiterers' stories about themselves, outward signs like the chalk dust in schoolmasters' clothes and eyelashes, the electrician's tiny half-healed pinpoint holes on the bulbs of fingers and forefingers due to handling sharp-ended strands of multicore wire, and the 'livestock' smell about farmworkers are all helpful. Doctors and dentists, says Mr Powis, are marked by a 'certain confident arrogance'.

Finally, the manual gives advice to police in the witness box faced with sharp-tongued barristers. It tells young policemen to bear in mind even the humblest of peace officers has a 'dignity and wholesomeness' above that of the lawyer. 'To be blunt about it . . . the size of their annual income depends upon their reputation for success . . . just let these facts fortify your resolve when your integrity is unfairly attacked.'

16 December, 1977   **Alec Hartley**

Trading blow for blow

Three strokes in the Isle of Man are degrading treatment. Two hundred in Saudi Arabia are the Sharia law of the land, calling to mind Professor Trevor-Roper's dictum that the beginning of wisdom in foreign affairs is to recognize that they are foreign. There is a slight remedy, short of cancelling defence contracts, sending the pound into a spiral, and starving the

West of oil (for as the frantic Foreign Office knows to its em-barrassment King Khaled pays pipers and is thus able, in the world as constituted, to call tunes). The remedy is to assist the Saudi Government, and perhaps others of the same confession, to uphold in every particular the requirements of the Koran. Alcohol and gambling would be forbidden to Saudi, and like-minded, potentates abroad. Adultery, an offence not unknown to some of the West End escort agencies, would be visited by physical penalties of a severity which we forbear to describe, although those who are interested could watch them being carried out. Doubtless there are other requirements and prohibitions which the Arabists of the Foreign Office, by a diligent search of the *ipsissima verba* and the *summa*, could com-pile for the guidance of distinguished Saudi (and comparable) visitors. Indeed it could be pointed out that any dereliction from them would amount to apostasy, and that unfortunately the Islamic punishment for that is death.

16 June, 1978   **Leader**

Flying high

If you want to poke fun at Parliament, all you have to do is read the account of Parliamentary proceedings in Hansard. To prove my point here is an example from last week's Hansard:

'The Earl of Clancarty asked Her Majesty's Government: whether they are aware that Monsieur Robert Galley, the then French Minister of Defence, in his radio interview on the France-Inter radio on 21st February 1974 stated that the gendarmerie are playing a very large part in official investigations into unidentified flying object sightings and alleged landings; and whether our police have been likewise officially instructed to collect reports and investigate these unidentified flying objects.

Lord Harris of Greenwich: the Government has no knowledge of either the radio interview to which the Question refers, or the role played by the gendarmerie in investigating unidentified flying objects. The police in this country have not been asked to collect reports, or investigate unidentified flying objects. The jurisdiction and power of the police are normally confined to terrestrial activities, but I have every confidence that should an occasion arise where there is evidence that an unidentified flying object has landed within a police area, the police force will investigate it with its customary vigour. However, until there is some clear indication that the frequency of such occurrences is likely to impose a significant burden on the police, I doubt whether it will prove fruitful to issue guidance on this subject.'

8 December, 1977   **Peter Hillmore**

Max Ernst's novel without words

Adventures of the Lion of Belfort, whose deadly element is mud; as a representative of the law, he apprehends the woman whose head has turned into a flower as she makes off with a fan of spoons. Turned refuse collector, he hooks an interesting decapitee out of a hole: the basket on his back is full of wings. Next, he shoots his lover and awaits the guillotine with leonine impassivity, since he knows he is, in reality, the executioner himself. Transfiguration and apotheosis follow.

That is Book One of *Une Semaine de Bonté*, one of the great novels of the twentieth century, although it is constructed not with words but with pictures. Book Two is about water, cities, bedrooms, sepulchres, all inundated. In the flooded drawing-room, a girl insouciantly plays with a ball. As for Book Three, the fire and dragon sequence, go and see for yourself.

Surrealism is a mode of perception in which the idea transcends both word and image and may be expressed by either. *Une Semaine de Bonté* is one of the great masterpieces of surrealism and now, happily, accessible at a reasonable price so that it may go and spread its virus of the imagination at a time when, God knows, we need it. The reproductions are a wee bit muddy but you can't have everything, not at £3.20.

For this novel in collage, the reader may provide his own narrative line from the anxiety, paranoia, and disorder of the senses for which Max Ernst's pictorial text provides such abundance of material. Everything is magnificently, serenely, blackly, sacrilegiously funny. Each malign little picture, those grainy engravings that invert the visual language of the nineteenth century, insinuates itself so mercilessly into the consciousness that it is the real world that soon seems peculiar and *Une Semaine de Bonté* starts looking like what it really is, a snapshot album of the here and now compiled by the unconscious.

Ernst's collages have been the source of innumerable imitators who faithfully obey the letter but, like the followers of Joyce, have a fatal incapacity for reproducing the spirit – here, the infernal, heroic gaiety of an absolute lack of belief, of a passionate and positive faith in nothing but the power of the imagination to transform itself and the world. It sits on the special shelf that, besides, contains only *Ulysses* and *The Trial*.

2 March, 1978   **Angela Carter**

The inland sea of pleasure

Obsession is the key to the Floating World, a phrase for the Ukiyoe tradition that included literature, Kabuki theatre and the art that is now on show at the British Museum. It was a tradition dedicated to the study of beautiful women and meant 'floating on a sea of pleasure'. It started in the courts of the Emperor's city, Kyoto, and spread in the seventeenth century to the new urban boom town, then Edo, now Tokyo, described even then as 'new and brash'.

Just how far the feeling of floating differed from what we call erotica can be sensed in the definition given in Asai Ryoi's mid-seventeenth-century *Tales of the Floating World*: '. . . living only for the moment, turning our full attention to the pleasures of the moon, the snow, the cherry blossoms and the maple leaves, singing songs, drinking wine and diverting ourselves just in floating, floating, caring not a whit for the pauperism staring us in the face, refusing to be disheartened, like a gourd floating along with the river current, this is what we call Ukiyoe . . .'

When the West discovered the art of Ukiyoe in the last century it was with the hunger of a Puritan plunging into a feast of erotica. Thus began the first chapter of a confused history of incomprehension about another culture's sensual traditions. It rambles on today in a general failure to grasp the difference between what we call erotic and what for the Japanese was deep obsession.

In fact it is one face that emerges out of this floating sea of trees and gourds. It's the face of the courtesan made most famous through the prints of Utamaro. The face gazes at her own image in the mirror, as obsessive as the cult that surrounds her. At the same time she is the ideal subject for an artist keen to display superb skill of line, breathtaking dexterity with the delicacy of fine fabrics, and a worldly eye that must idealize the inhabitants of this floating world. This line, that curve, the play of material and the fold of a robe take the place of the nude body. It's a world of carefully-designed interiors, and oblique suggestion.

The artists who illustrated the books, painted the scrolls and then came to the notice of the West with prints were servicing an obsession born of the dullness of arranged marriages, of the frustrations of the samurai deprived of the chance to fight and of the restless craving for pleasure of a rich merchant class hemmed in by the isolation policy of Japan.

It was a world of almost enforced leisure that created its own rituals and kept its own order. It ranged through the tea houses and the geisha to the great prostitutes who occupied a rank of their own quite inaccessible to even the middling rich. These were the courtesans idealized by the artists and worshipped by the sons of rich fathers like the exotic actresses of the nineteenth century.

The artists documented each hour of their day in the high class brothels – the Green Houses. These ran in orderly fashion through 24 hours with a time and place for everything. Only Utamaro hinted at the weariness of it all when the last client had finally gone and the courtesan's shoulders could slump beneath the studied landscape of her robes. Occasionally an artist gives a glimpse of a cynical face above the flowers. Usually the pleasing effect is achieved through flow of design in which delicacy of silk and the tracing of patterns takes over from the figure they cover. So much so that the image of the courtesan became a way of advertising textile design: a practical twist in the Floating World.

Suddenly Utamaro shattered the delicacy of the courtesan's world with an image far removed from the constrictions of those little interiors. For the urban men of Kyoto and Edo it must have come as a well-aimed shock. The most sensuous women in all Japan were far from reach, out on the rocks of Ise, great Amazons diving for the abalone shells. He showed them without a trace of ingratiating fashion, big naked women among women with children at the breast and not a sign of the men who appear in Utamaro's most overt Green House scenes.

8 June, 1978   **Caroline Tisdall**

Durrell's Egypt

This must certainly be Gippy tummy I feel. That legendary indisposition. What a treat not only to see the country but succumb to it.

Lawrence Durrell's Egypt (BBC-2), to be shown on Sunday but released in advance no doubt so that we may better prepare ourselves with prayer and fasting, was the sort of long, elaborate meal during which men drop off like flies.

I would like you to test the validity of Banks-Smith's second law of television, which is that it is not possible to listen and look with equal attention. Hence the difficulty of getting a camel through the eye of a needle. The two humps are the trouble.

Durrell and Egypt were continually getting stuck in the same doorway. One must say that Durrell (looking exactly like W. C. Fields, which was distracting for a start) had the better of it. Sometimes he read from his own books. I would say very badly, if I believed an author could read his own work badly.

Like Eliot, his delivery was flat and uninflected so that the prose unrolled like some long Eastern carpet whose complicated patterns and soft colours you tried to interpret on your knees. While at this pious exercise, you were distracted by what Durrell called 'bits of cinema film, flap, flap, flap'. It was like trying to read a book in a train and being told to look out of the window.

When he had sweated from Alexandria to Cairo, Luxor-Thebes to Aswan, Durrell told Peter Adam, the producer, that the only way to capture the spirit of the place was to close your eyes and see it. I cannot say if Adam appreciated the advice.

I am inclined to think it was a mistake to use the novels at all. Within minutes I was chasing a hare. 'The muezzin's voice,' read Durrell, 'was hanging like a hair in the palm-cooled upper airs of the city.' In my mind's eye I saw a sort of skinned rabbit swinging and it took some yoicks and whipping in to drag me whining away from this image.

Just gossiping, he could be beautifully Beachcomber. 'I have vivid memories of Diana Gould (now Mrs Menuhin) doing an entre-chat on the roof.' Well one would, wouldn't one? Though I should mention that the roof, being Alexandrian, was flat. And while we are on dancers, so to speak, there was the navel disaster of the belly dancer who, spinning from end to end of a barge 'like an enormous top' turned the whole boat over, tipping host, guests, and Durrell into the Nile. A story clearly on the run from Durrell's Esprit de Corps books.

There were striking and memorable images like the Egyptians in long white nighties and latticed lifts going up and down like mechanical angels but they seemed independent of Durrell's commentary.

It is easy to criticize. I know. I know. As Durrell says in *Justine*. But he doesn't. And it isn't.

6 April, 1978   **Nancy Banks-Smith**

Letter from Kazakhstan

The jagged line of lightning flitters across the distant steppe where the border starts with China. But here the sun is a blowtorch at noon when the wind blows from the red and black sands of the Karakhum and the Khiselkhum deserts, a wind that blows through a city of towering new apricot-colour apartment blocks, boulevards, department stores and theatres. This is Karaganda, the city that sprang into being in the days when Stalingrad was under siege and the Russians were shifting their industries to safer places eastwards in the 'Forbidden Land' of the Kazakh steppe.

It has a population of half a million of 98 different nationalities. The land all around was bought for the princely sum of 250 roubles by a French Count Karno just 100 years ago, when a wandering Kazakh shepherd found some lumps of coal to burn on his campfire. You can still see, on the edge of the city, a few abandoned hovels piled around with earth against the Siberian frosts and with stones clapped on their turf roofs to hold them on when the wind roars out of Siberia.

But that is all that's left now of the days, not so long ago, when camels were used to transport the coal and men and women were tempted in from the yoor-ta tents of the steppe to work in the European-owned coal mines for a few kopeks in the hand before being driven off again, broken by malnutrition, TB, and nystagmus from chopping coal in crude candlelit mine tunnels. The memory is perpetuated in the way everything here is still reckoned in English feet and yards. Huge coal seam deposits are still called by the names that English mining engineers gave them, like the Mary-Anna.

The steppe soil is so salt, so sour, on these flat salt-pans, that extra earth has to be brought in to grow the poplar trees on the wide pink boulevards where the steppe wind cuts the smoke of swarms of Cossack-made motorbikes and drab green Russian lorries stencilled starkly Post or Bread or Petrol, while the militia wave them on with white batons.

This is a coal-mining city and a great many of its coal miners own new cars; stout-hearted Volgas or Moskvitches or the lighter Lada, and many have the small wooden dacha out on the steppe for weekends. Sons and grandsons of the old chaban sheepherders are the new mine managers: like Zholumbet Muhamedzhanov, a suave-suited Kazakh earning £10,000 a year.

'I still love the steppe though,' he says. 'I go there hunting. Oh – for saigak or the kashkara – the wolves.' The saigak is a sort of antelope and its dried meat is highly prized in the gourmand restaurants of Paris and Berlin. 'Sometimes the saigak herds come so close to the city we have to fight with them,' say the Kazakhs. There is a German influence here too: descendants of the German miners who migrated here in the 1920s, and so you meet a Comrade Fischer and a Comrade Littmann.

Rheinhold Littmann, blond, Teutonic-looking, is a 'brigadier' team leader of coalface workers, as well as being deputy to Kazakhstan's central Soviets. Giant coal seams all of fifteen feet and more thick, and busy export of coal from here as far as France and Italy, give these steppe miners a living standard to make our British miners wince: 30-hour working week, and new flats with bathroom, heating, lighting and phone, all for 12 roubles a month out of average earnings of 350 roubles a month, and some coalface workers pick up, with bonus, the equivalent of nearly £1,000 a month: income tax only 8 per cent.

But, once outside the city, and that old steppe is just the same that Marco Polo and Genghis Khan saw (they proudly call him Chin-ghiz Khan): as you travel down the old Silk Route road that leads from Samarkand into Outer Mongolia and China, cunning swarms of midges raise bumps like pickled onions on your face, and mandarin-bearded Kazakhs, in sable fur hats, jog on horseback or on their big black-maned camels.

Far out, towards the Karakal mountains that rise blue-white springing like Chinese dragons off the steppe, you can still see the famous yoor-tas used, the Ghenghis Khan goat-hair felt tents of the Silk Route, but the goat-hair felt for them has to get turned out in two factories down in Karaganda and Alma-Ata these days.

The yoor-ta is still the only practical thing for the chaban shepherds faring with their flocks from one end of the great steppe to the other: a yoor-ta costs only about £500, will last nearly for ever, and can be dismantled and packed on the back of a horse or a lorry in just 25 minutes. Cool in summer, snug in winter when the kashkara are howling outside, it's like living under a trilby hat somebody has set down on the steppe. And in a yoor-ta you must still eat boiled horse washed down with the Genghis Khan drink of kou-miss, mare's milk, while squatting round the one low circular table with its red star painted on it. Even the chabans have their brand-new cars and lorries now, and they use solid gold teaspoons to stir their hot sweet milky Kazakh tea – 'We do not like Russian tea; this is Indian tea to make Kazakh tea; Kazakh tea chaksai – very good – chaksai!' They eat their horsemeat off plates decorated with the word Sputnik, because it is right here that Russian cosmonauts get guided back to earth.

There are still mosques and there are Musselman graves out on the steppe. Each grave with its little wall to keep out the kashkara. The chabans no longer retain their single tuft of hair by which the faithful were to be lifted up straight to Paradise; instead, they say, they get their uplift now from acting in translations of Shakespeare.

'We are doing Richard Three tomorrow night!' – and learning English and reading Defoe, Dickens and 'John' Priestley; and they have just started to get enthusiastic about that Western game of 'rugger' and are planning to send a team to Britain. (Welsh rugby fans will be intrigued to know that the Kazakh national anthem is titled 'Land of My Fathers.')

5 December, 1977   **John Aeron Summers**

Rubbing shoulders with the mighty

It is one thing, as all Wales takes for granted, to have God on their side – and the fact that Gareth Edwards is at scrum half absolutely clinches it. Not to mention the astonishing J. P. R., quicksilver Gerald, that pit-a-patter pinball merchant Bennett, and one or two other handy coalface toughs who look awfully big in scarlet.

England have beaten Wales but once in the last 14 years. This afternoon the bedraggled homesters go out again at Twickenham all in white for what has become a ritual slaughter of the innocents. Every two years the Welsh particularly relish committing if not murder, a pretty open-and-shut case of manslaughter at Twickenham – and with Gareth celebrating his historic 50th cap they propose no mistakes today.

Neil Kinnock, MP, had been rabbiting on all week about not being able to get a ticket. Hard cheese. A few million other Welshies were in the same boat, but they were not kicking up a fuss about it – just drinking themselves dopey in dingy taprooms and miners' welfare bars, with the unfairness of it all. Kinnock says Twickenham will be full of English society women who can't tell a forward pass from an elbow in the groin and will probably not see another rugger match as long as they live. Yesterday a policeman who is involved in a real murder case gave Kinnock his ticket. 'I will,' said Labour's loudhailer, 'back every police pay claim for the rest of my life.'

Rumour has it there was an ad in last week's *South Wales Echo* which read: 'Wanted Desperately. Two Stand Tickets for Twickenham. Offer Rolls-Royce Car in Exchange.' Next day there was a reply ad saying: 'Will yesterday's advertiser please state what year is the Rolls-Royce.'

Not that the cocky crinkly-haired Gwent and Powys jinkers are as *absolutely* confident as usual this year. The longtime bragging over their rugby football stuck in their larynx during the summer when the British Lions, captained and coached and overbalanced by Welshmen, came an awful cropper in New Zealand. Though, mind you, Gareth, Gerald and J. P. R. were not there. They will be this afternoon – so hang on to your hats, for it must be said that in their singular ways the three of them represent just about the most zanily exciting talents that the great old game has ever seen.

England have had their usual week of whistling to keep up their spirits. They have a doughty bunch of forwards, to be sure, one of whom, Beaumont, is this year's new captain. He said yesterday that he was 'looking to the lads to get stuck in early'. That's at least more of a defiant pep talk than that of an England captain not so very long ago whose exhortation to his team consisted solely of 'Bugger me, fellows, I'm bloody nervous . . . Anyone got a fag before we go out?' – which he followed, once out, by winning the toss but then, his nerves still all a-jangle, allowing the Welsh captain to have choice of ends *as well as* the kick-off.

The last Henry V to captain an England rugby team was also in on the act this week. Eric Evans, all red rose with face to match, whose side in the 1950s was beaten only once in 13 internationals, thinks the English crowd at Twickenham doesn't cheer loud enough these days for their white-kneed chaps. Evans said he would be bellowing from the stand today even more whoopingly than he used to when leading the pack. 'I just cannot understand anyone who is not proud of his school, town, county, or country,' he barked yesterday.

Certainly there is enough reasonable plonk going in the car park beforehand to inspire more than the odd clap for a chap. The same sort of sentiment as Evans's was voiced in a letter to the editor of *Rugby World* last year.

'Sir,' wrote A. R. C. Westlake, from stockbroker Surrey. 'I suggest that at Twickenham the following words should be sung to the National Anthem: "God Bless St George's land/Mighty of heart and hand/God bless our land!/England's the land we love/ Let's give a mighty shove/Raise her all lands above/God save our land!/ England! England! England!" (Shouted). Inspired by this, and with more practice in passing and kicking, England might even win. Yours, etc. . . .'

It's that 'passing' bit that worries me. Anyway, today, as well as new men at fly half, wing forward and a green young centre, England's selectors may well have been accidentally inspired by picking a fiercesome big West Countryman called Nelmes for his first home international. For Nelmes, who sells hand tools around the valleys, has not only been Cardiff's vice-captain for five years, but lives only a couple of hundred yards from Gareth Edwards! He has played countless times against the dreaded Welsh front row, so England will have one at least who is not overawed by the terrible tough trio from Ponty.

Nelmes, with a yeoman's face and oaken thighs, is, they say, the most charming and gentle of chaps both before and after matches. In between times though he is mighty uncompromising. He puts you in mind of that line by a massive Irish forward who, asked by a waiter what sort of omelette, replied: 'An *egg* omelette, of course, you daft twit!'

Actually, to understand better what the fuss is all about, switch on BBC-1 at 1.40 to see Elaine Rose's film *It Remains to be Seen!* in which that splendid Thespian nutter Kenneth Griffith sentimentalizes on his very first Twickenham visit with his headmaster in 1952. Wales won that day too: Lewis Jones was hobbling, I seem to remember, but helped send his namesake, the Olympic sprinter Ken, to bring home the bacon.

In the film, Griffith relives his journey up to town from his beloved Tenby. When the train hits Paddington, the band is playing Land of Hope and Glory. Methinks the English can forget the Glory bit for yet another year.

4 February, 1978   **Frank Keating**

Pressure waves

Sir – I write to draw readers' attention to the new British all-comers record set on television on 31 January at about 11.55 p.m. This is the third time in three months that the 'Dynamic Weather Forecast' record has been broken.

The record for the greatest number of symbols added to or

removed from the weather map in a single forecast for so long held by that great stalwart, Jack Scott, was broken in November 1977 by Michael Fish. He increased the score from seven to an unheard of eleven – best in the world last year.

Fish was unable to equal this until 26 January, although several scores of eight or more were achieved in the intervening period. However, Bill Giles has shown rapid improvement over the last few months, and his average has risen from 5.38 to an astonishing 7.62 in the first month of the new season.

Then Giles scored an unequivocal 14 in the late evening forecast which must surely have ensured his place for the Commonwealth Games. It is to be hoped that the heat of international competition will not lead to a repeat of the early evening performance through his uncertain temperament –

Yours faithfully,
Peter Meredith Williams
Vaynor Lane, Cefn Coed,
Merthyr Tydfil, Mid Glamorgan.

3 February, 1978

Sorry, Brian

Over the years now, snugly incognito in a pack of confident questioning reporters, I have watched Brian Clough operate. Once I asked him for a quote and he thought for half an hour that I was a minicab driver. Now I try not to catch his eye, for regularly it is he who is asking us the questions. He is said not to tolerate shy men or shirkers and, seeing I am both, I safely keep my distance, enjoying his hale heart on his sleeve while my pale one is in my boots.

He once did tell me that he and his wife woke up to my byline picture every morning. I did not know whether to take it as a compliment or an insult, whether to smile or smirk. Because English soccer managers, you see, are not meant to read The *Guardian*. It is very confusing.

So are most things about Brian Clough. What impression, for

instance, will he give when he walks out at Wembley for today's League Cup Final? He will be leading out an astonishing Nottingham Forest team. Will he be the bouncy one-of-the-boys in his tracksuit? Or his suited I've-seen-it-all-before swagger? Or will his very real wide-eyed awe and justifiable pride show through on this day of days?

Last week Clough did what, to my knowledge, no other manager has done. He asked the League if his assistant, Peter Taylor – they go together like Bosanquet and Gall, Hobbs and Sutcliffe – could walk alongside him in the parade. The League refused – which says a lot about the Football League, sure, but even more about Brian Clough. His enemies say he is generously nutty. His friends say he is nuttily over-generous.

Clough and Taylor have been together now for 20 years, more than half Clough's life. They met when Taylor was transferred from Coventry to be Middlesbrough's first-team goalkeeper and immediately twigged that a raw roustabout reserve who had just finished his National Service was making his gloved hands sting something terrible during practice. Aye, aye, thought Taylor, who is this nut? He is still wondering. Taylor was the only person who persuaded the young centre-forward that he had a future. Nobody else at the club even hinted at it and Clough usually asked for a transfer every other day; and on every other day Taylor would calm him down.

When the youngster finally bagged the first team's red shirt he went totally and gloriously bonkers and in Middlesbrough's next 271 League matches Clough scored 251 goals. By the Easters of 1958, '59, and '60 he was cracking his egg with well over 40 goals in the bank. These days famous international centre-forwards are pleased to have potted a quarter as many. Only the legendary Dixie Dean (283 in his first 300 League games) keeps Clough out of the record books.

In his second of two appearances for the Football League in 1959, Clough scored five out of five against the Irish League in Belfast. A week later, Walter Winterbottom put him in the full England side, between Greaves and Charlton for the games against Wales and Sweden. He did not score: Wales drew and Sweden won. In 1961 he went to Sunderland and in 1962, at

Bury, he did his knee and that, most effectively, was that. He was 26, an unqualified Second Division has-been.

Like Don Revie, an older man in whose plodding footsteps he has danced, Clough was born in Middlesbrough, the very nub of England's soccer nursery – if you do not count Scotland, that is. In 1935 the depression was still depressing when Clough was born. Six sons and two daughters stretched dad's sweet-factory wages to the limit. His father lived to be proud of his son. Mam, as mams are there, was always his greatest supporter. If tears are channelled around that snubnose this afternoon as he sniffs the Wembley atmosphere, the first two will be for them . . .

He says he cried too when he failed the 11-plus. He left Sec. Mod. at 15 to serve a term as office boy to the local firm. For two years he was post boy and junior clerk in ICI's work-study department. He kicked balls about on Saturdays and Sundays (opening bat in the summer) and before his National Service, Middlesbrough had at least made a note of how to spell his name.

Tears too when he was told, finally, that he would never play soccer again. George Hardwick, one-time England captain, was manager of Sunderland then. George not only organized Clough's testimonial but encouraged him to coach the junior side. He was on his way. (He does not forget: half a dozen years later, when Hardwick was trying to make ends meet at insignificant Gateshead, Clough took his championship side from Derby to play a match to pay off the little club's debts. Stories like that punctuate even the most skimming read of his career).

Still under 30, he knew his only hope as a soccer buff with importance was to start at the very bottom. He did. Of the 92 League clubs, the very bottom of the Fourth Division then was, wouldn't you know, Hartlepool United (bless them, they are still, as ever, looking for re-election). So Clough became the League's youngest manager in 1965.

Hartlepool's local journalists felt silly when sometime Saturdays they had to telephone over the gate receipts in shillings, not pounds. Soon the club's long-term benefactor, Ernie Lord, gave up the ghost and without his support Barclays bilked. Clough withdrew his own salary. He dismissed the team's bus driver and drove the thing himself. Bells ringing for the first time, he went cap in hand to pubs and clubs, to the Rotary and the Darby and Joan: he raised almost £10,000 and kept the club solvent. All to persuade the forgotten manager of faraway unknown Burton Albion to become his assistant. He was Peter Taylor, one-time Middlesbrough goalie.

At the end of the 1967 season, Hartlepool won promotion for the only time in their history. (Their two previous claims to fame in the century were to make the FA Cup Fourth Round, in 1955, and to concede the record number of 109 League goals four years later). By then Clough and Taylor had left for Derby County, languishing at the bottom of the Second Division. (With them, by the way, they took John McGovern, an ungainly fawn, who will be captain of Nottingham Forest at Wembley today, leading the parade right behind the trumpet major.)

To my generation Derby County have always had a ring about them. It did not last. They won the first Cup Final after the war with a marvellous team ('Stamps Has Scored! Stamps Has Scored!' I can hear Glendenning shouting it still). By the end of the sixties however, they were anonymous sluggards and on the way to the Third Division. How Clough and Taylor transformed them is already entrenched in the legend. They arrived to a players' revolt; they thought Clough and Taylor were too young. Clough turned the place inside out. When they won the First Division championship just four years later only three players of the original staff of 28 survived (Durban, Webster, and Hector). After six years the two of them left to another revolt – only this time the players threatened to strike because they were going. There were unparalleled town-hall meetings to get them to stay.

They had become too big for the club. As Clough put it in one of his more considered speeches at the time: 'Suddenly the board were not as big at the golf club as they used to be. People were saying to them, "Who's running Derby? You, or Clough?" In the old days when we were floundering in the Second Division they used to answer "Clough, of course, that's what we pay him for." But recently everyone knows the answer before they ask the question.' As well as this, five of the seven doddering directors found it hard at the golf club to defend Clough's Labour Party canvassing, his free tickets to picketing miners and his docking of players' wages for a regular contribution to Oxfam.

By then Clough was a national television star. What had started as a vibrant and refreshing view of soccer had now turned into an act in which the likes of Coleman and Parkinson were actually nodding earnestly and wondrously after asking him opinions on socialism, Biafra, Vietnam, Watergate, and the Common Market. By that spring the nation would not have been surprised to hear him discussing the Budget with Robin Day. Serious television critics suddenly and at last woke up with hatchet in hand. As David Sylvester said in the *Sunday Times*, 'He exhibits the brand of egotism we associate with bright children whose emotional development has not kept pace with their brain.' When they could get a word in edgeways, the nation uttered a heartfelt 'Hear, hear'.

From Derby they went to Brighton. Clough never took to the South (and vice versa: it is hard still to find a good word for him there) and soon our pierrot left Taylor to run the show and took cap and bells to the then mighty Leeds United. He was to succeed Don Revie. This time there was yet another players' revolt, and Clough, ambitiously trying too much too soon, was left high and dry by a weak-kneed board after a disastrous month and a bit. He slunk off to count his pay-off, which was finger-lickin' good, but his heart was hurt badly by the steely bum's rush Revie's narrow-eyed team had given him.

He joined Forest in 1975. At once Derby asked him back. He hummed and hedged but finally turned them down. He felt he was on to something at Nottingham, even though they then languished, as ever, among the dead men of the Second Division, lower even than their next door neighbours, County.

Taylor inevitably joined him at Nottingham – and just as inevitably they immediately won promotion last year. Within a month of this new season they were clear at the top of the First. They are now an astonishing six points ahead and with games in hand. Just for fun, too, they play at Wembley today.

And it is fun. Hark to this, from the usually staid and studied and responsible *Sunday Telegraph* last month. Their football correspondent, Colin Malam, was stirred to write, 'They have entranced half the nation. Reports of people with only a casual interest in football altering their daily routine to catch Forest's latest outpouring of pleasure on television suggests the team has captivated the affection of the public in a way not experienced since the Busby Babes ... It is not surprising. Forest's beguilingly simple and devastatingly effective style, allied to a transparent honesty of purpose, communicates a sense of pure joy. They make you feel good to be alive.'

Clough does not allow his players to cheat. Or even niggle the ref. Nor grow hair long. He asked Nottingham's supporters to stop singing obscene songs: they stopped and flew banners the next week saying, 'Sorry, Brian.' Like one of his heroes, Muhammad Ali, he himself has lately taken a vow of silence: there was a genuine surge of popular groundswell enthusiasm for him to get the England managership – but he and Taylor were happy to run the national youth team under Greenwood. He knows his time may yet come. So do we.

He is kind to his lovely wife. He loves his children kindly. He can up and take a week's holiday in Torremolinos at the very peak of the championship season (though I wonder what he would do if his centre-forward thought the same). If the mood takes him he has been known to buy a slap-up meal for a seemingly impoverished student who happened to be eating at the same restaurant. He can be witheringly dismissive and rude to autograph hunters, reporters, or players – as well as directors, dukes or minor royalty. On the other hand he can be charming to rogues. He can send a huge bouquet of flowers to Mrs Frank O'Farrell when her husband was sacked from Manchester United, or make a long out-of-his-way hospital visit to see a sick journalist who has been giving him stick for years.

If he ever stood for Parliament he says he would do it in a safe Tory constituency – just to show them. He is said to be more worked up if Yorkshire lose badly at cricket than when his football team wins well. He graciously replied to The *Guardian*'s northern soccer correspondent, Paddy Barclay, who had written asking him for an interview, saying he would love to play squash with him 'as long as there was no mention of soccer'. I bet, come to think of it, he is a darned good squash player – they are all introverts trying to be extroverts, or is it the other way round? He likes drinking, but hates drunks. For all his talk of Rolls-Royce or British Leyland he still drives a Mercedes.

His longtime pin-up has been Deborah Kerr. His longtime buddy has been Geoff Boycott. See what I mean? How can you possibly pin down in print a geezer who fancies the rosy English Deborah and the thorny English Geoffrey, I ask you?

It is as well he is letting his team do all the talking for him these days. So I reckon we could be in for an extremely eloquent afternoon at Wembley.

16 March, 1978   **Frank Keating**

Theresa finds a gap in the FA's defence

Theresa Bennett, aged 12, the clever, ferocious and frustrated girl footballer, was awarded £200 damages yesterday because she was deprived of the opportunity of playing with a boys' team last season, and £50 for the injury to her feelings. Deputy Circuit Judge Michael Harris decided at Newark County Court that she was a victim of unlawful sex discrimination by the Football Association and the Nottinghamshire FA, which refused to register her as a player with Muskham United under-12 boys' team.

This judgement applies only to the particular case of Theresa. But a precedent is always seen as a precedent, and hundreds of girl footballers must now be thinking of exploiting the decision. The Football Association cannot even guess what will happen. It stands like a defensive wall of players awaiting a free kick, with its hands nervously crossed over its masculine privileges.

Theresa, of Little Carlton, Newark, said after the hearing that she would happily play for the under-14 boys' team, 'if they will accept me.' For their part, the two FAs asked for a stay of execution while they considered an appeal. Sir Harold Thompson, chairman of the FA, said afterwards that the case raised all kinds of issues. 'I have no idea whether there will be a flood of girls applying to play with boys – I am not psychic,' he said. 'We shall have to wait and see.'

One possibility the FA will consider is whether an age limit should be set for girls wanting to play in and against boys' teams. Sir Harold was only joking when he said: 'We may have an application from Diana Dors – I don't know.'

Any future cases brought by older girl footballers would have to be judged in the light of Section 44 of the Sex Discrimination Act of 1975. This states that sex discrimination is not unlawful where 'the average woman' seeks to take part in a game, sport or other activity of a competitive nature where her physical strength, stamina and physique put her at a disadvantage with 'the average man'. The judge accepted medical evidence, given for both sides, that physique under the age of puberty was not significantly different between boys and girls. As for the Act's reference to 'average woman', he said it would be farcical to define this as a national average woman aged 42.43 years, or whatever it was. For the purpose of the case he took 'average' to mean average boys and girls under 12.

Outside the court Mr Glyn Jones, an official of Muskham United, said that the under-12 boys' team, deprived of Theresa's tigerish skills, finished next to bottom of the league. The team would certainly have done better with Theresa.

During the hearing Theresa chewed bubble gum 'because I was a bit nervous about what would happen'. But on the whole she found the case a little boring and kept looking round the room 'because they were talking about what could happen when I was 19 when we were really on about things now, when I am 12'.

She supports Manchester United. For what it is worth – and it is always well to follow anyone on a winning streak – she tips Argentina to win the World Cup.

16 June, 1978   **Michael Parkin**

The political football

The profession of politics is a peculiar game. It is not so much dirty in the way that World Cup football is dirty; more often it is just plain brutal in the way that top-class rugby is brutal. What might look like a particularly savage foul under the rules of normal life is accepted as part of the game at Westminster. As a result, quite nice people do very nasty things to each other without the expectation of complaint on either side.

Mr Reginald Maudling, one-time Chancellor of the Exchequer and Deputy Prime Minister and twice a serious contender for the leadership of the Conservative Party, has been on the receiving end of quite a few cruelties from his colleagues as well as from fate. Now on the back benches after a long career as a senior Minister or shadow spokesman for his party, he wanly accepts in a new volume of memoirs* that the only sensible time to kick a man in politics is when he is down. There is not much doubt that Mr Maudling is down.

And yet . . . how different things might have been. It is true that there is little profit in speculating about what might have happened to the course of modern British politics if Mr Maudling had not been narrowly defeated by Mr Edward Heath in the election for the Tory leadership in 1965. But I believe there is some genuine relevance in considering what might have happened if Mr Chancellor Maudling's economic policies – the famous (or to some notorious) 'dash for freedom' – had not been cut short by the 1964 General Election. Such speculation is relevant to the present economic argument because Mr Maudling's dash for freedom was probably the last full flowering of the Keynesian approach to economic management, just before the shades of monetarism began to close round Mr Maudling's successors at the Treasury. Attempts on similar lines were made by Lord George Brown in the later

* *Reginald Maudling: Memoirs (Sidgwick & Jackson).*

60s, but never got off the ground.

Mr Maudling rightly makes this controversy the centre-piece of his book, and defends his position vigorously. He introduces it with an illuminating annex about his chief, Mr Harold Macmillan, which is not only amusing but also enlightening about the essence of the argument which is now taking place between the new monetarism of Mrs Thatcher and Sir Keith Joseph on the one hand and the unreconstructed Keynesians on both sides of the party divided on the other. He records that Mr Macmillan called him to the then Prime Minister's residence at Admiralty House to offer him the Chancellorship. Having won Mr Maudling's delighted acceptance, the Prime Minister then went on to give his new economic Minister a short lesson in the nature of his job. His instructions were that Mr Maudling was to seek to break out of the familiar cycle of stop-go which had bedevilled successive post-war governments, and to take steps to deal with the drift of an increasing shortage of international financial liquidity.

Mr Maudling writes: 'I remember him describing it quite clearly in an analogy which I still think is a pretty good one. If a lot of people are playing a game of cards and using cowrie shells for money, the game can progress so long as all the participants have some shells to spend. But if the whole supply of shells is collared by one or two participants, then the game will come to an end. No doubt it was a crude analogy, but it was a pretty effective one, and his desire, which I fully shared, was to see that the supply of internationally acceptable cowrie shells was sufficient enough in total, and adequately distributed in particular, to ensure that the game could continue.'

The analogy is exact and it goes to the heart of the present controversy over the growing imbalance in international trade.

'So we went for expansion, quite deliberately and with our eyes open, recognizing the dangers. The prize to be obtained, the prospect of expansion without inflation, the end of stop-go and a breakout from the constrictions of the past was a glittering one. No one could guarantee success, but the chances were high, and the alternatives were drab and depressing.'

120

In the event, the 1964 election intervened. Mr Maudling had unsuccessfully urged the new Prime Minister, Sir Alec Douglas-Home, to go to the country in June. Sir Alec preferred October, and was beaten by a hair's breadth. The incoming Labour Government, faced with what then looked like a gigantic balance of payments deficit, was driven back into the stop phase of the old stop-go cycle.

Mr Maudling reveals that it was he who prepared, as a contingency, the import surcharge scheme which the Labour Government eventually adopted. But he is deeply critical of Mr Wilson's reaction to the deficit, accusing him of making the crisis infinitely worse by an all too public panic.

There is something in what Mr Maudling says. But it proved to be the pinnacle of his own career. Although he was to be runner up to Mr Heath in the 1965 leadership contest, and held high office again after 1970, a rich architect called Poulson had by then entered Mr Maudling's life. The ramifications of that episode effectively began the process which eventually dumped Mr Maudling back on the back benches.

The final kick came in 1976, when he was sacked as shadow foreign secretary by Mrs Thatcher. He records that interview in the following words: 'Without beating about the bush, she told me in the most charming manner that she must ask me to relinquish my responsibilities.' Mr Maudling asked why and was told there was criticism of the lack of public speeches from him. Mr Maudling goes on: 'She suggested that I might like to write a letter of resignation, but I said that as I had not the slightest desire to resign I did not see why I should. We then parted with mutual, and I believe sincere, expressions of personal goodwill.'

Mr Maudling has at least had the personal satisfaction of being vindicated in the Poulson affair by what amounted to a vote of confidence from his colleagues in the Commons following a sharply critical report from a select committee of MPs.

Perhaps the most poignant passage in the book is Mr Maudling's picture of himself sitting alone in the smoking room of the House of Commons with a large whisky and water, waiting for the result of that division on the closed circuit television screen over the bar. He had decided to resign if he lost the vote. In the event, that did not prove necessary. But it is unlikely that he will hold high political office again.

29 June, 1978   **Ian Aitken**

Hair apparent

There will soon be a new word in the language; to heseltine, meaning to build up a monumental pile of blonde hair, fix it in place with a complicated system of scaffolding and webs, and then spray it with lacquer. It would be advertised in hairdressers': 'Unisex shampoo and heseltine, £3.'

Young men would have their hair specially heseltined for their first speech at a Tory conference. Mrs Thatcher has hers heseltined every week. Unfortunately, something has gone wrong with the display mounted on the original owner.

Mr Michael Heseltine is the Environment spokesman, and by now probably the most popular single figure for the Tory faithful. Yesterday he was supposed to be talking about local government but this got only a short look in as he produced instead a mighty anti-Socialist diatribe designed, no doubt, to show what a great Tory leader he will make.

It was being said that he had been put into the slot just before lunch in order to punish him for being so overwhelmingly popular last year. The idea was that if he overran the delegates would get angry about missing their lunch and he would be driven from the platform by the concerted rumbling of tummies. In the event they loved it so much that he could have gone right through lunch-time, dinner, and into breakfast this morning.

But to the detached observer the fascination lay in the terrible things that were happening to his hair. Something had gone dreadfully wrong with the engineering system holding it up. Great chunks of it crashed down, like cliffs falling into the sea, covering his forehead and sometimes blotting out his eyes.

Now and again he tried to shore it up in mid-speech, but then

'The natives are restless tonight.'

a bit would sheer off and crash around his ears. By the end the whole noble edifice was in ruins, a sad reminder of the frailty of man-made things.

What makes him so popular is, I think, the air of controlled lunacy. He manages to appear as if he is so outraged by socialism and by the present Government that it is only by supreme self-control that he can prevent himself from picking up the lectern and smashing it on to the nearest Socialist. Once, on a famous occasion, the self-control did snap, and he started swinging the House of Commons mace. But this, of course, looked just silly, and the caged tiger routine is far more effective.

Sometimes he even loses touch with his voice and weird involuntary squeaks creep in at the top of his vocal register. All in all, it is amazingly effective, and it is no wonder that they stopped the conference ball to applaud him when he walked in last year.

One young man who had obviously had his hair heseltined for the day was a 16-year-old from the Rother Valley called William

Hague. One hesitates to say too much about the young men at this Tory conference, except that there are an awful lot of them and they are terrifyingly confident. Young William had a surprisingly elderly-sounding Yorkshire accent which made his voice sound almost exactly like Harold Wilson's, to the obvious confusion of delegates who had their backs turned. He had, however, a far greater command of the cliché than the former Prime Minister, and he marked the economic debate with phrases like 'rolling back the frontiers of the state', 'home-owning democracy', 'large and progressive cuts in public spending', and 'a society where effort and initiative are rewarded'. The sight of these aged saws coming from so young a head had the entire conference on its feet at the end of his speech.

The most disconcerting thing of all was that William did not even look surprised as Mrs Thatcher herself leant over from the platform to applaud him. He merely seemed faintly pleased, as if he had won the hundred-yard dash or the school prize for diligence.

13 October, 1977   **Simon Hoggart**

Boyson's law gets lordly rebuke

A lively clash between Lord Longford and Dr Rhodes Boyson yesterday stirred diners at London's Dorchester Hotel from their post-prandial doze. The peer was thanking the MP for his address on law and order to a Foyles literary lunch. But his thanks were laced with barbs.

'It would be going too far to say that the speech was total clap-trap,' he said. 'Well, a little too far anyway.' But he made it clear that the doctor's medicine – a return to hanging and the wholesale sacking of social workers – sounded to him more than a little round the bend.

Dr Boyson had told his audience, which included the Israeli ambassador, Mr Abraham Kidron, that life was only made possible by defence and the good life by law and order. Britain had allowed its law and order to decline continually. Social workers had been arrested for throwing stones at the police and, astonishingly, had been allowed to keep their jobs. 'Indeed, for all I know, they have been promoted for their great ability in attacking the police,' said Dr Boyson. 'We must punish those who threaten our order. Punishment is for the correction of the evil-doer, a warning to the potential evil-doer and for the satisfaction of the law-abiding.'

Lord Longford, looking perturbed, said that this doctrine, especially the reference to satisfying the law-abiding, was absolutely un-Christian. 'The idea of hanging people to satisfy others is really horrible,' he said. 'Dr Boyson should spend more time in joining me on doing something for criminals' victims.'

This riled the MP, who sprang to his microphone and said that Lord Longford's comments were quite unacceptable.

'Don't get testy,' said Lord Longford, as Dr Boyson seemed about to advance on him over the Israeli ambassador's lap. But then the chairman, Mr Norris McWhirter, intervened.

'I think that ends this happy lunch,' he said.

The guests of honour, including the ambassador and Dame Rebecca West, looked inscrutable during the exchanges, but the audience, which paid £7 a head for tickets, was divided.

Dr Boyson was applauded when he praised the Isle of Man for keeping the birch. But Lord Longford won a mighty 'hear hear' and considerable applause for his theological points about crime.

28 June, 1978   **Martin Wainwright**

Problem people

Michael Mogg is the chief social worker in the psychiatric social work department at the Park. He is 41, and had been threatening to give up social work to be a painter for as long as anyone can remember. My first day with him was not promising: he had just returned from an unproductive painting holiday and sat around his office as if forced by circumstances to engage in a nine-to-five occupation when he would far rather be doing something else. Mogg hates paper work and the telephone, and the increasingly bureaucratic Health Service set-up depresses him beyond words.

He makes all his own visits informal, rarely fixes appointments in advance, relies on some extraordinary intuition that clients will be at home and in need of him when he calls; generally speaking, they are. Often they are slumped in their armchairs in a state of abject misery, without even the energy to greet him when he arrives. In ten visits I made with him in three days, nobody was out.

The first family we went to see presented a Dickensian scene: eight people huddled together in the dingy front room of a small terraced house in Headington. Grandpa, recovering from a serious operation; his daughter who was agoraphobic and so never went out; her coloured husband who was unemployed; another daughter under severe emotional strain due to bonding problems with her son who was a confirmed epileptic; the first sister's daughter, a 13-year-old nymphomaniac who had recently broken her leg; the epileptic son himself; another daughter who was a school avoider; another young child who cried incessantly . . . one of Oxford's most famous problem families, said Mogg.

From Headington we drove to a council housing estate outside the city to visit a heavily tattooed young criminal, awaiting trial on a car stealing charge. His wife seemed unable to manage their two children; they were about to have their power cut off for not paying the electricity bill. The couple were having a serious argument and the husband was about to strike his wife.

From here, pausing only for a depressed lunch, we visited a worried-looking little woman, recently deserted by her husband and struggling with three children; and then to see a dwarf woman with a husband, a Cowley night worker, who had once threatened to beat Mogg up but was now extremely polite to him. They had a problem son, a Park Hospital referral, and a charming little girl.

That was Day One. On Day Two, on the depressing housing estate of Blackbird Leys outside Oxford, we went to see a severely crippled woman whose husband was a milkman. The younger of their two sons had behavioural problems due to his mother's pressures on him in early life, and shortly after our visit we learned that he had been severely injured by falling off his motor bike.

We visited a Scotswoman who had had eight children by her lodger, including a mongol child, and an elderly old-fashioned strict Baptist couple struggling to cope with an epileptic grandson (their son had disappeared without trace) when he came home from the Park at weekends.

On Day Three we answered an emergency call to a woman whose child, who had a history of epilepsy, had developed a severe nose bleed. And we went to see another dwarf wife, a religious fanatic, who had an alcoholic husband: their son had been removed from a school for severely disturbed children as too disturbed for the school to handle. Lastly, Mogg wanted me to meet a widow whose severely brain-damaged son had recently been beaten up by some Oxford louts who couldn't bear the sight of him walking the streets.

During these meetings, Mogg himself said little, apart from the conventional 'You know where we are. Give us a shout if you want anything', while we were leaving. His interviewing is unobtrusive to the point of being non-existent, although it is usually followed by action when he gets back to his office. Perhaps his presence alone was a benediction, I thought. How does Mogg, who has conducted interviews on stairs, in hallways and even, on occasion, through letter boxes, achieve this effect?

'Well,' he told me, 'the old watchword is: "Start where the client is": if you are aware that he is anxious, angry, sad, start with those feelings, even if they are apparently unconnected with his or her real problem. You have to listen to a client's silences as well as to his words.

'Interviews are not done just for the hell of it, though it may have seemed like that to you these past three days. To most people, the office interview situation only increases their feelings of vulnerability. One of my workers conducted good interviews with children through her dog. She wasn't a

ventriloquist; the dog merely provided an eloquent vehicle . . .
Children, if one can make any generalization at all about them,
talk most through their activities. The smallest shared event
can provide a heaven-sent opportunity to communicate.'

Mogg had not set out actually to reassure any of the people
we had visited. 'To say to someone, "Don't worry," is criminal.
Even when the worry to your own eyes may be quite trivial, to
your client or patient you immediately reveal how little you
have understood their feelings and, if the worst does come to
pass, you may actually have caused damage. Anyway, re-
assurance is usually given to lessen the anxiety raised in *us*
rather than to help *them*.'

I had not heard him giving much advice to anybody, either:
'One is always being asked, "What would you do about so-
and-so?" "Do you think he should be in bed by seven o'clock?"
That foxes you: if you say yes or no without fully understanding the implications of the question, you stand in danger of
causing undreamed of rifts. It is important to decide if the
advice required concerns matters of facts, or opinion. I tend
to avoid opinion like the plague.

'The social worker is like a farmer in that, although living
by the clock and by the calendar, he makes hay while the sun
shines, i.e., he works where and when he can, yet he must
structure his work within the rhythms that nature offers. He
may be part enabler, part trouble-shooter, or plain transport
officer, but these are all opportunities for helping clients to
work out their problems. In the end, he must be a demonstration of the community's concern: a concern that is not based
merely on sentimentality.'

28 June, 1978   **Wilfrid De'Ath**

Jerry's way

My friendly neighbourhood doctor died suddenly the other day. For once both the adjectives are accurate: he was my dear friend and he lived round the corner. There is something very grievous and wrong when a doctor dies unaccountably and unexpectedly, especially when it is the doctor who twice saved me from the same thing, at great pains to himself. He rescued me; when the time came, I could not rescue him. There was one moment when he was having dinner quietly at home, and the next he was gone. I shall miss him very much, and not I alone.

There cannot be many in our North London bailiwick, who did not know Jerry Slattery, or were not part of the entourage of which he and his wife Johnny were the nucleus. He was probably one of the best-known family doctors in London, and loved for a great deal more than his medicine. And probably by hundreds of people who had never been ill in their lives but who tried to be, in order to have a private word with Jerry.

Dr Slattery was Irish, therefore convivial; he was a doctor, therefore skilled; he was kind, and therefore loyal. I should know, since I forced catastrophic complaints on him that were not to be dealt with by pills. I think this originally brought Jerry Slattery and me together: that a man in such a mess as I was in could not only be brought together but bounce back good as new.

'Come, me boy,' he would say calling at the hospital bed, 'we'll have a small one on the survival of your living soul, and we'll get the Sister in.' Thus I lived, and Jerry died.

I am making this piece about Dr Jerry Slattery because to me he represents something the medical profession could ill afford to lose, lost it though it has. He was a celebrity, in his way. In another age I suppose he would have been called a 'fashionable doctor', which in a sense was true, since he created his own fashion. He ran something between a surgery and a salon. If you called in at one of Jerry and Johnny's almost innumerable parties you were almost certain to find yourself in the midst of the Dr Slattery Repertory – a very miscellaneous and rewarding company, since Dr Jerry Slattery rejoiced in the company of actors and writers and professors and comic singers and lunatics.

It might be Peter O'Toole, Olivia Manning, Michael and Jill Foot, T. P. McKenna, Llew Gardner, everyone you can think of, even me. In some way or another all of us had been preserved by the ministrations and comradeship of this extraordinary versatile man. And throughout these occasions Jerry was always on the line: he was a doctor, and went where a doctor was needed. Once, I remember, I called in in the middle of the festivities with a rather bad pain; instantly he broke away and summoned an expert to give me a cortisone injection, which was totally horrible, and then soothed me by saying: 'Now we'll have a small one to make it better.' As it happened it made it worse, but it was well intentioned.

I am writing about Dr Jerry Slattery not as a local GP but as almost a national figure. He was passionately interested in politics, which made him a pleasure to talk to for me at least. We met long years ago on one of the early Aldermaston marches, so we had much in common from the start. Thereafter we in consultation abandoned the symptoms very quickly, and got down to the nitty-gritty.

One time he came to see me on what we supposed, without much rancour, to be my deathbed, since I was frankly in a pretty poor way. 'You're somewhat down,' said Jerry. 'In fact, we'd better get you to hospital right away, without delay.' (Which he did). 'But while we're waiting,' said my beloved doctor, 'by the way, what did you think of that *Times* leader today? Was it not an outrage? Now I'll tell what I feel about that situation, *The Times* should be ashamed of itself . . .'

And thus I drifted into consoling oblivion and thus my life was saved.

My doctor was unusual in his profession in that he did not accept sickness as a thing in itself; he argued that there were only sick people. Many doctors argue that illness is a condition to be found in this patient or that; Jerry argued that there were patients who happened to be ill, and that their emotions and circumstances were as important as their temperatures or their blood-count or their ECG. Not more so, but equally so. Several eminent consultants have told me that they have been obliged, or even forced, to listen to a brief life history of the customer before they knew whether they had a paroxysmal haemoglobinuria or an in-growing toenail.

This may have exasperated the consultant gods, but it did the sufferers much good, as well I know. As I say, Jerry Slattery believed that illness was something that happened to people, not something to be examined by itself. This is not as common as you might think.

This is such a wholly personal memoir that I am sorry to have inflicted on those who were not friends or patients (it was hard to be one without being the other) of the archetypal family doctor, a dying race. I do not use doctors very much, but when I do, by gum, I stretch them. My creed is that I believe in the Holy Ghost, if you insist, but I worship at the shrine of the National Health Service, and I shall not forget Dr Jerry Slattery.

You cannot really say less for someone who saved your life, and who lost his.

28 November, 1977   **James Cameron**

Body politic

Some curious relics of Napoleon were auctioned in Paris last week. Clippings of his hair and beard and a tendon from his left arm, all removed from the body soon after death, fetched £1,250.

But there are other Napoleon memorabilia, or is it paraphernalia, adorning collectors' tables rather than Napoleon's body. The Paris sale last week prompted me to find out the fate of the Emperor's mummified penis, death mask and other relics that are known to have survived. They were last auctioned at Christie's in 1969. The idea of selling a penis was a bit much for Christie's to swallow, and afraid that more had been bitten off than the auctioneers could chew, it was described in the catalogue as 'a small dried up object, genteelly described as a mummified tendon,' with a hasty assurance that 'the authenticity of the macabre relic had been confirmed'. (How? Mind you, the fact that the 'tendon' survived its cutting off from the owner does prove the old adage that the penis mightier than the sword.)

These relics were sent for sale by an American stamp dealer, who oddly bought them back from himself.

2 November, 1977   **Peter Hillmore**

Up the Blue Creek with the GBP

I am on jungle patrol with the last of Kipling's men, the men of the Great British Presence. It is the Belizean Jungle in Central America, well south of Mexico, the sort of insect-infested terrain the British once patrolled, as their stiff-upper-lipped duty, all over the tropical world. But since this may be a quite extinct national activity in much less than a decade, I knew I had to be quick if I wanted to see this final sunset of empire for myself.

There are 12 of us. One of the two officers is the only one with live ammunition. The men all carry guns, but loaded with blanks. The main enemy is the weather. It is close to 100 degrees and the Blue Creek villagers stay in their wooden huts. All around us are the Blue Creek Mountains; palm or mahogany trees the best part of 100 feet tall; vast attap trees with their saw-edged leaves rising 40 feet like giant ferns.

My British Army jungle jacket, trousers and hat, loaned to me for the occasion, are already soaked in sweat and my throbbing head seems to have swollen three sizes so that the jungle hat cuts into it.

This Belize jungle, to the extreme swampy south of our former colony, and the nearest to where the Guatemalans have their frontier post, is now the only jungle in which the British can still be seen on their traditional jungle patrol – except for Borneo, which is purely a training operation, not a real assertion of British military might.

Immediately ahead of me, stepping over twisted roots of trees resembling snakes and cutting heavy boots against the large flint-like rocks, is the leader of the patrol, Second Lieutenant Niall Campbell, of the Royal Highland Fusiliers. On his stiff upper lip is perspiration and a moustache which would have pleased Kipling. Otherwise, he is cast in a rather more democratic mould. 'The jungle operations I have been on? All great fun,' he says. Some of his men stage-groan. He laughs and jokes with his men – up to a point.

Campbell does not come from the landed gentry, though his manners would pass in that role. He is the son of a hotel keeper in Perthshire. Today is his 21st birthday.

We are on the west bank of the Blue Creek River. Our patrol will scour the bank for Guatemalan mischief and stage some ambush practice. In the village behind us Maya Indians scrape a bare existence, living off rice, bananas and eggs and trading the spare ones for soldiers' surplus rations.

The reality of the jungle seeps through only slowly. From the RAF helicopter which had delivered me to Salamanca, one of the bases of the First Battalion, Royal Highland Fusiliers, it had looked rather like Salisbury Plain, a smudge of friendly green. Only when the jungle was all around me did the reality of the foot patrol really sink in. All the normal assumptions of safety conferred by living in a man-made environment simply disappear. A snake bite would mean being carried as quickly as possible to Miama; and Miama is rather a long way away.

Our patrol is arranged according to Second Lieutenant Campbell's assessment of the terrain. At the head, two fusiliers act as scouts, waving the rest of us on if the coast is clear. Well behind them walks the gunner, Fusilier Dalrymple. He carries a machine gun that weighs nearly 30lb. If anything happens to the scouts, he can make it very uncomfortable for the enemy. Dalrymple says he would like a lighter gun, but this one can fire from belts of ammunition holding as many as 200 bullets.

133

Fifty feet ahead of me the patrol leader turns and gestures at all to get down quickly. As I throw myself into the undergrowth, something moves near my right hand. 'Oh,' says Captain John Edwards, second-in-command at Salamanca who has come as an observer, 'there are a few frogs here.'

When the line of men comes to a halt again it is at a stretch of the river where it is possible to see the bottom. The bottom is white as if covered in chalk, and there are white rocks scattered over most of it. Second Lieutenant Campbell gesticulates to Corporal John Sweeney, his second-in-command, to get the scouts across the river and investigate the other side. They go one at a time, up to their navels in water and covered by rifles on our side of the water.

Then Corporal Sweeney, a man with a button-face, fair moustache and a repertoire of stories about snakes, scorpions and tarantulas, calls up all the other men to cross, snapping his fingers at them individually to indicate the exact moment.

It is my turn. I wade in. The river gets steadily deeper. It comes over the top of my jungle boots and seeps into my trousers. The rocks on the riverbed are loose and roll about under my feet. I twist my ankle (previously blown up to nearly double size through insect bites and the heat).

'The horrible bit,' admits Captain Edwards, 'is when you get the water in the crotch.' I am relieved to hear that there are 'comparatively few' alligators in Belize.

I am getting the symptoms of heat exhaustion. Irritability. A capacity to see things as wildly funny when they are really not all that funny, such as the fact that under my muddy and sodden jungle boots I am wearing a pair of monogrammed Harrods socks.

How long have I been in the jungle? Things are getting blurred. I cannot tell. My wrist watch is underneath the tightly buttoned jacket sleeve and I can't undo it without perhaps letting in the sand-flies (they give you a bump) or the beef bugs (they lay eggs under your skin which grow into hungry grubs the thickness of a finger while still inside you). We find a little time to talk. 'It's murder, sir, murder!' I am informed by Fusilier Tango Wilkie of Glasgow.

'Yes,' says Fusilier Wally Rae, 'and we've been losing £20 to £30 a month because of the drop in the value of the pound.' All this unrest in the ranks is too much for the patrol leader's stiff upper lip. 'Oh God,' says Campbell. 'All this has been said before, hasn't it? You'd rather this than Northern Ireland, wouldn't you?'

This, in turn, is too much for the fusiliers. 'At least there, sir,' says one of them, 'you can shoot people for your job. You have got a reason for being there. This is unreal.' A moment of stunned silence in which it occurs to me I would certainly rather have these sturdy reminders of empire on my side than against me.

Nursing its own thoughts, the patrol marches in silence back to Blue Creek. Some of the villagers have come out to say hello. But one little Maya Indian in a big straw hat ducks behind his hut as we approach. Is he planning something against the one remaining example of the British as jungle policemen?

I peep gingerly round to the back of his hut. What I see is positively encouraging from the point of view of British influence. The Maya Indian, in this most primitive corner of our former empire, where pigs and chickens roam as freely as fate and snakes allow, has not been plotting mischief against Kipling's heirs. He is merely oiling his gleaming Raleigh bicycle.

15 April, 1978   **Dennis Barker**

Jus' folk

> *I'm a stranger here*
> *Just blowed in your town*
> *Just because I'm a stranger*
> *Everybody wants to dog me around.*

Pete Seeger, the Harvard dropout who wrote 'Where Have All The Flowers Gone' and 'If I Had A Hammer', just blowed into town. And, at 3.30 a.m. at Heathrow, everybody still wanted to dog him around. Behind the barrier I waited for the banjo-picking troubadour of American radicalism whose tinny, terrific voice had virtually recruited me into 'the movement' back in the forties. The night he passed through wartime Chicago and one of his singing buddies invited a bunch of us eager kids to 'hootenanny' with him was one of the emotional high points of my adolescence.

I was amazed at how little he has changed. Coming through Customs with his part-Japanese part-Virginia wife Toshi, he still has that same long-necked, lanky amble, that same slightly preoccupied gaze fixed somewhere off into the middle-far distance. And, of course, strapped on the back of his tall, thin frame, that old battle-scarred black case holding the five-string banjo he had designed for himself.

He is as kind to dogging strangers now as once he was to a 16-year-old know-it-all who, on that long-ago night in Chicago, kept correcting him on the right way to sing 'Talking Union' – which he had probably written. Bone-tired after a six-hour wait at J. F. Kennedy due to a storm followed by a nine-hour flight, he agrees on the spot to talk over his life and old times.

Pete – as everyone the world over calls him – would rather talk about Woody Guthrie than himself. He'd met the wandering Oklahoma minstrel, seven years older but far wiser in the ways of the road, on the stage of a New York theatre where both were raising money for migrant workers in the thirties. 'I was naïve in many different ways, but I guess he liked my banjo playing. He let me bum along with him for a while. On and off for a year or two. What I learned from him lasted my whole life.'

Especially since Woody Guthrie and Leadbelly passed on to that great hootenanny in the sky, Pete probably has been the single most important catalyst in the post-war folk renaissance. (It runs in the family. The British folk singer, Peggy Seeger, married to Ewan McColl, is Pete's half-sister.) His personal and musical influence over younger folk musicians – from Joan Baez and the Kingston Trio to Bob Dylan – has been incalculable. Yet he insists on calling them all 'Woody's children'.

'Woody was their father. I was just the midwife. My main

function in life was to carry on the message I learned from Woody and Leadbelly to a new generation.'

He looks slightly disappointed in me when I ask what the message was. Suddenly, I feel incredibly out of touch with that 16-year-old Chicago firebrand I once was. 'Woody's message is,' Pete gently chides me, 'that the working class is the most important group of people in the world. The women and men who do their hardest work for least pay and get very little credit.

'The Spanish poet Garcia Lorca said it much better than I can. "All our art is but water drawn from the well of the people. Let us give it back to them in a cup of gold so that in drinking they may recognize themselves." '

But before I can erect a suitable defence against his homespun, poetic Marxism, Pete grins. 'Of course, Woody didn't put it into such fancy language. "Quit tryin' to be so god-damn o-riginal all the time," he'd say. "Just do a good job. Take over an old tune and put new words to it." '

Ah, that was the Guthrie – and Seeger – I remembered. The trade mark of their pioneering group, the bumptious and ragtaggle Almanac Singers (1940–2), was complete indifference to 'artistic integrity'. Constantly changing personnel, reshaping old songs and inventing new words to fit the idiom of any audience they met, the Almanacs loved freely adapting church hymns, dust-bowl ballads and black spirituals. Once, in a hootenanny for some steel workers in Gary, Indiana, I'd heard Woody Guthrie instantly revise his own song 'Worried Man Blues' (itself perhaps a jazzed-up hymn): 'It takes a steel-ladlin' man to sing a worried song . . .'

Purism in folk art still holds no appeal for Pete. 'Woody once said about another song writer, "Oh, he jes' stole from me but I steal from everybody. I'm the greatest song stealer there ever was." '

Only the other night, Pete says, at a New York City rally he did for striking coal miners, his partner, folk singer Barbara Dane, made 'some good changes' in 'Solidarity Forever'. 'Like many old union songs it was male oriented. Men here, men there, you never hear women mentioned ever.' Pete warmly approves of women who want 'to change a word here or there' to make their point in the old songs.

In 1969 in Washington DC he performed in front of 'the biggest audience I'll ever sing for' – half a million Vietnam protestors. A little reluctantly he tried out 'Give Peace A Chance', which he'd just learned from a teenage girl. 'I thought it was awful wishy-washy at first. I wanted a stronger song. But this huge audience was too diverse to latch on to anything stronger or to follow the rhythm of a quicker song. However, this very slow song – written by an Englishman – worked. I'd shout out a few lines in between, to make it more pointed.

'All we are saying
ARE YOU LISTENING, NIXON?
Is give peace a chance
YOU BETTER LISTEN, AGNEW!

'I just sang it over and over, and pretty soon Peter, Paul and Mary – even Mitch Miller – jumped up and joined in.'

The main thing, he insists, is to use songs to reach as many people as possible. And then getting the audience to partici-pate – 'getting them involved'. Tonight in London's Royal Albert Hall and tomorrow night at City Hall in Newcastle – both concerts for 'the people of Chile' – he will undoubtedly entertain by slinging in sly jokes and virtuoso displays of his amazing banjo-playing alongside the social comment, and pretty soon he'll invite everyone to sing along with him. This may be, as he suggests, an old Woody Guthrie technique. But it also suits his 'cultural guerrilla tactics'.

Being blacklisted during most of the 1950s was no laughing matter for the Seegers. Ironically, it was the refusal of res-pectability-seeking labour unions to hire Pete and his People's Songsters which led to their biggest commercial success as the Weavers – an indirect out-growth of the earlier Almanac Singers. 'We simply wanted to sing for the labour movement. But when the unions began purging their radicals, they got scared of hiring us. We hadn't set out to be a pop group. Yet in the very year Senator McCarthy was getting into his stride – 1950 – there we were selling two million records of "Good Night Irene".'

Temporarily, the Weavers became a top performing group. 'All of a sudden we had a manager, and a record contract and a hit record. We saw some of the plushiest night clubs in the country - but also it was the most corrupt and decadent part of the country. A poet friend of ours used to like to say, "Everything is grist for the writer's mill". Some nights Lee Hays and I'd sit in a Reno, Nevada night club and look around us and just say "Grist".'

The Weavers kept going for a couple of years. But due to the blacklist they couldn't get any decent jobs. 'So we took a sabbatical from each other, which turned out to be a Mondaycal and a Tuesdaycal.' Pete was indicted by the House UnAmerican Activities Committee for refusing - on grounds of conscience, not the Fifth Amendment - to talk about his politics. Instead, banjo on his back, he offered to sing a song. A Federal judge didn't think this was funny and sentenced him to a year in jail. Pete eventually won on appeal - and vividly remembers how English supporters raised $1,000 for his legal expenses.

The fifties were grim. 'Yet it also was a wonderful time for us. It could even be fun. I'd come into a college town - nobody else would hire me - and I'd go knock on the door of the local radio station. And the disc jockey would say, "Oh yeah, you sang that 'Good Night Irene', I remember that, c'mon in and we'll talk for a minute." And I'd talk on the air with the deejay for five minutes before anybody had a chance to protest. And then I'd be off. Cultural guerrilla tactics.'

Re-acceptance came with the slow return to reason after the Korean war ended. Pete used his blacklist period to almost singlehandedly open up American colleges to folk songs. 'They were the only places brave enough to hire me. I was relatively unknown, so I could sing at liberal colleges like Oberlin. Paul Robeson couldn't sing anywhere.'

Pete has never reneged on his past friendships or beliefs. He readily acknowledges political debts. 'According to some, it was unregenerate Stalinism. To others it was noble Marxism. To others it was just common sense. Whatever it was, we were all caught up in learning how to put art at the service of the working class and not just for profit. What I learned from the Communists has lasted my whole life – that an artist has a responsibility as a citizen. This is what Paul Robeson taught us all.'

But he wouldn't be who he is if he didn't lighten his lecture a little. 'Of course,' he grins, 'as Rockwell Kent joked, "Art is a weapon. But remember, a bread knife is also a weapon. And it cuts bread."'

I could go on talking all night in nearly-deserted Terminal 3. Pete, though eight years older than me, exudes such youthful charm and sincerity, that if only for a few moments, I feel like jumping up and daubing Forties slogans like OPEN A SECOND FRONT NOW! and END JIM CROW! on the walls.

But, as he is quick to remind me, this is 1978. Pinochet's military junta arouses him today as much as Franco's rebellion against the democratically-elected government of Loyalist Spain did in the thirties. And Pete Seeger is here for a few days to continue what is, for him, that same struggle against fascism.

In the words of one of his best sellers, he is singing out a warning all over this land.

7 March, 1978   **Clancy Sigal**

News from the pulpit

I went to mass on Sunday in San Salvador to hear the leader of the opposition. Once a week, from his pulpit in the cathedral, Archbishop Oscar Arnulfo Romero gives the congregation the latest news. 'We are not claiming to make martyrs,' he said in the message I heard. 'But the facts are the facts, and they will not be published by the official press.' He then announced that a young catechist had been murdered a few days ago as he was working in a country village: an unknown group of political thugs had killed him by the roadside. As he does every week, the Archbishop went on to reveal some items from his voluminous postbag. One was a letter from an elderly woman

140

who had lived as a tenant on a small piece of land for 48 years. Suddenly her landlord told her to leave. When she tried to sit out her eviction, her five sons were arrested.

The congregation, which heard the Archbishop's message (it was read out by a colleague; he was away at a conference that weekend in Costa Rica), came predominantly from the crowded back streets of this city and its nearby villages. Even the choir was in T-shirts. You will not find El Salvador's establishment at prayer in the cathedral any more. The Archbishop broke all official links with the government some months ago and vows not to renew them until human rights are restored.

The polarization between the Archbishop and the military regime which runs El Salvador was reflected in the farcical elections for the country's national assembly which were held while we were there. In Guatemala in spite of all the controls on the presidential election campaign, the Christian Democrats saw fit to put up a candidate. In El Salvador, the Christian Democrats boycotted the elections, along with two left-wing parties, the Movimiento Nacional Revolucionario and the Partido Union Democratica Nacionalista.

El Salvador seems well on the way to becoming the nastiest country in Central America. In Guatemala and Honduras there is a kind of political stalemate. Nicaragua is slowly but indubitably opening up. But in El Salvador the signs point to an explosive level of violence as the regime steps up its repression in the face of tremendous tension mounting from below. The country has long been the most densely populated in the region. An antiquated system of land-holding which effectively keeps most of the land in the hands of fourteen families – 'los catorce' – has made thousands of Salvadoreans look abroad for work. They have been the great migrants of Central America. Nine years ago tension between Honduras and the large population of Salvadorean immigrants led to war between the two countries. In the last few years low farm wages and rising inflation have added to long-standing problems, and helped to politicize the peasantry. Country priests have increasingly found themselves moved to speak up for the peasants, as the government has clamped down on any kind of independent peasant movement. Last year the centre-left opposition (which was boycotting this year's national assembly elections) had hopes of winning the presidency. Thanks to a fraud, the regime's official candidate, Carlos Humberto Romero, was declared the winner. Anger and disappointment have made the opposition more bitter and determined.

The new regime has been carefully trying to distinguish itself from its predecessor. It sensed the mood of the new Carter Administration more quickly than its neighbours and began to tidy up its image. The recent elections were promoted as a showpiece of democracy. Although the opposition boycotted them, the regime found a paper opponent by reviving another right-wing party, the Partido Popular Salvadoreno, that had not contested any recent elections. As we drove through the country, every government radio channel was filled with identical commentaries praising 'the political maturity and sense of patriotism of the people of El Salvador in exercising their right to vote'.

In another piece of window-dressing, the regime recently took the gamble of allowing the Inter-American Commission on Human Rights to visit the country and take evidence. Its report has not yet been published. For the moment the Carter Administration claims to be convinced that things are going well. When Terence Todman, the Assistant Secretary for Inter-American Affairs, was in San Salvador, he urged the opposition to contest the election.

The regime's most significant act so far was the passage last autumn of a new decree 'to defend and guarantee public order'. It severely restricts the freedom of public assembly, prohibits words or gestures which 'tend to discredit' the government, and makes it a crime for a Salvadorean or a foreigner to spread 'tendentious' information about the country abroad. Church sources describe it as the most totalitarian measure on the books in Central America. Whereas the previous regime of Colonel Arturo Molina used to declare temporary states of emergency in the best Latin-American tradition, the new decree gives the government similar powers in perpetuity but without the stigma of having declared an 'estado de sitio'.

In the words of one priest: 'In the days of Colonel Molina, they used tanks and shooting' (the kind of tasks for which Britain's armoured cars would have been useful, if the Labour party had not stopped the government from going through with the sale). 'The new people are more subtle but the persecution is worse.' Church sources claim that the level of official and officially sanctioned para-military violence against the peasantry is rising. Homes are mysteriously set on fire, assassinations continue, people 'disappear'. The regime says it is facing a major guerrilla threat. Church sources reply that the amount of guerrilla activity has not mounted over the past 12 months. The government's unwillingness to tolerate democratic opposition is beginning to force the peasant movements 'to defend themselves'.

A year ago last February, when he took over the archdiocese of San Salvador, Monsignor Oscar Romero had a reputation as an evangelical but relatively right-wing prelate. His conversion to an increasingly political form of evangelism is one sign of the change in El Salvador in the past year. He calls El Salvador a rotten society 'which is being dragged towards chaos by the avarice and selfishness of a few and the incompetence of others'. A thousand peasants stir in their pews at his words. Each member of the congregation turns to his neighbour. They all grasp hands.

27 March, 1978   **Jonathan Steele**

Otello

The latest revival of Verdi's *Otello* at Covent Garden is a triumph. I would love to know how it compared with the Tamagno performances, at the turn of the century (if I may use the phrase), when my father and great uncle, unable to get seats, still found it worthwhile to stand outside the opera house in Bow Street. The great tenor's clarion notes penetrated the walls and the London fog and gave an idea of what the performance was like. I am not saying that the tenor, Carlo Cossutta, is necessarily one of the legendary Otellos, such as Zanatello or Melchior, but he is a magnificent performer of the great role. He is at the top of his form, noble, strong and immensely sure in gauging the effect of pathos he wished to achieve.

The new baritone, new to us at least since the Fianculla revival, the powerfully built Silvano Carroli, proved one of the best Iagos I have ever heard; cruel, striking, and with every word coming forward on an inexhaustible torrent of tone. Maria Chiara, a little nervous at first, made a lovely Desdemona, the part which Verdi and Boito managed to draw to a fuller size than the Shakespeare original.

Chorus, orchestra and the minor contributors gave of their best for the conductor Giuseppe Patane. One of those evenings when one found oneself saying, with Henry James: 'The real right thing.'

21 April, 1978   **Philip Hope-Wallace**

Americans

Seeing American footballers makes one realize that Othello was not pulling Desdemona's leg. These are the anthropophagi whose heads do grow beneath their shoulders. Built like American bison, their baffled eyes peering under great boney ridges, they strike fear into the enemy by widening and raising their already improbable shoulders. A device Joan Crawford used with much the same effect.

They harden skulls already impervious to punishment by repeatedly banging them against padded posts. The game itself appears to involve a lot of falling down on the part of the footballers and a lot of leaping up and down by the football coach. Further than that I am not prepared to commit myself.

Woody Hayes, the football coach of Ohio State University, the last in The Americans series (BBC-2) is a dead ringer for Donald Duck from the peak of his cap to his vertical take off rages. He has, says Desmond Wilcox, attacked photographers and referees, jumped on his own watch, even blacked his own eyes. This is pure duck soup, consommé de Donald.

Surrounded by herds of human buffalo he is immediately apparent by pure force of personality and flow of invective, shaking furious fists at these docile mastodons and threatening alternately to kick their asses to the ceiling or throw them off the squad.

Knowing full well that language is not their strong point (their strong point being the apex of the cranium), he takes them for Sunday morning classes in word power. Using as a text book Word Power Made Easy, as indeed it has to be. His method is rather along the Dotheboys Hall lines of say and do. Or say and don't. 'Apathy,' he shouts. 'Apathy, avoid it like the plague.' Apathetic students: 'Hell, they sit there and look at their shoes for an hour. Thinking great thoughts. They ain't going anywhere.'

He looks after his squad like a mother, for a duck must be somebody's mother, ensuring they see only wholesome films and not comedies. 'We don't want anything with too much laughter in it.'

Thurber went to Ohio State University. Thurber, whose men spread softly like uncooked cookies. For ever flown with wine or in ineffectual flight from wives. In a coup d'etat, Thurber drawings, found gathering dust, were hung instead of photographs of Ohio State footballers.

A sense of humour, avoid it like the plague. 'I've never seen a man make a tackle,' says coach Hayes, 'with a smile on his face.'

11 April, 1978   **Nancy Banks-Smith**

On the beach

President Carter promised yesterday, in his high-pitched, Sunday school voice, that the 2,000 American soldiers who died on this beach on 6 June 1944, would be vindicated by 10 times that number of American soldiers now stationed in Europe 'to make sure that this kind of threat is never before us again'.

The bare words sounded banal and diplomatic. Yet President Carter, speaking without notes, wearing his raincoat that looks as if it could have been picked up for a few dollars at Bloomingdales, with one leg of his again fashionable drainpipe trousers flapping in the wind, sounded as if he meant it. 'We are determined, with our noble allies here, that Europe's freedom will never again be endangered,' he said.

His host, President Giscard d'Estaing, much more formal in his waistcoated suit with no overcoat, confessed that he remembered that 'like all young men on that day', he had heard the news of the Normandy landing 'with great impatience and pride'. Now, under an American war memorial, before an assembly of war veterans and diplomats, President Giscard thanked the Americans for saving European liberty.

Getting these two disparate presidents, with all their security and publicity apparatus, from Paris to this remote beach and back again seemed scarcely less formidable a military feat than the original Operation Overlord: a combined operation, again, synchronized to the minutest detail, to enhance the political standing of two Presidents in difficult times.

Logistics included helicopters to get the two Presidents here, and more helicopters to escort their train back to Paris. More than 400 photographers, television cameramen and reporters had to be programmed, minute by minute, to arrive, operate, transmit their product and return to base, regaled by Rouen duckling with all the trimmings, white wine, vintage Burgundy, champagne and brandy. American security, with helicopters, walkie-talkies and exact timing, was reinforced by more traditional French methods, including gendarmes posted every hundred yards along the motorcade route, and armed riot police guarding every one of thousands of culverts, level crossings, bridges, and tunnels along the 100-mile railway route.

Combining security on this scale with a public relations exercise seemed to present the same challenge, in miniature, of combining detente with the defence of the West. If it worked it was largely due to the Carter smile, the homespun style which won round even the dour Norman burghers of Bayeux and the remote farmers behind the beach.

At Bayeux, the first town liberated by the Allies, a beaming Carter hand-shook his way to a rostrum. A small girl in Norman headgear offered him flowers. Sizing her up expertly, he decided that she was small enough to pick up, headgear, flowers and all, and carry her shoulder-high to a delighted crowd. Giscard looked on. He could never have done it.

Yet Giscard was won round in the end, like everyone else. Beaming, he answered his guest in English – an unheard-of departure from French diplomatic tradition.

Among more concrete results of the Carter visit, the first to emerge last night seemed to be a significant French concession to President Carter's determination to stop nuclear proliferation. French industrialists were reported last night as seeking to renegotiate their contract for providing Pakistan with a nuclear reprocessing plant.

The contract, opposed by the State Department, would give Pakistan access to plutonium which could be used to make the same bomb that India made in 1974. Yesterday's reports said Pakistanis were being asked to switch to a 'coprocessing' technique, producing a mixture of plutonium and uranium, instead of 'reprocessing' which would produce pure plutonium.

6 January, 1978   **Walter Schwarz**

Power play

If, like me, you used to get a little nervous during the Windscale inquiry into nuclear power as expert after expert went on to the stand and assured everyone quite categorically that nothing, but nothing, could go wrong with nuclear power, here is a story to set you thinking.

A whole team of nuclear power experts in California has just managed to install two nuclear reactors into a power plant *backwards*. It seems that engineers from the giant Bechtel Corporation installed the reactors for units two and three of the San Onofre nuclear power plant near Sacramento back to front, and now have to make sure that, when the reactors are capped,

'The way I look at it is that Windscale is nearly 300 miles from London as the crow flies – incidentally, could you get one of your boffins to work out just how far a contaminated crow can fly.'

the caps are put on backwards as well.

Such is the expertise of nuclear experts that the boob was only noticed when inspectors for a US regulatory commission saw that a reference mark on the reactors was facing north instead of south. 'It's more an engineering embarrassment than anything else,' is how an (embarrassed) spokesman has described the mishap. I hope he's right, and I also hope that all British nuclear reactors will have signs saying This Side Up in large letters.

8 December, 1977   **Peter Hillmore**

The journeyman's return

'When we first came up here we studied every Utopia the world has ever known – to avoid their mistakes,' said Remy, a bit pretentiously. The senior member of Longo Mai hill commune is known to malicious outsiders as the 'guru' because he talks a lot and is the only one over 40. He was trying to impress a visiting professor of sociology from Paris. It was true all the same: five years ago the pioneers had taken time off from house-building, rock clearing and ploughing to read up some famous Utopias since Plato's *Republic*.

Today Longo Mai (Provençale for 'long may it last') is too much like hard work to be Utopian. It is a workmanlike attempt to attack some social and ecological problems while making a decent living in the open air.

They call it a co-operative because 'commune' suggests drugs and the far Left, and it is important to be accepted in a conservative countryside. Everything is done and owned in common: you take clothes and money when you need them. The farms have been attacked by thugs from the Marseilles Mafia, so every night someone is on guard and others sleep in the woodcutter's hut on top of the mountain.

Aneka, who loves peace and quiet, is a frequent volunteer for duty at the hut. She is 16, the latest recruit from Germany. She likes looking after horses and reading Brecht. She looks windswept and radiant as a new convert to a religion. In some ways Longo Mai could be called a kibbutz if it were not stuck on a steep hillside in Haute Provence.

Drugs are forbidden but not much else. The first pride of each year's crop are the new babies, and then the lambs. Some people get married, others don't bother. The music is terrific, thanks to Willi, who sings Brechtian songs in German accompanied by violins and guitars. He could hold his own in a sophisticated Berlin nightclub. The food is home grown down to the black bread made from their own flour and their own wheat in the old ovens they found under the ruins. They make their wine too, but consumption exceeds production and the rest has to be brought up from Forcalquier. A visiting ecologist remarked that they appeared to live in a state of biological symbiosis with the sleek Malinoir wolf hounds they use as sheep dogs.

Five years ago they arrived: Willi and Jakob, who helped to start the movement off in Vienna a long time ago; Remy, militant social worker turned ecologist; Andrew from Scotland, now chief shepherd; Kathi from Austria (she also sings), Françoise, Herve, Pierre and the rest. They bought three picturesque ruins and 600 acres of derelict scrubland. Today they are as excited as the day they came – conceited too, about the two ruined farms rebuilt, the third going up soon with the help of summer volunteers; a flock that migrates on foot to high summer pastures, just as flocks used to do in the old days: the first wheat and barley crop to grow up here for decades; the new pines, maples and fruit trees on a decaying hillside.

They are unshaken in their futuristic ambition to restore old fashioned sense to the way people live in Europe. Longo Mai itself, acting on the local peasants, is meant to be a starting point – a catalyst for change. 'The starting point,' said Peter Hill, 'is that a third of Europe is overcrowded and two thirds turning into a desert.' Peter is fund-raiser and unofficial PR man for the movement known as European Co-operative, Longo Mai. (Cheques to his office in Basle,* please – but from Britain he prefers volunteers). He is British but so European he speaks English with a Swiss-German accent. 'When we started up here, the average age of the local peasants was 55. Five years later it's 58. We chose this area because it was dying but not beyond saving.'

The chain of eight co-operatives in France, Switzerland, and Austria act as a single unit, swapping round people, produce and machines. Longo Mai's wool is spun at the once-derelict mill at Briançon, knitted into sweaters and blankets in the workshop at Forcalquier, sold in Basle. Remy calls this 'restoring

* *European Co-operative Longo Mai, PO Box 417, 4002 Basle, Switzerland.*

the original chain of production – destroyed by mass-produced clothes and food.' The prevailing system makes for single-crop, subsidized farms in the plains 'actually in a state of fiefdon to industry', while hill farmland turns into desert. 'It is anti-ecological in the profoundest sense – and immoral too while there is hunger in the world.' Remy thinks the social malady is more serious than the ecological because the system marginalizes people as well as land, in towns as well as villages.

It was, indeed, marginalized townsmen who started the whole thing off in Vienna in the disillusioned aftermath of the 1968 uprisings. Willi, Jakob and others were trying to run a union for oppressed apprentices. 'It was frightful,' Kathi remembers – she was a militant Viennese schoolgirl at the time. 'Whatever the apprentices tried to do they were locked up in Borstals.'

The group began travelling and conferring. From a splinter group at an international youth congress in 1972 the essential Longo Mai idea emerged: it's no good trying to improve your life in a pernicious economic system and the best way to start a new one is to do it yourself. Longo Mai was taken up by the Swiss authorities and fund-raising was public. 'The Swiss are the only Europeans who understand the importance of hill farming,' said Peter Hill. 'They learnt it in the war when a brilliant plan brought all the high farms back into use and fed the country. They are also the only people, bless them, rich enough to put up the money for this kind of thing.' Donations from Swiss individuals and town councils now total a million pounds a year. Later some ecologists, the ILO, FAO, and the EEC became interested because if the movement succeeds it will have found a way of employing young people, increasing food production and repopulating moribund areas. Longo Mai plans to triple its present active membership of 100 next summer and to start more settlements – including a fishing co-operative in Britain with its own processing and co-operative urban marketing to bypass the big food chains.

The money behind Longo Mai is considerable and it arouses suspicion. A reporter in *Le Meridionale* concluded it must be either international terrorism or a plot by Swiss bankers to speculate in land. Two settlements in Germany had to close after being hounded by police looking for terrorists. The original investment has been calculated by the ILO at around £4000 per settler, and, divided among 100 settlers, the charity income from Switzerland comes to £10,000 a year each. But Peter Hill says most of the money is not spent on the settlers. 'It goes out in loans to farmers: old ones trying to stay in business and new ones starting up. And Longo Mai is basically a school for volunteers who will go and start other settlements. This summer we shall have thousands of holiday volunteers from all over Europe, and we think at least a hundred will want to stay on.'

The array of machines – a bulldozer bought from the Swiss Army, an old German combine harvester, a fodder and flour mill and a fleet of cars, lorries and tractors – all are shared with the local farmers. The sheep shearing team works for everyone and is paid in wool that goes to the Briançon mill. Herve set up the system after taking a course in sheep management. 'The price of wool had dropped so low nobody bothered any more,' he said. 'People went in for conveyor belt varieties of sheep reared only for meat. The mills closed down and wool used in industry now came from New Zealand.' Now they find wool can be profitable if taken through all its commercial stages – and some local farmers are beginning to agree. Longo Mai has reintroduced the old varieties and operates a sheep bank, lending ewes to farmers and getting paid back in lambs.

When the settlers first arrived, people expected another hippy commune, and when they brought in costly machines the police and secret service took an interest. The first Swiss and German settlers asked for a residence permit; instead they were told to leave France in eight days. The resulting articles in *Le Monde* put Longo Mai on the map and produced a crop of French volunteers. Now the authorities are watchfully neutral and the farmers accept the settlers as odd, useful, a bit conceited and certainly 'serious'.

The most spectacular happening has been the summer sheep migration, on foot to high pastures. Herve insists this makes economic as well as ecological and cultural sense – keeping herds healthier, eating free grass for four months of the year, and staying in contact with other villages. It is also enormous fun. Last year they drove the flock all the way to Eastern Austria – to the consternation of traffic police and Customs men, and the tearful delight of older villagers, hearing those tinkling bells after decades of silence.

The Austrian migration was meant to advertise the fact that Longo Mai is determinedly European. 'At the EEC they've been trying for years to define a legal status for a European co-operative,' said Peter Hill. 'We have actually set one up.' He is now trying to organize a new brand of volunteer as 'journeymen of Europe' – wandering from one settlement to another 'just as journeymen used to at one time – and indeed young people nowadays want to move about'. When the fishing co-operative in Britain starts, he insists that: 'the last thing we want is for it to be full of Britons. People from England have to come out here and be Europeans.'

19 April, 1978   **Walter Schwarz**

Frank Raymond Leavis

Leavis used his Mill Lane, Cambridge, lecture room in the 'fifties like an ideological slit-trench. Often he would snap off single shots: 'Milton is as mechanical as a bricklayer.' Sometimes he would throw hand grenades: 'There's something wrong with T. S. Eliot down there (pointing towards his waist) – or even lower.' Occasionally he would risk a full bayonet charge at the main critical enemy – the mandarins, the Neoplatonists, anyone whose seriousness about the fertilizing relation between literature and life seemed more dilettante than his.

When all the imaginary smoke and gunfire died away he was left standing – a bald, touchingly slender man, worn down by his own putdowns, his invariably and defiantly open-shirted neck mottled with sunburn like a gipsy's hand. He was the Max Miller of the lecture circuit, a one-line virtuoso.

Those of us from the enemies' colleges who crept across

no-man's-land on one morning every week to fraternize at his open, free tutorials at Downing College discovered that he had a truer secret weapon possessed by none of his great contemporaries – an instinct for academic democracy.

He treated adolescents like Trevor Nunn, Simon Gray and John Cleese as equals or potential equals. That was not a fad or an immaturity in him; it grew from his belief that a healthy literature nourishes – and is also nourished by – the roots of a sane society and that the study of it through a 'collaboration' between teachers, critics and citizens is an activity fit for grown men and women.

He encouraged his pupils to apply this yardstick not only to literature but to newspapers, television, advertisement hoardings, letters and common speech. He was ruthless in using it. He revered most of Shakespeare but, in tutorials, dismissed much of *Othello* and *Antony and Cleopatra* as an attempt to soup up emotion about the doings of great babies. In its time, it was heresy. Ten years later the interpretation surfaced through some indirect channel in Olivier's *Othello*, in a system of subsidized theatre which is now staffed by many of Leavis's former pupils.

Perhaps the most telling counter-assault on him was by C. S. Lewis, who said that the use of subliminal code words like 'maturity' and 'relevance' smuggled in an entire value system that was never made explicit for scrutiny. Others accused him of being a crypto-Marxist. Leavis never replied, which was a pity but then his weapons during his long career of humiliations in the Cambridge English faculty also included silence, internal exile and cunning. His most murderous and underestimated weapon was ridicule, which he deployed in lectures with the virtuosity of a music-hall star and with an insensitivity verging on paranoia. He once said of a decent and courageous contemporary whose gait was showing the strain of trying to work while suffering from a severe leg injury, 'it's not the fashion in my family to go senile at 60'. How the 'grads laughed.

He also alienated generations of pupils from the journalism of critics of integrity like Cyril Connolly and Philip Toynbee because he resented – with only some justification – the way they dominated the review pages. But any primary-school teacher who as a matter of course now pays sensitive attention to the speech and writing of children and of people outside school has Frank Leavis to thank for it, among others.

For all his spite and his congested prose style, he was the most creative, serious and influential literary critic since his Victorian model, Matthew Arnold. In later life, he wanted the Oxford professorship of poetry because Arnold once held it. To his grief W. H. Auden beat him in the election. Perhaps his personal tragedy was that he never got far enough outside Oxbridge backbiting to realize that a great cultural wine, as he was, never needs that kind of bush.

18 April, 1978 **John Ezard**

Ups and downers in Cologne

Cologne is a Heinrich Böll city. It is associated in my mind with his stories dating from the early 1950s describing the poverty and hunger that followed the Second World War. In these stories, soldiers came home to ruined towns in a mood of stunned bitterness. One looks out from the train window and sees that the front wall has been blown away from his house. Inside he can see men stealing the furniture.

Everything in these people's lives has been destroyed. One man is reduced to working in a circus as a knife-thrower's target. Another pursues a trade in contraband cigarettes. Another merely waits, inert, in a rented room, stubbing out his cigarettes against the wall by the bed: eventually he discovers that a girl in the next room who lives in seclusion since her beauty was destroyed by a bomb blast is a figure for whom, before the war, he had developed a vague romantic feeling. This is transformed by his present misery into love.

The early stories of Böll are bitter, wretched and, it has to be said, shot through with sentimental self-pity. As historical documents, though, they exert a fascination. They encapsulate

155

the feelings of the period.

If I were writing a brochure for West German tourism, I should mention this period of immediate post-war misery only in order to point up the miracle of modern Cologne: the restoration of the cathedral, the wonderful achievement of rebuilding the town centre, and so forth. I should recommend the traveller to go by one of the luxury inter-city trains, with its secretarial and telephone facilities, its superb dining car, and its friendly bar. And the traveller who took my advice would arrive on the outskirts of the city, and the train would skirt round the old centre, gradually losing its enormous speed, and none of the glasses would rattle and none of the passengers would be jolted in their seats. Nor might the passenger notice the bomb-damaged buildings at the side of the track – there are not many of them left.

But if, instead of leaving the station on the cathedral side, he were to opt for the rear exit and seek a room in the back streets, then indeed the traveller might be reminded of those bad days and might consider himself to have arrived at the city of Heinrich Böll.

It has changed, naturally, but a certain essence has been retained. There are still shells of bombed houses – one has a sex-shop operating on the ground floor of a ruin. Not all the damaged walls have been patched up. The inhabitants no longer belong to a defeated nation – but many of them belong to the defeated portion of the nation. Others are new arrivals, on their way up. This is the sort of place where people on their way up meet those on their way down.

A German-Jewish woman told me how she had come here on her way down. She had found herself staying in a place where the prostitutes lived with their pimps. This was difficult at first, but eventually they began to accept each other, only there was one Jewish prostitute whose grandparents were killed in Auschwitz. She and the prostitute had had a terrible quarrel. 'How could she, after that, how could she,' the lady shouted in the empty bar, 'how could she sell her body to Germans? To Germans!'

The prostitutes here get very cold and wet standing under

umbrellas in the early hours. Or they wait at the entrances to the bars, tilting their heads at the passers-by. Some of them are pretty, but many have that desperate, raucous manner indicating a dependence on drugs. Here is one playing a fruit machine. She puts the money in, then turns her back and hurries impatiently to the other side of the room. Then she begins to laugh and shriek at the machine from a distance. It is as if she cannot bear to be near the thing when it is in action.

The women have a choice between tentative old Germans and lonely young Turks - who are the dominant nationality in this area. Here is a couple having a Saturday night out. They are posed at the restaurant table, sitting both at the same side, in the manner of a Degas painting. She is German, with an elaborate blonde hairdo and a heavily powdered face. He is a Turk, younger than she.

He is being rather sentimental, he looks at her tenderly throughout the meal. But the trouble is they have nothing to say to each other - he clearly does not know enough German to sustain the conversation. And so she looks around the restaurant, paying sharp attention, it seems, to the impression she might be making on any other Germans present. It is clearly an effort for her to survive the boredom of the evening.

During the day the area is cheerful enough. The shops are mostly run by Turks, and cater for all the needs of the immigrant community. Second-hand clothes and furniture are on display. There are cheap charter firms, with groups on the pavement outside surrounded by masses of cardboard suitcases, waiting for the airport coach and the holiday with their families back home. There are lodging houses for the immigrant worker, and the landladies will give you a pretty frank looking-over before allowing you to cross the threshold.

In my street there is a rather dreary cheap pension and a very dingy middle-range hotel. I am staying at the rather cheap pension, but I drop by at the very dingy middle-range hotel for a drink. Here it was that I met the German-Jewish lady, sitting alone at the bar.

In next to no time she told me that she was married to an Englishman whose name I knew. Then it all came out: how her marriage had broken up, how she had ended up here looking for a job. She had found one today as a secretary in a Jewish firm, and was thus very, very happy. As she explained this she could not have looked more wretched if she had tried.

We discovered we had old friends in common, and talked a lot about the past. As we did so, I couldn't reconcile the circumstances of our meeting with the substance of our conversation. A few years ago, we would have been talking at a cocktail party. She would have been saying some of the same things: 'Yes, I found a nice little place, I've furnished it with antiques. Quite pretty.' But now, having seen those second-hand shops, I knew what she really meant by antiques.

And during the course of the evening that nice little flat turned into a terrible lonely trap, and this quarter of town, which for all its shabbiness had seemed in a way picturesque, became threatening, destructive – the real end of the road. As I say, I could not reconcile the fact that we had friends in common, had moved in similar milieux, with the present difference in our condition.

But she saw it vividly. 'Let's meet tomorrow,' I said. No, she said emphatically, we could have one more drink now, but after that it would be impossible. The next day? No. Well, I would be staying here for a week, surely we could meet again? No, it was all impossible.

The fact that I was passing through, and that she was here for good, made it impossible that we should meet again. The fact that we had friends in common made things worse. It was as if she suddenly could not forgive me for finding her here in such reduced circumstances, and knowing who she was – as if, all in all, there was nothing she could share.

10 July, 1978   **James Fenton**

Gone dancing

'We change people into couples' reads the advertising. 'Touch your partner, move as one.' Inside on the glittery central dance floor, couples were taking a turn, some with rapid complicated twirling steps, some with stiff and awkward shuffles. These were private lessons, with the young and beautiful teachers guiding and steering their pupils around with deftness and ear-to-ear smiles.

The Arthur Murray Dance School in the Strand has been in business since the early fifties and its trade is booming. The dancing is purely for pleasure – the pupils don't go in for competitions. The lessons are extremely expensive; people spend an average of about £500 a year for 30 private lessons and 60 group classes. Some spend as much as £1,000 a year. Many pupils have been going for years, several nights a week.

A large notice in the entrance proclaims 'Student-teacher Fraternization is Prohibited'. The teachers, men and women, are all young and attractive, most of them failed professional dancers, some of them ex-students who have graduated to teaching. They are like Redcoats, bopping and dancing around, cracking jokes, cheering things along.

In a side room a class was in progress. The young man conducting it kept up a line of jolly patter. 'It's a fun class, FUN! Now, all take partners, preferably men with women! Everyone grab someone else! It's a quick foxtrot. Big smiles on everyone's faces, please. I've never seen some of your teeth before!'

The group was a broad mix of ages. Some of them were quite old, but many were young. There was a young man from the French embassy who had been coming for several months. 'I came to learn to dance for a Christmas party, and I liked it very much,' he said. He danced with an impeccably straight back and a courtly air, bowing to his partner. There was a tiny Chinese girl, a small middle-aged Arab, and a young motor-mechanic. Several of the young men seemed excruciatingly embarrassed and stiff, concentrating on their feet with grim determination. Many of the young women also seemed shy and awkward.

The teacher lined up the men on one side, and the women on the other, and taught them a little routine. 'Forward, forward, forward, side, close! Remember, gentlemen, we're going to step outside the ladies if we want to avoid treading on toes! Come on everyone, it's National Smile Week!' Some of the men wore immaculate patent dancing pumps, some of the older women wore silver and gold evening shoes.

A large middle-aged woman was having a private lesson on the centre floor. Her teacher was a handsome young man with curly brown hair, and he wheeled her round, with a patter of tiny steps. He let go of one of her hands and she swung round, her free hand outstretched gracefully, and a beatific smile on her face that made her look for a moment as if she was floating on air. She turned again and he clasped her round the waist as they sped off across the boards. She was an executive in a travel agency and had been coming to the dance studio for five years. She had gone beyond learning to dance, and the 'lessons' were now just a long dance with a perfect partner, as the music floated on from rumba, to samba, to tango, to waltz for fifty non-stop minutes.

At the end of her lesson she came and sat by the side of the floor. She had booked herself two lessons that evening with her teacher so she was sitting out for one session to wait for her turn to come round again.

'Oh, it's wonderful,' she said. 'There are no places you can really go to dance without a partner. Here you can come on your own, and you are guaranteed a wonderful partner to dance with.' She explained that she had taken part in a number of Arthur Murray 'showcases', when the school hires a hotel ballroom and puts on a series of choreographed dances, each student with his teacher, to demonstrate to other Arthur Murray schools around the country. There is also a party at the studio once a week to which all students are invited. 'I try to come along as often as my work allows,' she said. She said she had friends there, but not people she met again outside.

An old man was shuffling slowly and watching his feet, as his lovely young teacher with luxuriant long curls guided him gently. At the end of his lesson he said, 'I'm 69 and my main trouble is remembering the steps I learned last time. I went for a holiday in Majorca and I watched people dancing and thought I'd like to learn. Before I only dared dance after I'd had a few drinks. I shall continue the lessons. Susan is a lovely girl, a very good teacher.'

A young man in a tweed jacket and cavalry twill trousers with hunched shoulders was having a lesson in the disco room at the far end of the studios, where lights flashed and the music was loud. His teacher was showing him one or two of the new dances from *Saturday Night Fever*, but he was a slow learner. His knees and ankles and hips seemed to be fixed at odd angles, and it didn't seem likely that they would ever quite come to terms with *The Bump* (where people's bottoms and hips collide at regular intervals), or *The Hustle*, or *The Body Language*, or *The Brooklyn Bus Stop*, or *The Tango Hustle*. He said, after the lesson, that he had been persuaded to come by his sister, and he had met his girl friend here. 'She stays with me now – I mean, of course, just socially,' he said.

Saturday Night Fever has brought in hundreds more students wanting to learn to dance like John Travolta, and the disco side of the business is growing rapidly.

A young soldier in a pin-stripe suit, who was stationed at Chelsea barracks, said he came to the studio whenever he could get away. He liked all kinds of dancing, but said he wasn't good at it. 'My friends tease me a bit about it but it doesn't put me off. They say they could teach me to dance for half the money, but I like it here. You meet a nice class of person.'

Arthur Murray founded his first dance studio in New York in 1914 on 42nd Street. He started out teaching his friends at school to dance. When he left school he invented those foot-print teach-yourself-to-dance sheets and went into business with a record company. The foot-print method was a great success, but the real dancing boom took off in the thirties. By the mid-thirties there were 500 Arthur Murray franchise-holders running dance studios around the country, and it spread to England and Australia. Arthur Murray is still alive and living in Hawaii.

The studio exudes an aura of respectability. The cost keeps the clientele select, though most of them spend a large proportion of their money on dancing. As one young man put it: 'It's so nice to be able to ask a woman to dance without it meaning you fancy her, or anything. The girls are pleased to go somewhere where they won't be pounced on. It's a very nice atmosphere to meet people in.'

They were solitary characters, many of them young people whose old-fashioned attitudes, shyness and sense of propriety made discos and dance halls difficult. It was almost as if dancing had become a substitute for sex, and there was something curiously asexual and fearful about many of the people there. The manager said they liked cleanness. 'So many discos these days are dirty places, full of people in jeans and tee-shirts. Our clients aren't like that. Hotels are all right, but you have to have a partner.' The studio is indeed spotlessly clean, perhaps a little too aseptic, with no bar and no refreshments.

It is a small, cheerful world of respectable people adrift in London. A pretty, immaculate, conservatively-dressed 19-year-old woman said: 'I think dancing is a social asset. I'm not very good, but I enjoy it. I would hate to go to places where dancing was just a preliminary to something else that might be a bit, you know, nasty. Here I dance with some charming people of all ages, very courteous. Yes, it is very expensive, but I come here at least three nights a week, so I don't mind spending most of my money.'

A middle-aged unmarried woman – a piano and violin teacher – had been at the studio for years. 'It's a lovely social world,' she said. 'No, I never see any of these people outside, but here they're real friends.' An extremely uncoordinated chartered accountant in his fifties had been attending regularly for four years. He was being pulled and pushed and tugged about the dance floor by an infinitely patient young teacher.

The manager watched him for a little. 'Let's face it,' he said. 'He's never going to be able to dance. He doesn't mix socially here, always sits in a corner, but he must get something out of it.

He's made real progress, I can say that.'

There is something charming and infectious about the atmosphere of the place. At first sight all those people paying out so much money for so little company was sad, but after a while the pleasure that most of them seemed to get from dancing, or at least trying to dance, began to shine through. It's synthetic fun, expensive company, but at least they are enjoying it.

24 April, 1978   **Polly Toynbee**

Beginning

'At the age of 10 I said I wanted to be an organizing female with a briefcase. I had seen someone looking like that. In fact, I've never had a life plan or an ambition. There was never a time when I sat down and thought, what shall I do to earn money? One didn't in those days. Coming from an academic background, it seemed natural to follow an academic path. So that was all I thought about – being a brilliant academic.

Both my parents were classical scholars and they wanted me to study classics. I had a great row over this because I wanted to read economics. I had become a Socialist very early on. I was well under 10 when a rich aunt used to give us summer holidays and take us out in a horse-drawn carriage for picnics. When we came to eat we sat in one place and the coachman sat somewhere else. I'm sure he was much happier that way, but I trace the beginnings of my socialism to that point. It was my first appreciation of class distinction.

I'm sure a good Freudian would say that my left-wing attitude was a rebellion against my mother who was a Conservative. Anyway, I didn't entirely win the battle. It was agreed that I would read classics for three years and then read economics for a year after that. I had no aim in view. I secretly thought that economics perhaps held the key to some of the injustices and miseries of the world by which I was then greatly troubled.

By the time I started on my classics course, I had already met Jack Wootton. He was a friend of my brother's and we became engaged when I was 19 and really all I wanted at that time was to marry Jack. Some of my friends were career minded. I had one particular friend who said she wanted to become a doctor, a research doctor, and so she did and rose to the sort of heights where the Japanese bowed to her. I was very impressed of course, but I never wanted anything like that for myself.

At Cambridge we didn't seem to discuss careers. We sat around in each other's rooms and talked. God knows what about. I suppose I identified with the group of girls who also had anxieties about their men. You see, the War was on and here we were surrounded by young men who were cannon fodder. It was difficult to think much beyond that. Jack got wounded in 1916 and was sent home for 14 months until he recovered. When he was passed fit for active service again, we got married and two days later he left for France. Five weeks after that he was killed.

It was a shattering experience, although my troubles were in no way unusual. What happened to me happened to thousands of my contemporaries. But my upbringing left no room for self-pity. I went on to finish my classics degree. I was unwell with tonsillitis and got an 'aegrotat' degree (the one they give you when you are ill) but a year later I got a first-class economics degree and was immediately offered a research scholarship at LSE. I accepted this because it was something to do. I would put it no higher than that.

My research came to nothing, but during that time I lectured to social science students at Westfield College. I did it only once a week, so it doesn't seem very important looking back. Most of the students were young women of means and leisure who wished to engage in various charitable activities, so they came in their cars and their pearls and their elegant clothes to hear what I had to say. God knows what I told them. I tremble to think.

A year later when I was still uncertain what I wanted out of life, Girton invited me back to hold the post of Director of Studies in Economics. This I accepted as much as anything because there seemed no adequate reason to refuse. I was also invited to give a course of lectures required for one of the compulsory papers in Part II of the Economics Tripos. As a woman I

164

was not, and could not be, a member of the university – women students were simply admitted as a matter of courtesy to lectures provided for male undergraduates.

I was terribly nervous. I wore a green suit which I had made myself. The skirt had an elastic band around the waist and I was so worried that it might break, that I made two skirts and wore one on top of the other.

This was one of the most materially comfortable periods in my life. I was free as never since of all domestic responsibilities and chores. Everything was laid on and the bath water was always hot. But my heart was not in it.

And then I saw an advertisement in the *Daily Herald* for a research worker in what was then the joint research department of the TUC and the Labour Party. This was the first job I applied for and I consider it a landmark in my life. Hugh Dalton was on the selection committee and was very encouraging. I had worked for him in his fight as Labour candidate in a by-election in Cambridge.

I nearly didn't get the job. They asked me why I had applied and I said it was 'due to a multitude of converging considerations' and what they wanted to hear was something about 'unbeatable injustices of our social system'. But I got the job and it was lovely. I was very naïve about the Labour Party. I remember arguing with one of my friends that Labour politicians never drank. God help us!

It was very unusual after university life where I was used to doing things in my own time. I took the starting time of the new job for granted, but I did find it odd that at 5.30 on the dot, in mid-sentence even, people would stop what they were doing and go home. But I enjoyed the work. I liked preparing wage claims for the TUC side and dealing with a bus conductor who would come in and ask for help with his income tax.

I didn't like election time. We would have to write notes for candidates and sometimes we would go along to evening meetings and listen to what they did with those notes. It put me off for ever of wanting to be a Parliamentary candidate. So phoney.

I was incurably serious-minded and still, I think, suffering from the emotional shock of Jack's death. I was absolutely whole hearted in my devotion to the Labour movement.

But after a couple of years I wanted a change. I began to want to speak for myself instead of always over the signature of others. That public men must be properly briefed was something I recognized, but I did feel at times that the research department went too far. So once again I began looking at advertisements in the press to see if I could find something else reasonably congenial to do.'

Baroness Wootton interviewed by
14 December, 1977 **Linda Christmas**

A country diary: Kew

In the last days of the old year, the primroses are in flower in the Queen's garden at Kew. There is still a blue borage and even the rose of Sharon holds a golden memory of the season gone. The flowers stand in their winter retreat in the small seventeenth-century garden that is being re-created behind the Queen's palace, a grand name for the Dutch-style house that lies by the bank of the Thames.

Every tree, every shrub, every herb would have been found here three centuries ago. The formal framework is made from an intricate pattern of clipped box hedges and banks of yew based on a French design. On the one side is an arbour of pleached hornbeam leading to an artificial mound erected as a viewing point, smothered with sedum and box and backed with elder.

The herbs are not only labelled but carry informative plaques with delightful quotations from the early herbalists like Gerarde and Parkinson to bring comfort to winter ailments. Borage used in salad will exhilarate you and make the mind glad. Put the leaves and the flower into wine and they will drive away all sadness and melancholy. The roots of those early primroses, sniffed as a juice, will purge the brain and allay migraines.

As for self-heal, one head still flowering in the dark days, it is so efficacious that it renders all physicians unnecessary. Then the yarrow, in flower everywhere on waste ground and wayside, the leaves chewed are a remedy for toothache. Even a crick in the neck can be cured with an infusion of wild tulip if drunk with red wine. Wrapped in such medieval mysteries, I walked across the park to the enclosed grounds around the Queen's cottage where a piece of old oaken England is left to its wild self and fed the pheasants as they stalked from the tangled undergrowth.

30 December, 1977   **John T. White**

France foots the Imperial bill

A jet cargo plane loaded with 20 tons of flowers is on its way to the Central African Empire to put the finishing touches to the coronation on Sunday of Emperor Bokassa I. The cargo should tip the cost of the extravaganza to well over £10 million, most of which will be paid by France as part of its aid programme to the underdeveloped empire of less than two million people.

Emperor Bokassa, a former French colonial army sergeant, self-promoted to Field Marshal, has left a trail of debts in France after ordering horses, carriages, coronation robes, jewels, cars, crowns, thrones and bathroom equipment intended to make him appear the most important ruler since Napoleon. Most of the bills are being picked up by the French Government after one of the creditors, a coachbuilder, said that he would not deliver the wheels of the coronation coach if it was not paid for. Only a clash with a religious festival prevented the coronation taking place on the anniversary of Napoleon's elevation in 1804, but the ceremony in Bangui on Sunday will far outshine the glitter of the first French Empire.

Preparations have been going on for more than two years, after an assurance to Emperor Bokassa by President Giscard that France approved his every wish. Apart from the fact that the despotic multi-married leader known as Papa Bok has a sentimental attachment to France – he calls de Gaulle his father – the Central African Empire is the French President's favourite big-game hunting ground. Two of his relatives are also in charge of an operation there to exploit uranium reserves.

As a result of President Giscard's open-ended promise, interpreted as a pledge to foot the bill, the emperor has spared France no expense. Among cargo freighted at France's cost (more than £1 million) are more than 100 cars, 75 motor-cycles, 35 horses, 100 tons of food, 140 tons of wine, more than 400 tons of furniture, and 100 tons of fireworks.

But weight is outshone by magnificence. The Empress Catherine will wear a 20ft-long train encrusted with nearly a million pieces of gold. The emperor will wear a robe embroidered with pearls with a 30ft-long train in imperial purple. The imperial crown, which like all the finery has been made in France, has 5,000 precious stones and there will be two imperial carriages followed by a fleet of landaus. The three-ton imperial throne is a golden eagle whose 800 feathers have been plated in gold. The emperor's bath is encrusted with gold and silver and bears the imperial 'B' under a crown. The 35 grey horses trained in Normandy to pull the coaches and landaus are expected to live only four or five weeks in the local climate, and the coach drivers have also been warned that their lifespan will be short if they make any mistakes. The emperor's reputation, second only to Amin's for precipitous executions, has meant that he has failed to attract a white chauffeur despite the promise to pay in gold. But President Giscard has sent a dozen security men to protect him. The biggest French reward for his largesse is exclusive TV rights for what Papa Bok has called 'the most important news event of the century'.

The French Government, which prefers not to mention trifles like 300 refrigerators and 200 stoves that have been expressed to Bangui, prefers to stress the enthusiasm of the local population for the ceremony. After all, despite a subsistence standard of living in one of the most impoverished countries of the world, nobody appears to have refused contributions for the coronation of Papa Bok's toll booths set up every eight miles across the country.

Nor are shopkeepers refusing to offer their entire stock as a tribute with hardly a thought for the £200-a-day fine if they don't.

2 December, 1977   **Paul Webster**

The boat people

Refugee officials and diplomats call them 'the boat people'. Some are indeed fishermen, but most are city folk who, before they slipped away from their homes in Saigon and other towns with hearts knocking and gold and dollars sewn into their clothes, knew nothing of the ocean or its dangers.

Nobody knows how many have drowned or been murdered by pirates. But more than two years after the fall of Saigon, they are still coming, and in increasing numbers. They run the gauntlet of the pirates to the Thai coast where the Thais, their camps already full of Cambodians and Laotians, are beginning to turn them away. They arrive hopefully off Singapore which, until recently, they have wrongly seen as a haven, to be ordered out – at gun-point if necessary.

A few blunder down into Indonesian waters, and some head for the Philippines or Hong Kong. But for those who go south, there is now one preferred final destination – Australia, where the arrival earlier this week of a modern trawler with 180 people aboard, including seven Vietnamese soldiers who were overpowered and locked up, has caused political consternation and a diplomatic incident.

The lush little island of Tengah, eight miles off the Malaysian coast, could have been the setting for *South Pacific* and, indeed, a neighbouring island was the location for that film. Now its palm trees and white sand beaches are the scene of a genuine drama, for the Malaysian government has set it aside as a concentration point for Vietnamese refugees.

For anyone who worked in Vietnam, nostalgia is unavoidable. There is the quacking sound of the language. There is the little girl in the pink dress washing her knickers in the sea who giggles, and then hides the giggle with her hand in a gesture that could only be Vietnamese. There is the very Vietnamese fact that refugees are cutting down timber on this Malaysian island and selling it as firewood to Malaysians, and most of all, there is the familiar impact of the Vietnamese ego – sharp, strong, selfish, and shrewd, but rarely unmixed with charm and usually compelling respect.

The refugees' stories have a sameness that can be summed up in the word 'incompatibility', although they also reflect badly on the Communists' failure to find some role for the old South Vietnamese middle class other than agricultural labour. The elected camp chief, Nguyen Hoang Cuong, is a case in point. A businessman and university lecturer, he was given a job in a firm of which he had been a part owner before the liberation. Then the police took him away. He spent nearly a month in detention on the charge of having assisted a former associate of Air Marshal Ky to leave the country. The charge was true, but it had happened before the fall of Saigon, so he was released. 'But it was enough for me,' he says in his fluent English; 'I realized that people like myself would not have any place, any job, any future with the regime. Sooner or later I would be taken to a re-education camp. So I determined to escape.' After four attempts, he succeeded.

Malaysia is looking after nearly 5000 of these 'boat people', Thailand probably has a similar number and there are smaller groups in Hong Kong, the Philippines, and Singapore. None of the South-East Asian countries is prepared to let more than a handful stay permanently, and some, like Singapore, won't even let them stay on a temporary basis. The current American quota of 15,000 for Indo-Chinese refugees falls far short of the total of 80,000, most of them not sea refugees, in camps mainly in Thailand. Thus Australia has become 'the last hope', according to Nguyen Hoang Cuong. The Malaysians have not taken away the refugees' boats and, if they want to go on, they are not stopped. On Tengah, refugees are working now to refurbish four for the long trip to Australia. They are capable of carrying 120 people. They delayed sailing after promises from Australian immigration officials, under urgent instructions from the harried Fraser government in Canberra, that they will be considered as normal migrants. But if the promises are not kept, they vow they will set off.

As the Australian immigration minister said recently: 'The

potential is there for large numbers of people to reach Australia in small boats now that the trail has been blazed.' Nearly 800 refugees, including the latest batch aboard the big trawler, have already reached northern Australia. Given the care with which Vietnamese apparently continue to listen to the BBC, The Voice of America, and Radio Australia, the new 'trail' to Australia will already be general knowledge back in Vietnam.

'When will it all end?' a Malaysian diplomat asked plaintively, back in Singapore. The answer is almost certainly that it will get worse, and that diplomatic difficulties with Vietnam, largely avoided till now, are going to become a dimension of the problem. The Vietnamese have already demanded the return of the refugees aboard the trawler as 'pirates'. The Australians have refused. Vietnam has made a similar demand that the Philippines return a cargo vessel they say was hijacked in June. The Philippines government intends instead to try the alleged offenders in Manila.

The almost certain result of the increasing number of sea escapes is that the Vietnamese will intensify security measures. There will be more guards on shore and on the boats and future escapes will inevitably involve more violence and even killing. Where there is violence the question of hijacking arises. Already several governments, including that of Malaysia, have announced that escapees from Vietnam will henceforth be treated as illegal aliens rather than refugees.

One can sense the growing irritation of South-east Asian governments. Why don't these people accept their fate instead of, however heroically, crossing the sea to park themselves in countries that don't want them and can't cope with them? Australia, partly replacing the United States and France as the end of a painful transmission belt, is equally annoyed. But the refusal of the Vietnamese to accept the inevitable is the characteristic which, on both sides, prolonged their civil war beyond all expectation. And there are reckoned to be some 100,000 boats up and down South Vietnam's long coastline, so this is one problem that is not going to go away.

3 December, 1977   **Martin Woollacott**

Bank holidays while you wait

Not for everyone did festivities mercifully close on Tuesday. Yesterday was listed as Nepalese National Day, when whoever at the Foreign Office drew the short straw (the duty celebrant? the skeleton bon viveur?) will have put on his decorations and trundled to 12a Kensington Palace Gardens, there to down yet more scotch. Trundling is not suggested by any disregard for the Royal Nepalese Embassy, for whom anyone who has seen military service must (and had better) have the highest respect. It is suggested by the relentless press of national celebrations which occupy one night out of three throughout the diplomatic year. Not even at times of manifest surfeit is any rest allowed: Haiti, Cuba, and Sudan all celebrate on New Year's Day, and a small but select gathering will take place off Berkeley Square three days later to honour the independence of Burma.

These 21-gun days are only a tithe or less of the bank holidays which most countries allow themselves, but the myth that Britain has fewer than anyone else is not sustained in a searching examination of the subject which has lately come to hand. The Morgan Guaranty Trust Company has listed for the convenience of businessmen the holidays observed in every country it can think of, including even the People's Democratic Republic of Yemen which puts aside June 22 as, not surprisingly, Corrective Move Day. Malaysia is the outright winner with 45, not all celebrated at any one place, with Switzerland trailing at 38 distributed among the cantons. The UK, allowing for regional variations, has closed banks on 21 days of the year. Romania closes only five times; so did the Republic of Guinea until it decided that November 22 deserved some rejoicing as the Anniversary of Portuguese Aggression.

Thus a salesman seeking excuses not to sell, or a foreign correspondent not to correspond, could so construct a year's itinerary, travelling every day, that he never found himself in a working capital. Indeed he would have a choice of itineraries. On

June 24 he could s pend the Battle of Carabobo Day in Venezuela, St John the Bapt ist's Day in countless Catholic lands, New Constitution and Fishermen's Day in Zaire, or what is called Feriado Municipal A ngra in the Azores. A perversity among the Uruguayans closes t he banks from March 20–24 to celebrate Tourist Week (and t hen, come April 19, is the Landing of the Thirty-three Orienta les). But there is some foundation for the myth about British h olidays. If Antigua, Dominica, Grenada, Montserrat, St Kitts, St Lucia, and St Vincent can all observe the Birthday of Prince Charles, why cannot the people of Wales with whom his name is perhaps more associated closely? And if July 13 is Organic Action Day in the Virgin Islands, please can we have one here?

29 December, 1977 **Leader**

'*I quite agree, it's a rough ride – but it might get us to the garage!*'

Diary of a skier

Long before the papers and the milk these inky January week-end mornings, Britain's ski exodus begins. The jets line up at Heathrow, Gatwick, Luton, Birmingham, Manchester, and the rest, for the zipped-up people padding to their 6 and 7 a.m. check-ins in fur and moon boots, only the unwary in slippery leather.

Heathrow at six is blasted from its overnight torpor by an anoraked army bristling with sticks and skis. The check-ins quickly become road blocks of amiable British confusion. Half-a-dozen Greeks, with as many words of English between them, jam our check-in while the queue lengthens 30 yards. The Greeks turn and stumble over poles and bags, minds frozen. I hope they got to Athens.

Our British Airways 300-seater Tristar is chock-a-block, one of 54 planes transporting 6000 packaged people this week-end – many more are making their own way – of the 15-week season. Our party of six is bound for Italy, which for the first time last year poked its ski tip in front of Austria as the most popular winter sports country among British visitors. Just why that should be, we are hoping to find out.

The jet purrs over the Alps to Milan in less than an hour and a half, a change from the pioneering days of 20 years ago when Major Walter Ingham rattled us across Europe in his Snowport Special, dancing half the night before the train landed us bleary-eyed in the Arlberg. Walter is happily retired to Elba (and why not?), Inghams people tell me.

His successors have other problems. Four coachloads bound for the central Alpine resorts of Bormio, Livigno, Santa Caterina, and Aprica descend simultaneously for a restaurant stop to break the five-hour drive. A meal of spaghetti, roast chicken and swigging wine is on everyone's table within minutes. We pass Como, but for the 45 minutes it takes many of us are simply comatose, our early morning catching up on us.

Bormio, at the foot of the Stelvio Pass at the far end of the wine-growing Valtellina valley, welcomes us with the news that the snow is the worst within living memory. Italy has often been spared the snow famines of recent Alpine winters, but not this season it seems. Alfredo Cantoni, our host at the Hotel Girasole, Bormio 2000, halfway up the 10,000-feet Cime Bianca ('White Peak'), works hard to conceal his despair.

Ten years ago Bormio, like so many Italian resorts, was almost unknown to the English speaking world. Elizabeth, his wife, Lytham St Annes born, tells proudly how Alfredo set out single-handed to woo us after the cable car was built here seven years ago. 'London, Birmingham, Manchester, and everywhere they had a ski club, he would take his projector and film. Then New York. Every English speaking person on the slopes he brought here.'

It is a formidable accomplishment. Americans are demanding. 'You must treat them like grown-up children,' says Alfredo. 'They want an explanation for everything. The English are much easier. They accept things more, put up with things when they don't go quite as they should.' US visitors arrive from New York on packages basically costing £240 a fortnight and consider them a huge bargain. The English are paying an average of £175 for travel and half board.

Americans get nut-and-bolt lectures from their leaders. 'Without making value judgements let me say you'd be in big trouble packing a drug.' On the slopes, an English leader, skis at a muscular angle, roars his young people on, barrack room style: 'Come on you 'orrible little Klammers you!'

Bormio is a square kilometre of ancient house and church, its forum intact from Roman times, no cars in its narrow, cobbled shopping street, where moon boots can be bought for under £10, and the lira at 1625 to the pound purchases a good deal more than the schilling at Kitzbühel or the franc at Wengen. This, of course, is one of the big reasons for Italy's rising popularity.

For the first two days we play dodge-the-rock skiing. Christopher, 20 years a skier, gives up halfway, and carries his skis down in numbed defeat. The vertical drop is 5870 feet, one of Europe's biggest, and there should be seven miles of run from the peak to the valley. This is like the M1 with two lanes blocked and the third scattered with rock. The sun is wonderful, but in the churches they pray for snow. We sauna and bathe in Bormio's thermal pool, nipping nakedly from 80 degrees Centigrade to the eight-jet massages, until we realize that the open arch is open to the ladies' section.

During an hour's run north to Livigno, hard on the Swiss border, we see the Stelvio Pass, a huge glacier open only for summer skiing. 'Five thousand people ski the sixty square miles on a good summer's day,' says Alfredo, planning his next assault on the English market. 'It's so nice to mix with mountain walking, barbecues and summer things.' At Livigno ('Little Tibet' from its remote situation) we ski in better snow, and buy Italian brandy from its duty free shops at 75 pence a bottle. On the mountain, I slip and slide on the icier patches. Our Bormio ski hirer won't sharpen the edges because he's frightened of wearing them out prematurely.

White Christmases happen, they really do. We wake on the fourth morning to an unangry silence. We throw open the shutters and it's true, the snow is falling, has fallen throughout the night. Italian knees sink to the ground; their season is saved. 'This will last until the end of February,' Alfredo says confidently. 'But the snow cats will be careful. The snow must be beaten, spiked, and rolled. Then we need a cold night. Then another day's snow.' Bormio gets all this and more. The half-dozen tractormen are prepared to work on the slopes by headlight all night. Sixty degree slopes don't worry them. Fog does, and they have to call it off.

The first day of powder snow is fantastic. Even novices turn with a flick of the skis. The second day brings trouble – two broken legs as the deep snow catches people out. Skiing is a strange sport, mentally and physically so hard in its first stages, the simple act of putting on your boots at 6000 feet an ordeal. Out you come from your personal tunnel and the sense of freedom and release is sublime. Christopher has made an

176

almost bombastic comeback. 'Never skied better in my life. Even kept up with Alfredo.' Thus the day of shame is redeemed. Italian skiing has a convert.

28 January, 1978   **John Samuel**

Rainier check

It was Somerset Maugham who once described Monte Carlo as a sunny place for shady people. It is a bit difficult to judge whether he was right about the place the whole year round, but he certainly had a point as far as this week goes. The town is now so filled with shady people it is surprising that it is not in total darkness – and most of them are journalists.

This is quite a week for royal weddings. In this republic-minded world these are events that do not happen all that often, so to have two of them in the space of a few days is quite an event for monarchy-minded people. Today Princess Caroline of Monaco is going to marry a French businessman, Mr Philippe Junot, and on Friday our own Prince Michael of Kent is going to marry Baroness Marie Christine von Reibnitz in Vienna.

It might come as a bit of a blow to those people who place the British monarchy somewhat higher in the prestige stakes than that of the Principality of Monaco, but Caroline's big day is considered more newsworthy than Prince Michael's. His might involve some constitutional issues between Church and State but on Friday he will no longer be 16th in line to the throne, while this afternoon Her Serene Highness Princess Caroline, Mrs Philippe Junot, will still be second in succession to all 400 acres of Monaco.

The press has been banned from all the events surrounding the wedding. They have not been invited to the ball that was held last night for 600 special guests, nor to today's civil ceremony in the throne room of the royal palace, nor to the religious ceremony in the palace chapel. The fact that the religious ceremony is in the palace and not in the local cathedral has added to the speculation that the bride's mother, a former film star from Philadelphia, objects to the fact that the groom is a mere commoner.

The only journalist who will attend the festivities and ceremonies on behalf of the world's press is a personal friend of Prince Rainier and officials have told us that his report might be a little late 'because it will have to be read and approved by the Prince first'. ITV's camera crew were taken to a police station and questioned on Monday for the heinous crime of filming, without permission, a man putting up official flags.

This has inspired the other journalists to frenzied attempts to gain entry to the palace and get the scoop of the year about the wedding of the year. One American scandal sheet has flown in no less than 12 journalists, who have spent the past few days scouring Monte Carlo with handfuls of money trying to buy an invitation to the ball or better still an invitation to the civil ceremony, which will be attended by less than 50 people.

Three helicopters are reported to have been hired by this newspaper giving rise to the rumour, now denied, that Monaco has hurriedly formed its own air force to press uninvited helicopters into the nearby Mediterranean.

The Royal Family might approve of the difference in style between the 1956 wedding chaos and the relative decorum of 1978, but the local population do not. Shopkeepers who live on selling souvenirs to the tourists – the Principality made over £4 million from the sale of postage stamps last year – have been actively discouraged from putting up pictures of the happy couple and there are not many signs in Monte Carlo of an impending wedding, the presence of the shady people excepted.

The decision to have a reception for all native Monagasques this evening after the half-hour civil ceremony was a late addition to the arrangements and very much a concession to local feeling. The only other occasions on which the ordinary people can share in the celebration is a lunch given by Caroline for all people born in Monaco the same year as she was, 1957 (and such is the size of the population that this means 43 people will lunch with her) and a hastily arranged walkabout of a couple of hundred yards.

It is not quite clear whether the local residents would have preferred a big public affair, rather like we had when Princess Anne married a commoner, out of their affection for the royal house of Grimaldi or because it would have brought in more visitors. The hotels of Monaco are not full this year.

But last night's ball at the palace did help swell the hotel bookings. About 600 people from all over Europe received the precious silver-lined invitations – and a sociological lot they were. By my reckoning, there are only 10 reigning families left in Europe (and that list includes such places as Liechtenstein and Luxembourg). But by the reckoning of the palace of Monaco there is a King of Romania, an Archduke of Austria and a Prince of Egypt, all of whom were dancing last night away. American royalty was represented in the ageing shapes of Frank Sinatra, Cary Grant and Ava Gardner (by now it should be becoming clear why the passing-out parade of police cadets seemed a preferable event for Prince Charles).

In fact, the Hollywood royalty have managed to present us shady people with the only event of the celebrations so far (unless you include my game of roulette with Ringo Starr). Film star David Niven gave a party for his old friends Princess Grace and Caroline in his Riviera villa yesterday lunchtime.

We all rushed around outside trying to get such newsworthy information as the menu, and some journalists hired a boat to see if they could get in through the garden (they couldn't). And Gregory Peck's car rammed into the back of Cary Grant's in their desperate attempts to avoid us.

And, while we are on the subject of nobility, and this is a royal wedding after all, is Caroline really marrying a commoner? This may seem an irrelevant question to pose in a liberal democratic newspaper dedicated to the equality of all people and the breaking down of class barriers, etc, etc, but it is a topic of conversation in Monaco.

Mr Junot's father, a deputy mayor of Paris, has long claimed family links with a general whom Napoleon made the Duke of Abrantes. But the present Duke has spent 20 years contesting the Junot claim and is preparing to take the matter to court. The whole argument centres on esoteric genealogical claims

179

about collateral family lines and the like.

This is of academic interest to British readers, but the Junot family has found another claim to noble lineage: that they are related to a former King of England. This turns out to be Etienne of Blois, King of England from 1135 to 1154. This Etienne is better known to us as King Stephen, one half of the Stephen and Matilda partnership.

I am in no position to argue with this claim (one listens to the arguments of one's hosts politely), but it does pose an interesting question in this week of royal weddings. If on Friday Prince Michael stops being number 16 in line to the throne and presumably slips back to about 53,000,000th in line does not Mr Junot leap above him in the succession stakes in Britain? There is after all a road in Monaco called Avenue de Grande Bretagne.

28 June, 1978   **Peter Hillmore**

Good works of Cobden, Bright & Co.

There is not much left at Dylife except gravestones and mystery. There is a notice board by the roadside explaining that the Romans may have mined here and that, during the nineteenth century, this grey-ash spoil heap littered with rubble was a bustling mining village, perhaps the most prosperous in what was then West Montgomery.

Up the hill at the Star Inn, the landlord tells you that Cobden and Bright once owned the mine. 'They built 100 cottages for its expansion, you know, but by the time they were built there was nobody left to live in them,' says a bird-eyed farmer's wife. 'Cobden and Bright owned it all right and they made a mint. But it didn't close because there was no lead left: it closed because of the poison.'

Dylife mine, prophetically close to the village of Staylittle, reached its peak output of 2,571 tons of lead ore sold in 1862, 12 years before legislation brought the child-slaves in these so-called 'miscellaneous mines' to work on the surface, and long before pit cages and lifts replaced the exhausting ladders which, since Roman times, had been the only route in and out of the workings at the beginning and end of each shift.

The coal mines led the way in the improvement of conditions: the old metal mines remained primitive to the end of their days. By that time the miners of Dylife were going down to a depth of 120 fathoms by ladder.

David Bick, industrial archaeologist and historian of the old mines of Montgomery and Cardigan, explains how Cobden came into this grim picture. For 40 years, between 1818 and 1858, the mine was owned by Williams and Pugh. Hugh Williams was a businessman whose plane of operations intersected with that of Richard Cobden and, in 1840, Cobden married Williams's daughter, Catherine Anne. In 1858 when Williams died, Cobden became one of the trustees of Dylife and another mine slightly further north.

The trustees disagreed about the future ownership of the mines, and it was decided to sell them. Cobden, scenting a quick killing, tipped off his political friends, Bright and Milner Gibson. Together they formed a company which bought the entire operation for £24,000. Cobden, Bright and Co. set briskly about the task of making it pay.

Published histories emphasize that the first steps included the revolutionary introduction of colliery tramming, direct to the surface, for the lead ore at Dylife and inspectors' reports confirm enthusiastically that Dylife was one of the first mines – if not the first – to provide changing rooms for miners. Output soared, and at the surface the hundreds of tons of ore to be dressed grew to thousands of tons.

In July, 1860, Bright confirmed to Cobden that the mine was doing well. By 1862 the profits were around £1,000 a month. Underground ventilation was bad – excessively bad in places even by the standards of the time – and boys were employed turning the handles of blowers. At the surface, in grossly over-crowded cottages, fever raged.

The 'fever' lies at the centre of the mystery. 'Come with me to spend a day in these glorious hills away from your diplomatic and my party tortures,' Bright had written to Cobden in 1860, suggesting a visit to the mines. Would these men, so vocally concerned about the condition of the poor, have done nothing about gross overcrowding and the decimation of their workforce by fever?

There were plans, as the locals but not the history books tell us, to rehouse the miners in new cottages that were built but never occupied. 'Fever' in the sense of ague, shallow breathing, a fast weak pulse, and delirium – as it would have been diagnosed at that time – can cover many conditions and many sins.

The few remaining legible gravestones tell us something. Between 1859 and 1877 there seems to have been an unusual distribution of death. Many children died, and that you would expect. But the normal pattern of the times, in which the women tended to die young, either in childbirth or because of the excessive burdens of repeated pregnancies, is not evident.

Those who died between 20 and 40 were mainly men. The experts on occupational medicine hold that lead mining has no toxic hazards for the miners, and that seems odd. Was Dylife an exception that has been overlooked?

The initial anaemia of lead poisoning would certainly predispose the mining community to disease: the abundance of lead dust at the surface might have served not only to increase infant mortality but possibly also as an abortifacient, sharply reducing the birth rate of the community. Dylife, it seems, might well have died from the lead it mined, simply because the increased production resulted in massively increased exposures to metal-rich ore dust.

That certainly is the hypothesis favoured by some in the area whose roots go back to and beyond the era of Cobden, Bright and Co. Cobden had died in 1865 and, by 1872, production at the mine had fallen to below 1,000 tons a year. Recognizing that Dylife was on its last legs, Bright and Co. sold out for an astounding £73,000, making almost £50,000 on their initial investment plus the trading profits in between.

Mining histories tell us that, by that time, the mine was so worked out that there was not a single end capable of producing 'one cwt per fathom'. But could Bright have sold a worthless mine for £73,000, and would any mining company have bought it? In any case under the weight of a depressed lead market, Dylife mine went out of business in 1884. Its grey ghosts and gravestones pose the unanswerable question of whether the profits can ever be said to balance the human losses.

Somewhere buried in the historical documents of mid-Wales are the parish records of the vanished village. Perhaps one day a skilled and patient epidemiologist will comb them for the answer to the mystery. Or would it be better and kinder to forget?

30 August, 1977   **Anthony Tucker**

Live and let die

One Friday evening recently, the TV newsreader mentioned in a jolly sort of way that a cloud of fall-out from a Chinese nuclear test would be passing over New York some time on Sunday. Nothing to worry about, he said, unless it rained. I stayed in bed on Sunday; it rained all day.

According to a Staten Island Zoo official, the bobcats sleeping à la belle étoile in the great New York outdoors have higher levels of lead in their blood than the big cats living inside. The New York Medical College treated one of the zoo's black leopards for lead poisoning – his second bout. His twin brother had already died. 'He was loaded with lead,' the official said.

There are nights when I stare up into the dark haze where the stars should be and wonder what's killing us now. You can't pick up a New York newspaper without finding some new titbit of horror.

A family was desperately ill for two years; there was arsenic in the rubber sealant with which they'd patched up the dishwasher. A local politician is fighting to prevent trucks carrying radio-active nuclear waste from driving through Manhattan. A Federal report confirms that a small mishap 'could cause 10,000 immediate deaths and 1.3 million late cancer fatalities'. A paediatrics professor estimates that up to 400,000 children a year are taken ill because of the lead-laden air. And so it goes. No wonder

New Yorkers are paranoid; they are threatened.

Most of these reports blur in the mind. Occasionally one stands out. The *New York Times* said briefly that in a routine screening of 55 children of battery factory workers in Raleigh, North Carolina, some had high lead levels. Seven children were taken to hospital for treatment.

Raleigh is the state capital, peppered with references to Sir Walter. At night you can hear the trees yawning; it's a relaxed, gentle, Southern town. Caroline and John Jones live with their three children in a huge trailer park in the suburb of Zebulon. The two-bedroom trailer cost 16,000 dollars: 900 down, 130 a month. Mrs Jones is particularly proud of the living-room with its red and black fur loveseat, console stereo and airconditioning. The place is clean and tidy.

On April 7, 1976, after being out of work for a year, Mrs Jones got a job with the E.S.B. Wisco Division which makes batteries for motor-cycles. She drove to the small, brick factory out on the highway in her own car. Four months later, her husband got work there too; her mother took care of the baby, Samantha, during the day.

'After I'd been there a week, I decided it was too dirty; sometimes when I left it looked like I worked in a sawmill. I'd take my clothes home and wash them but John's clothes were getting holes like they'd been burned. So I asked for uniforms. But we didn't get any.' Without realizing it, every time she drove home she was taking lead dust with her.

'My hair started to break off and fall out, so I bought some scarves. When I got home, I used to be so tired and for five months I had a headache and constipation, and I used to swell in my stomach. The nurse at the plant said it was because of my new baby. Then for two weeks Samantha would wake up at night just crying. I didn't know what was wrong. She wouldn't eat, wouldn't drink. She just cried.'

In January last year, under a Federal Early and Periodic Screening Diagnosis and Treatment programme, the local health department screened a two-year-old boy. He had no symptoms, but he had a high level of lead in his blood; his mother happened to be in hospital with lead poisoning. She worked at Wisco. When Samantha Jones was screened along with all the other workers' children, she, too, was found to have a high lead level. So was her mother. Headache, constipation and irritability are the early signs of lead poisoning.

Samantha was taken into hospital for treatment. The injections were painful. 'It hurt so bad, she cried and cried. It was terrible.' Samantha will be kept under observation for some years. A young child with high lead levels over a period of time can have development problems later.

Mrs Jones has kept the three pamphlets given to her when she took the job. She is sure that no one ever told her of the dangers of working with lead. Yes, they took a blood sample at the plant regularly, but she says that she didn't know why or what it showed.

Robert Morgan, the plant manager, has worked at Wisco for 25 years. Fatherly was the word that sprang to mind when I met him. 'Now, I don't want to raise any skeletons that have been laid to rest' were his opening words. According to Mr Morgan the factory hasn't had a problem. Workers, he said, have always been given a thorough explanation about lead and its hazards. The difficulty, though, is knowing what people who aren't too well educated have absorbed. 'You can't hold each person's hand. It wasn't dangerous if they followed company rules. It's like automobiles; driving's as dangerous as hell.' He also suggested that only the children of workers who weren't too careful about personal hygiene were affected.

Uniforms? Everyone handling lead has always had them. Now everyone does. If security precautions were good enough, why have they tightened them up so much since last January? 'If you're going to be like this,' he said, 'I'd rather close the meeting right now.'

Carolyn Jones left Wisco last month; she managed to get a job at Westinghouse. 'The dreadful thing is that I don't know whether Samantha is going to have something wrong with her or not.'

How does one know, let alone prove, whether a child who turns out to be a slow learner and difficult is suffering from early exposure to lead or the effects of coming from a fairly uneducated family? The situation is complicated by the fact that the Joneses are black. Rightly or wrongly, Mrs Jones now feels that it wouldn't have happened to her if she had been white. 'Jobs are so hard to find, I wouldn't have minded about the lead for myself,' she says, 'but I would never do a thing to harm my children. I still can't believe that anyone would let you do anything that's harmful to your kids without your knowing. Now I'm scared of what else is going on. How do I know that there aren't a whole load of other things that I can't see that's making them ill?'

In Kellogg, a small mining town in Idaho, 98 per cent of the children living near the local smelter were found to have dangerous lead concentrations in their blood. A lawyer is fighting to have the smelter closed. Parents are fighting to keep it open. That's how badly they need the jobs. Good morning, America. And how do you feel today?

25 November, 1977 **Linda Blandford**

Androids for the chores

A small company in New Jersey claims to have developed a household robot which can vacuum the house, serve meals, babysit, answer the telephone and speak 250 words including 'Well, how do you do?' Detractors, including robot researchers, are sceptical.

The company, Quasar Industries Inc., insists that it will start mass-producing the robot or 'domestic android' within 20 months and will sell them for $4,000 each.

The prototype, which can be seen now, is 5ft 2in tall, weighs 250lbs, is conical in shape, 'walks' on three wheels, has two arms with tripincer hands and a circular head without features. It is electronically propelled and can be recharged by plugging it into a wall outlet.

Quasar says it is getting an enormous number of inquiries from people who want to order the robot as soon as possible. The company has already produced 32 androids which are used for promotional purposes – they roll around the streets, spouting information and astonishing people.

The director of Stamford University's Artificial Intelligence Laboratory told the *New York Times* he thought the domestic android a 'preposterous fraud. The state of the art is nowhere near this – not in voice recognition, vision recognition or motion.'

'They put Marconi down,' replies Quasar's president. 'They put Newton down. To everyone who has put us down I say "just wait and see, buddy".'

What the robot said to a reporter was: 'Well, how do you do?'

12 December, 1977   **Jane Rosen**

Sole of honour

Exclusiveness is all very well; but this was excessive. The members of the grandly-titled West End Master Bootmakers Association who sat down to their 70th anniversary dinner at the Ivy on Friday could hardly have been a more exclusive gathering. Precisely six of them.

There were 30 before Britain's social revolution began in 1945. Some of the members at the Ivy thought there might only be three by the turn of the century, if that.

Hand-made shoes are becoming the prerogative of the very few; and not usually the British few. The rich Americans who used to order two dozen pairs at a time, at about £150 a pair, have largely dived into their economic funk-holes; while you are about as likely to find a British hand-made bootmaker in the provinces as you are to discover a gibbet and stocks. It is the Continentals and the Arabs who now decide they will have a few pairs of shoes in crocodile at £350 or so.

There was some lamentation on Friday that the more eccentric demands of the rich clientele have passed largely into history. There was once a man (a Scotsman, moreover) who owned a boxer dog which got run over. The vet made it a wooden leg to replace the one cut off, but the end wore down rather fast. So the owner asked a West End bootmaker to make a boot for the dog's wooden leg. The owner used to send it back to Belgravia for re-soling (though not frequently, as a top quality boot, worn two or three days a week by a human, may not need re-soling for ten years).

It has sometimes been suggested that the size of feet say something about the owner – small feet denoting feminine sensitivity in men and large feet a marked sexuality. The master bootmaker moves in sensitive areas. One of them swore me to anonymity when he showed me the drawing of the large feet of a well-known romantic and maidenly-modest woman author.

James Agate may have had a large ego, but he had very short feet. Bela Lugosi, the villain in dozens of Hollywood B horror movies, had enormous feet. Chaliapin had the largest recorded: they were about size 13 and his foot drawings always roamed off the edge of the paper. Lord Olivier's feet are of average size and unusually well proportioned.

Friday's chairman for the evening was the president and chairman of the West End Master Bootmakers Association, Eric Lobb; at 71, he is one year older than the association itself. The firm of Lobb has been in St James's Street since 1850 and has the Royal Warrant. Eric Lobb, who wanted to be a farmer and drives a Range-Rover because a Rolls-Royce would be 'ostentatious for me', is always reticent about his Royal clients. But I sneaked a look at the Queen's foot drawings and found she has small-to-average, well-proportioned feet. Her grandfather, King George V, had small feet, not entirely in accordance with his bluff naval image. The Duke of Windsor also had well-proportioned feet, as Eric Lobb discovered when the Duke rang up from Claridge's, asking a Lobb man to come and measure him. 'Royalty always make it more easy than any-one else,' said Lobb.

The remaining West End master bootmakers (or most of them) have two *bêtes noires*: the National Health Service and the ladies. The NHS can't pay enough to get quality shoes and boots at their sort of prices. As for the ladies, one bootmaker put it this way in a somewhat strangulated upper-class voice:

'They *are* a bit difficult to please, you know.'

The youngest master bootmaker in the West End, John Wildsmith, whose family made boots for Lord Palmerston (big feet, as many ladies would have testified), took up the point. 'Ladies today are very fashion-conscious,' he said. 'They do not *want* their shoes to last.'

Wildsmith, in the business since he was 16, and rather resentful that his view is 'so narrow – I have known little else,' is one of those who believe in making friends with the current trends. 'Deep down, I think the craft is dying out,' he said. 'I think it must do, especially the very expensive sort.' But Eric Lobb couldn't have disagreed more with this sentiment. 'People like us,' he said, 'will survive by being ourselves. We have more young men interested in becoming craftsmen than ever before. People are fed up with machines and the get-rich-quick philosophy. They like to be associated with quality. The people who have gone under have been those who tried to compromise.' Perhaps the future battles of Waterloo will be won in the boot shops of St James's?

29 May, 1978   **Dennis Barker**

Loving neighbours

Last year, for the first time in my life, I abandoned the big city and took up residence in the country, in a community that was somewhere between a large village and a little town. My stay taught me a lot of things, among others the truth of the slogan 'small is beautiful', which applies to many aspects of life and has huge implications thereunto. Of these, more anon.

But I offer one such implication now for your consideration and views. I will call it, pompously, the question of the polarization of people. First the working background. In a village, a small number of people represent a microcosm of the city, like a provincial repertory company that produces Julius Ceasar with a cast of ten instead of thousands.

There are the professionals (doctor, dentist, solicitor, MP, vicar), the tradesmen (butcher, baker, candlestick maker), the tycoons (a property man, a stockbroker, a lord), the bohemians (a writer, a painter) and an assortment of others young and old, ill and well, saint and sinner. The vast difference between this small group and their myriad equivalents in large towns is that in a village, you get to meet them all and in the city you do not.

In London, my next door neighbour is a stranger. With the butcher, the baker, and the candlestick maker I exchange good mornings and little else. I live in NW, I work in EC, and never the twain shall meet.

In the country there were few shops and the faces behind the counters quickly became familiar. I met them on the High Street doing their own shopping. I met them after working hours in the local cinema, at the local festivals and at the local locals. My neighbours were the postman, the lady who helped at the pub, teachers at local schools, a singer who performed at the local concert hall. Some had lived there all their lives, some had migrated, but they were the human beings I had for company if company was what I wanted.

We choose our friends from amongst the people we meet, and if we meet many we can afford to be selective. This sounds as if it were an urban advantage, but is it? Given the chance, most of us choose friends who are, on the whole, birds of our own feather. The same age, the same income, the same interests, the same beliefs, the same type of work. We avoid those who are different because in towns there are many available who are like us, go to the places we go, and hold the views we hold. Simple inertia does the rest.

In the country, this selectivity is impossible. If you want to be with other people, you take what other people are there – older, younger, poorer, richer, smarter, dafter, atheist or holy roller, socialist or high Tory, conformist or non-conformist. Going out to a party or a jumble sale, a pub or a promenade, you meet them, you talk to them, and you bloody well get on with them or languish in a well of loneliness.

And what does this mean? That in the country you encounter a much wider, though thinner, spectrum of fellow human beings than ever you do in town and, in doing so, something significant happens which has to do with polarization. City friends, carefully picked for similarity of background, ideas, creeds, and politics, continually reinforce each other. If I am a Blimp, the chances are that I shall work with Blimps, play with Blimps, and not only become more of a Blimp but inevitably cut myself off from all those who are not Blimps. Result: I shall assume that everyone who is not a Blimp is, to some extent, my natural enemy. Soon, I will only ever hear or read un-Blimpish views on television or in the newspapers, and if I do happen to meet someone diametrically opposed to Blimps, I need only make an excuse and leave.

The same exactly would happen if I were a Trot, a high Anglican, an anti-vivisectionist, or a flat-earther. I would spend my time with my own kind, and join shoulder to shoulder in sneering at all those others outside.

Almost the opposite happens in a village. If I wish to spend any time at all with other human beings – and most of us do, being a gregarious species – I must approach them tentatively. Because extreme, or even definite, opinions may alienate us from each other, we must first establish our common humanity. So we talk, to begin with, on the broadest common denominator, the things that affect us all – the weather, the recent plague of greenflies, the lateness of buses, the noise of the drills repairing the high street.

Next, we venture into the personal non-specific. You describe your operation, I tell you about my sprained ankle. You talk of your children's school. I mention that my sister-in-law is visiting. Later, as we feel each other out, we may mention neutral world disasters – a hurricane, a famine, a hijacking. If either of us senses a buried mine, we veer hastily away.

And the result? By the time we actually touch on intimate beliefs and opinions, a miracle has happened. We like each other too much for opinions to divide. We need each other too much to come to blows. If I stand for abortion on demand and you are a member of the pro-lifers, we would, in a city, hardly be likely to meet and if we did, would immediately fall out. In a village, the issue would be much less clear-cut because by the time I've lent you my pruning scissors and you've given me a cutting of rosemary, we have forged a common bond and mutually, if silently, agreed to disagree. Polarization has not taken place.

The moral of this story is not clear-cut, as it may seem. The village way is more human, warmer, gentler, and much more tolerant. The city way is factional, abstract, colder, and a breeding ground for intolerance. Country people love their neighbours, and dislike the stranger. Townspeople dislike their neighbours, care nothing for the old lady next door and march in solidarity with unknown prisoners half the world away. Which is better? Which gets more done? Or are there advantages and disadvantages in each?

23 March, 1978   **Jill Tweedie**

Dog tired

A large Great Dane was delivering an elephantine turd on to the middle of the pavement, its owner pretending to gaze with fascination into the newsagent's window. Should I, in a shrill and bossy voice, rebuke this man? He looked as large and fearsome as his dog. Out of cowardice, well aware of the passions of dog-owners, I said nothing and walked past on the other side.

I've never particularly liked dogs, but I was not a dog-hater either, until having children. But the countless occasions of scraping dog messes off the children's shoes, and sometimes their clothes, has made me hate urban dogs with real passion. With other parents I indulge in fantasies of setting up dog-hunting vigilante groups to roam the streets and pot at the creatures, even as they stroll on their leads with their owners. I read with glee the stories of the Chinese rounding up city dogs and herding them into electrified fences, since all pet dogs are now banned in China. (Dog is still eaten there though, selling at 20p per lb). I hope that in a few years' time we will look back on the phenomenon of the urban dog with the same amazement as we now regard the urban pig.

Dog-control, we have always been told, is the biggest and

hottest of political hot potatoes, something no sensible politician would dirty his hands with. But it looks as if the tide of vocal public opinion is beginning to turn. 1978 could mark the year of the anti-dog. Burnley council, following continued complaints from park users, lead the way last year by passing by-laws banning dogs from 120 acres of public parks, playgrounds and ornamental gardens in the city centre, out of a total of its 600 acres of parks. Angry dog owners left with a mere 480 acres of parks and recreation grounds to defile with excrement started organized dog walk-ins (or walkies) through the dog-free parks, challenging the right of the local authority to curtail this 'basic human freedom'. Other councils all round the country have begun to designate dog-free parks and some have appointed dog-wardens. Dog lavatories in places like Brighton, Kensington and Eastbourne haven't worked. (According to Dennis Barker, children play in the Kensington one as they think it's a sand pit and the cats have taken over the one in Brighton.)

There are an estimated 5.5 million dogs owned in this country, only half of which are licensed. Licences cost a ridiculous 37½p. When anyone suggests raising this sum the cry about old age pensioners goes up, though old age pensioners are expected to pay television licences. Then people say what about guide dogs for the blind? But their owners don't pay the licence fee, and a lot of blind people don't have guide dogs anyway. I hate to think how many dog messes they must tread in. In 1976 an Environment Department Working Party made one or two very timid suggestions, none of which has any hope of being implemented by the Government. They suggested the licence fee should be £5, payable to local authorities to finance dog wardens to enforce the law. This year the cost of collecting the licences will be greater than the revenue from dog licences.

More than 50,000 tons of dog excrement is piled on to pavements and parks every year. In 1976, 200,000 pedigree dogs were registered with the Kennel Club, compared with less than 600,000 human babies registered at Somerset House – and, of course, many hundreds of thousands of puppies are not registered.

In the past 15 years Professor Alan Woodruff of the London

School of Hygiene and Tropical Medicine has produced reports about the danger to health from worms, toxocar canis, and toxocar felix, equally dangerous diseases which can invade the body from the intestines and cause serious damage to the brain and eyes of children.

Professor Woodruff found in the course of his research that 2 per cent of the population have had the parasite at some time. This figure rose to about one in 20 children who lived near parks and open spaces. He took soil and samples from 800 public places all round Britain and found that 24 per cent of these were infected with toxocar canis eggs, which can survive in the soil for up to four years. Professor Woodruff sees about 30 people a year in his laboratory suffering from severe eye damage due to the parasite. Since it is not a reportable disease there are no countrywide statistics. The Health Education Council gives some pretty complacent counselling, advising against kissing dogs and cats and suggesting the washing of hands after handling them. But since many of those who suffer damage from the parasite never owned a dog or cat, that seems somewhat irrelevant.

The House of Lords indulged in an enjoyably silly debate about dogs just before Christmas. One Lord de Clifford, dog champion extraordinary, complained of the action of Burnley and 30 other councils in banning dogs. 'There are a great number of people who suffer from the attempts to ban dogs in parks and public places. Many of us remember not so long ago we fought a war for freedom. The banning of the use of public parks by a third of the population at any one time seems a gross interference of the freedom of the individual.'

Lord Houghton of Sowerby said, 'At the conclusion of our proceedings before the Christmas recess, we seem to be going through an animal phase. We have discussed otters; yesterday it was sheep, today it is dogs and a little later on today it will be horses: in between we have discussed trees.' He made an impassioned plea for the Government to find parliamentary time for raising the dog licence fee and creating dog wardens.

Lord Mowbray made a plea that action should be taken 'against irresponsible dog-owners and not against innocent dogs'.

Lord Somers said indignantly, 'I wonder why it is that local authorities always seem to attack the unfortunate dogs. I notice that they do not say anything about uncontrolled small children, of which there are many, who go into food shops sucking their fingers and then go round handling the food. I consider that to be far less hygienic than a dog just sniffing.'

Lord Willis gave a message from his Labrador Lucky. 'It is a race between myself and Lucky every morning as to who opens the post. The other morning Lucky happened to open the post and discovered that your lordships were debating this particular subject. His view on it was, I must say, rather dim. "How typical," he said, "of the House of Lords that just before Christmas, they should be so un-Christian as to criticize dogs." His views can be summed up very simply. He believes that humans are a health hazard to dogs. With those words Lucky asked me also to wish your Lordships a very happy Christmas.'

Baroness Steadman for the Government gave a dull and lengthy on-the-one-hand answer, and rattled out all the stuff from the old Working Party on Dogs, and in a great deal of time said nothing at all. The House then went on to discuss horse-meat trade with EEC countries.

Probably no other newspaper cutting file is full of such extra-ordinary contradictory material as the dog file. Looking back over 1977 all the dog articles are revoltingly cloying dog interest stories about funny/charming/lovable/loyal/naughty/clever/tragic doggie-wogs, or else quite appalling tales of people, children in particular, being savaged, often to death by mad Alsatians or packs of greyhounds.

'Homeless for love of a dog,' schoolgirl Lorraine and her family faced eviction rather than part with Curly. 'Divorce wife seeks custody of a pet dog,' but the judge didn't give it. 'Is Dudley the World's Worst Dog?' asked the *Mirror*, who told of Jack Russell Dudley's dirty deeds, and invited readers to write in if they had worse tales about their own pets.

'Villains flee as hero Bob dives into river to save his Denzil,' said the *Express*. Bob was a policeman, and Denzil his dog, and Bob got a medal for saving him.

A basset hound called Mary Poppins ate an unbaked loaf of

bread and 16 bread rolls and blew up like a balloon but survived.
'Petra, the pet every child knew, is dead,' and the BBC had to
tread gently in telling *Blue Peter* viewers that she'd been put
down.

Superdog Bruno was brought back to life by being given blood
transfusions from his fellow police dogs. Over 3,000 postmen
were bitten by dogs last year, and there was an outcry when the
postmen were advised to kick the dogs in the head. Then came
Bionic Dog, on all our screens shortly, so 'It's Tails Up as Max
the Canine Superstar gets ready to Grab the Ratings', says the
Mirror.

There was 'A Stray Dog walks 300 miles home,' and 'Dog's
Vigil Saves Life.' There was 'Every Dog's day is in the stars,' an
article about a dog astrologer called Sirius. And 'Tailwaggers
grant for dog kidney research' which wasn't about eating dogs'
kidneys, but setting up a fund for kidney machines for dogs.

All that, I suppose, you might put on the plus side. On the
other side there was an eight-year-old boy who was at a special
school, and couldn't read the notice at a scrap-yard gate saying,
'These dogs bite. Don't enter. You have been warned,' and was
bitten all over his body. Under the extraordinary headline,
'Fight to save death kennel dogs,' the *Mirror* told of the death of a
10-year-old boy savaged by four Alsatians, and the dog owner's
fight to prevent his animals being destroyed. Then there was the
death of a five-year-old, savaged by eight greyhounds who were
excited by the teddy bear he was clutching. And many others.

There was much prolonged drama about a kennels full of
beagles bred for experiments which went bankrupt. Two canine
crimes got much publicity, 'Crossbow fiend attacks Alsatian,'
said a *Sun* headline (I haven't found such violent language used
against dogs attacking children); the story starts, 'An Alsatian
survived a horror attack with a crossbow yesterday as a four-inch
bolt thudded into his head right between the eyes, just missing
his brain.' Then there was the two-year-old Alsatian, Major, who
urinated on a live electricity junction box and was blown into
the middle of the road. His owner took the council to court to
claim damages for his dog's changed personality. He didn't get
any.

We spend about £240 million a year on dog food, which is probably the most revolting fact about dogs. They consume vast amounts of meat and fish and until about six years ago used to eat whales, a dying species. Compared to the starving countries, our own food consumption is dreadfully wasteful, but the food consumption of pets is obscene. However, I have 'a modest proposal'. Let dogs eat dog meat, thus rapidly reducing the dog population. Eventually there would be just one dog left, which could be put in the zoo.

Please do not write me letters comparing dogs with human beings, comparing the atrocities committed by the human race with the innocence of dogs. I have not a moment's doubt that the life of one human being is worth the whole species of dogs. For this reason the threat of rabies alone should be reason enough for the doing away with dogs in cities, where most of them live.

9 January, 1978   **Polly Toynbee**

A country diary: Keswick – 1

Last night was no night to wait patiently for the badgers to come out, but it was no night either, in spite of the cold, to be in a house, so I went to a quiet badger sett long before dusk (one's eyes need that interval to adjust slowly) and found a stout holly for shelter. Just as eyes take time to adjust so, too, do noses – and ears: the smell of young, crushed nettles rose from under my feet and small sounds fitted into a pattern. The blackbirds sang themselves into drowsiness, into sleep, and the dark tracery of oak branches overhead stood out ever more clearly against the sky. Snipe began to 'jicker' on the bog and a very big flock of grey geese went over, babbling quietly, to settle there too – surely a mouth-watering sound for every fox on the fell? Nothing stirred at the sett and it was almost wholly dark when there was a sudden rush and rustle in the holly at my shoulder and a furious explosion of sound that not only made me leap but which must have startled every living thing anywhere near: an unsuspecting magpie had come in to roost and was utterly panic-stricken but, being a magpie, over-masteringly curious. It hopped above in the holly turning its head down this way and that and cursing loudly, telling the world that something was out of joint. I know when to give up – and went.

17 April, 1978   **Enid J. Wilson**

The case of the disappearing fritillary

Armed with a bramble basher, Janet Forbes and her friends are hunting down the meadows of Southern England. Thanks to the crop-spray, the re-seeder and the plough, the traditional grazing lands of counties like Hampshire and Kent are getting fewer and fewer. When they vanish, a little life system which many people would think of as traditionally English finds itself in danger too.

'In the early summer,' wrote Richard Jefferies, the naturalist and author, 'there is not an inch of the meadow without a flower.' The ragged robin, the cowslip, and various kinds of buttercup are fairly common and well-known. But rarer breeds like the fritillary and adder's-tongue fern use the hayfields and pastures as a last resort.

The Nature Conservancy Council, which gets £8 million a year from the Exchequer to look after Britain's flora and fauna, is getting increasingly worried about the fields. One field near Cricklade which is full of fritillaries, has been created a national nature reserve and others are now sites of outstanding scientific interest. Miss Forbes, her basher, and a team of helpers are the latest initiative to preserve the remaining ones.

They started work in April, selecting Sussex, Kent, and Surrey for their meadow search. Leaflets showing a cowslip and saying 'Do you know where they are?' were distributed and old land-use maps were dug out. The project ran into some early difficulties, partly because of the public's confused attitude to nature matters. Members of a Women's Institute, circulated by the NCC, rang up in alarm to say that they had always been told never to let on about the whereabouts of any orchid or rare creature they happened to find. But the news came filtering in and by early June, with the flowers coming out, the field expeditions were ready to start. Knocking on doors and clambering over farm-gates, the meadow-hunters began to compile their list.

Working in pairs, financed by the ubiquitous Job Creation Scheme, they should complete the tally in the next month. Each meadow will then have a card, equipped with computer codes and showing which of some 360 species it contains. The whole collection will then be collated and published as a survey by the NCC.

Last week, Miss Forbes, who is aged 26, and Miss Margery Deed, aged 23, were on their hands and knees in a damp meadow at Tonbridge. A sample of earth was bagged and taken back to the Nature Conservancy Council's base at Wye. Four stakes then marked out a square metre of meadow, which the girls, both university graduates, began to comb for plants. Like monkeys picking at fleas, they pushed aside the long grasses and a white flower called Sulphurwort to show the densely-packed mosses and ferns underneath. Seventy species or more can be found in a square metre and they give a good idea of the meadow's past. This one, reckoned Dr Barry Meteyard, of Tonbridge School, who told the girls about the meadow, had not been under the plough since the early 19th century. Miss Forbes, who can sum up a meadow as soon as she sees it, according to her colleagues, rated it 'medium interesting'.

The key thing about meadows, she said, was that they had to be managed to survive. A lot of conservationist talk these days gives the impression that if only mankind would disappear, the natural world would be quite all right; but with meadows that is very much not the case. On the way to this one, we saw a small ring-tailed plover examining the edge of a gravel pit. The gravel lorries grinding past looked the picture of a conservationist's nightmare. But the plover, said Dr Meteyard, had only started breeding in England when gravel pits became widespread. In the same way, said Miss Forbes, the meadow had to be grazed and cut to survive. 'Some farmers think that a wild area, one that's completely left, is the only thing that interests us,' she said. But a wild meadow, ungrazed or with no haymaking, would soon be invaded and finally overwhelmed by rank grasses and scrub.

28 June, 1978   **Martin Wainwright**

Mother and daughter

Down a green lane drenched with cow parsley, the herd turns in at the gate of Mill Marsh Farm. It is between three-thirty and four. The Guernseys are drowsy and docile in the heat. A figure with dark curly hair and a crumpled check shirt bolts the gate and coaxes them into the milking shed. Since she was a child, Joy Chapman's life has been dominated by milking time.

In the kitchen of the cottage adjoining the yard, there is a fire in the open range and a smell of soot. An old lady with a stiff arm is trying to hold a hot water bottle to her shoulder. She is fretting that a scald is keeping her from seeing the cattle safely off the road. Since she was a child, dairy farms have dominated Win Chapman's life.

Mother and daughter live landlocked in a green loneliness of fields and hedges; it is traversed only by the road outside their farm; the cars that stop mostly do so to let the cows cross, morning and evening. Mrs Chapman is seventy-six, Joy is forty-four and the likelihood is that the second part of her life will be spent on the same ninety acres which the two women have run together for twenty-one years.

Land represents continuity of the binding kind. It is handed on to sons who in turn marry and have sons, and so families staple themselves to the parish map. When there is a crop of sons, it is saluted as a tradition. But when there is a daughter, and when she is an only child who does not marry, it is a less rosy living.

And when there are no men, either husbands or hired labourers, to work the farm, the burden falls to women quite as relentlessly, for the seasons and the crops and the livestock make no allowance for the fact that a woman rather than a man may try to rein them.

The Chapmans have leased Mill Marsh for thirty-five years, which is a generation rather than a dynasty. When Charlie Chapman died in 1957, there was no question of giving up the lease; mother and daughter ran the herd, and even though mechanized milking had come in, Mrs Chapman herself was never at home with it. She learned to milk by hand when she was thirteen.

Until a few weeks ago when she was scalded, Mrs Chapman would be out in the road, seeing home the cows, or up in the fields holding sticks while Joy repaired the fences. She is small, bright-eyed and talkative. The kitchen is her burrow. She furrows through a drawer in the dresser, packed with brown envelopes; the miller has come for his money. She knows everyone's due, from the paperboy's to the landlord's. His is the biggest, £700–£800 every half-year.

'I do the cooking. Joy don't have the knack I do have for using this oven.' There are cats and puppies on chairs, a television on top of a chest and an old Singer sewing machine in one corner. 'It baint filthy, it baint dirty, but it baint what you call clean,' she says. It is a working farmhouse, mostly her domain now, since she is restricted in getting out.

Outside, anyway, is where Joy prefers to be. 'She lives for animals,' says her mother. 'There isn't much Joy can't do with the herd.' Milking takes the best part of three hours morning and evening, with a start between six and seven. Then there is mowing and bailing the hay, tending the calves, and the lapses between seasons when odd jobs expand to fill time.

'This time of year, you work till the daylight gives,' says Joy. She is red-cheeked and slender and her hair is beginning to grey. At the moment, there is fencing to be mended, then it will be haymaking. 'I do all the mowing. I do everything to it bar the bailing of it. We usually mow between forty and fifty acres.' And twice every day, year in, year out, there are about fifty cows to be milked.

Now is the time when life can best be lived out of doors.

November is the saddest month, though neither mother nor daughter says they get depressed. Too busy for that. 'In November, it's terribly foggy. We have to take the cows on the road, and that can be a problem.' Winter evenings. Cleaning up after milking. A warm room and tea and the telly about eight. Dozing until maybe midnight. Day after day.

What keeps Joy here? 'It must be the liking of it. I'd be quite happy if it took me all day to milk, it wouldn't worry me.' In one sense, there isn't an acceptable elsewhere. When she left school, Joy chose to work at home, rather than work away – her mother in fact was in service in Bournemouth before she married.

'I couldn't work inside: I couldn't stand being in a factory.' There are few enough of them around the Frome-Shepton Mallet area, anyway. But three evenings a week, Joy works in a village pub; it is about their only contact with the nearest village. The routine of milking keeps them away from feasts and festivals; they occasionally see a few relatives in the district.

Her mother still has two weeks' holiday in Bournemouth, but for twenty-one years, since the father died, there has been no holiday for Joy. One of her pleasures is breeding Palomino horses; she has five, and a yellow and purple rosette from the breeding society to mark their registration. She used to take them to shows but doesn't have the time now.

They manage without men, partly because the jobs are fairly routine, though Joy says there are certain jobs a woman couldn't do. Her mother chimes in: 'Joy can put the knives in the machine for mowing, though.' And Joy says 'If you keep your eyes open and see what other people are doing, you can do it if you've got a bit of sense.' She is unassuming about her ability, which must be very considerable.

The one time they did hire a youngster – because Mrs Chapman was not well – seems, if anything, to have reinforced the self-sufficiency which they have come to live by, for their patch of Somerset is not glowing with neighbourly acts of goodwill. 'You couldn't trust the little devil,' says Mrs Chapman. 'When you weren't looking, he'd be down on his arse smoking.'

'I wouldn't care to have anyone full-time again.' Another time, the old lady crept into a field to see if the lad had repaired a fence. 'When he saw me he said "Watch the fox". "Damn and bugger the bloody fox," I said. There he was sitting in a hole in the hedge with his arms folded, doing nothing. I gave him notice.'

Mrs Chapman was married when she was twenty-five; it was seven years before Joy was born, an only child. She was told she could have no more children. And why didn't Joy marry? 'She don't care a hoot for the trousers. She lives for the animals. Men don't enter her head. Joy don't take any notice of that.'

That is said quite straightforwardly; a sinewy kindness operates between the two women, and running parallel to the mother-daughter bond is one which links each separately to the farm. So Mrs Chapman says, 'I don't never interfere with Joy. I don't make any difference to her life. If she wants to go anywhere, I would say "Do you think you could get there and back in time for the cows, because I can't lift up the pails". '

Joy accepts the way life has turned out, for her without marriage and children. As for men, 'I've never had no interest'. Her mother says: 'Some of your old-fashioned nurses, they do have no inclination either.' For her there is an existence involving the farm and her mother. She isn't paid a wage; there is money when she wants it. She does have a bank balance separate from her mother. And she fulfils a daughter's duties endlessly, and good-humouredly, though sometimes they say they are both a bit grumpy.

Worries? 'Right now my biggest worry is mother. Then there are the cows and the farm.' They present themselves as just managing to get by financially. And will her daughter carry on Mill Marsh when she has gone? 'I've said to her: "Get rid of it". But she said I'm not going to get rid of it. But she's done it for her father and she's done it for me, so I suppose she'll go on.' And Joy says: 'I've no longing to live anywhere but here.' The last thing they see themselves as is prisoners.

6 June, 1978   **John Cunningham**

A country diary: Machynlleth

It is an accepted belief that our sand dunes, especially the
oldest ones, are a product of the Middle Ages when, so the theory
goes, the weather became much stormier and produced gales
which quickly piled up the extensive dunes we know today. The
evidence for this in Wales comes from both pre-history and
history. In modern times along the Glamorgan coast, when gales
have scoured away the sand down to the original soil level, quite
a number of pre-historic artefacts have been revealed. There
also a medieval settlement is reputed to have been overwhelmed
by sand. Similarly at Newborough dunes in Anglesey, a tradition
has come down of a village of the Middle Ages being abandoned
as the sand advanced and smothered it. Such legends are an
enjoyable part of our folklore but they take on an extra dimension
if someone stumbles on evidence that shows them to be true. This
has happened at the now pine-covered Newborough dunes and I
was happy this week to join a party of students from Salford
University when, under the guidance of the Forestry Commission, we were shown the substantial remains of a cottage recently
excavated out of a sand dune. It was quite moving to see these
long-buried walls and to speculate on their age. And also to sense
that many more such buildings, each with its story to tell,
probably lie beneath the sands all around.

8 April, 1978   **William Condry**

Roman courage

When Thomas More entered the service of Henry VIII the king
urged him, look first unto God, and then unto the king. But then
Henry was married to his older brother's widow, Catherine of
Aragon, and the waters of his reign were calm. Maybe it was the
memory of Henry's first advice that prompted Thomas More on

the scaffold twenty years later to proclaim himself 'the king's good servant, but God's first'.

More's faith is an inspiration to Catholics still; his Roman courage an example for all kinds and conditions of men. On the scaffold he behaved impeccably. When the Duke of Norfolk told him that his attitude to the king's divorce placed his life in danger he remarked, 'Is that all, my lord? Then in good faith between your grace and me is but this, that I shall die today and you tomorrow.'

Time and the passing show cannot dim the meaning of More's act. Yet he could be taken in by the impostures of the Holy Maid of Kent. His moral rectitude is unquestioned, yet his portrait on behalf of the Tudors of the murderous Yorkist Richard III predated Grub Street, and was responsible for the stereotype Crookback.

Like any other period, this was a time of wrack and confusion. Nothing was as clear-cut as it appears in hindsight. More's friend Erasmus wrote in *The Praise of Folly* a joyous attack on monasticism, the Holy Roman Church, the episcopacy, and on Pope Julius II himself: '. . . this notorious Madness for Zeal, and Piety, and Fortitude, having found out the way how a man may draw his Sword, and sheath it in his Brother's Bowels, and yet not offend against the Duty of the Second Table, whereby we are obliged to love our Neighbour as our Selves.' And this book was written in More's very house in Chelsea, where Beaufort Street now runs down to meet Battersea Bridge.

The title is a Latin pun on More's name, Moriae Encomium, for, as Erasmus confessed in a prefatory epistle to More, the idea for the book was implanted by his friend's surname, 'which comes as near to the Literal Sound of the Word, as you yourself are distant from the Signification of it, and that in all Men's Judgements is vastly wide'.

In truth the book is much more entertaining than More's own *Utopia*, though that sustains the notion of Thomas the saint: it advocates, in an age when yeoman and labourer alike were subject to plague and the violent fluctuation of harvests, a six-hour day and a primitive form of Christian communism.

The *Utopia* shows no real divergence between More the

Christian and More the Renaissance man. Nor did his heroism in death. And yet his resistance to Henry's Act of Supremacy was an anachronism for a man as intelligent as More. He must have seen the force of Erasmus's satire against the Roman Church; and long before the dissolution of the monasteries Wolsey had suppressed a number to take over their incomes for the foundation of the Cardinal's College, Oxford (now Christ Church). Before that, small corrupt monasteries had been abolished to no great accompanying outcry.

But reformation was the great political thrust of the time, and it was easy to see how politics were polarized, and how the king's own desires muddied the waters. What the National Portrait Gallery exhibition does is to illustrate the flowering of the Renaissance in England in the heat of the nation's politics: no surprise this, since the politics of Florence and Rome and Venice were hardly havens of security; from Savonarola's sanctions to the sack of Rome in 1527, the period is littered with violence and intolerance. And yet this same Julius II, 'Il Terribile', satirized by Erasmus, was the great patron of Raphael and Michelangelo; and Leo X, who conceded the title Defender of the Faith to Henry VIII, was the Medici who commissioned the wonderful family chapel from Michelangelo in Florence.

In England, More was the Renaissance and so was Henry himself, a scholar and linguist of fair achievement, taught by the poet Skelton: education had moved out of the monasteries into the universities and the inns of court. The prodigious child Elizabeth, later Queen, was a natural summation of the age's approach to learning. But the outward and visible sign of the Renaissance was Hans Holbein the Younger.

With Holbein, the wheels mesh. He was a friend of Erasmus and stayed with him at More's house. The three of them were friendly with the great printer Froben, who produced the Basle edition of *The Praise of Folly*, with Holbein's woodcuts. Holbein painted More and Froben (pictures of both are in the Portrait Gallery show) and Erasmus. In Basle he might have become a great religious painter. His native skills were as great as Van Eyck's, and unlike Dürer, his knowledge of his contemporaries did not sit artificially on his work. In England, the Reformation nipped in the bud any demand there might have been for great religious compositions (ironically, Holbein had left Basle because of the dispute over reformation). Instead, Holbein became a portraitist.

To say that is to say nothing and everything. It was a great age of portraitists. Even the mediocre portrait painters right through the Tudor age expressed something about character and the strain of sixteenth-century politics that no painter in succeeding centuries has matched. Torrigiano was here (there's his poly-chrome bust of Henry VII in the exhibition), having disgraced himself in Florence by breaking Michelangelo's nose. Cranach painted Luther, whom he much admired (the fine portrait from Bristol Art Gallery is in the exhibition); Michiel Sitow, Johannes Corvus, and a host of other minor painters worked in England. But Holbein dwarfs them all.

In Holbein painting found its greatest portraitist. In him art and nature reach a perfect conjunction. If you want to know what manner of man was the Duke of Norfolk who warned More of his danger, and who himself survived the vicissitudes of Henry's temperament, look at Holbein's portrait loaned by the Queen; and for evidence of More's father, as witty and courageous as the son, there is Holbein's portrait drawing, also from Windsor (together with the others in the remarkable series of studies for the lost group portrait of the family).

Here, too, is Henry VIII painted in his maturity (from the Baron Thyssen-Bornemisza collection in Lugano) painted in 1536, the year after More's death on the scaffold, three years after the birth of the Elizabeth whose rule was to consolidate protestantism in England. This is the cruel face of brute power muscled like a vast arm.

In Holbein each line and each accent is placed with a security that looks inevitable: and consequently is unequalled. Here too are the miniatures, of More, of his daughter, and her husband Roper, of Holbein himself: the self-portrait whose engraved replica is in *The Praise of Folly*. For Holbein alone *The King's Good Servant* is worth repeated visits; but even without him this exhibition of pictures, documents, gold and silver ware, and memorabilia is a splendid evocation of Thomas More, Philospher, lawyer, Lord Chancellor, and saint.

28 November, 1977   **Michael McNay**

Images of history

In Yeats's play *The Land of Heart's Desire*, which was once very popular, the heroine's house is infested with little folk in green, come to beg a sup of milk or a crust of bread, and all intent on filching her away to the 'vague mysterious world' on the painted back-drop. It sounds pretty awful, but it is in fact a good play because our sympathies are throughout divided.

The girl has oppressive in-laws and a boring life as things are, but all the fairies can do is kill her quicker – the dreams they bring are empty dreams. When she dies their tinkling music has an icy, uncharming ring. Jeffrey Wainwright's *Heart's Desire* (Carcanet Press) offers a similarly compassionate but disenchanted view of the frustrations and contradictions involved in our longing for a better life, but in a style that belongs wholly to our own time – no fairies.

Much of the book has to do with history, but it is a history brought to focus in eloquently brief juxtapositions: the drowned mill-girl whose 'bloodless fingers / Nudge the drying gills' of dead fish in the polluted canal of 1815, the bodies of 'the deep-chested rosy ploughboys' dead on the field at Waterloo, where Wellington ('No flies on Wellington') feels free to joke about the 'white bellies' of the French.

The restraint and accuracy of the best imagist poetry are here admirably allied with a moral concern which offers no easy answers. When the mill-owner dies 'his fat body clenches – Mortified at what is happening'. The poet doesn't let his pun triumph over a victim – it figures as a suggestion only, not a judgement, that a certain kind of pride, the pride that established England as a great industrial nation (we're still in 1815), was

208

death itself, and so we are still allowed a measure of human sympathy for the dead man.

There isn't room to praise adequately this, certainly the best first collection to have been published in the last ten years. It ought to have been the Poetry Book Society's choice for the quarter, not merely a recommendation. Its longest poem is about an early Protestant reformer, Thomas Muntzer, and his involvement in the Peasants' War. Wainwright's irony is neither evasive nor callous, and permits the splendour and the pathos of Muntzer's discovery to ring out in the line 'I find I am a god, like all men'. The poem is a masterpiece, and the book indispensable.

20 July, 1978   **Martin Dodsworth**

Master of the Fence

Albert Finney did not look as if he was going to practise dying a dozen times that day. As he collected his mail at the stage door the other morning he had some 'Wotcha!' banter for one and all, indeed looked as mischievously cheery-trim as when Tom Jones first clapped eyes on Susannah York all those long years ago. The large white capitals ENIGMA were stamped across the back of his royal blue windcheater. Not a bad rehearsal rigout for the Thane of Cawdor.

But apparently Finney had refused point blankety blank to let me see him going through his 'orrible throes at the business end of Macduff's brandished steel. 'No way! Albie'd go bananas!' was the official statement issued by a National Theatre spokesperson when I asked if I could watch rehearsals. And I had said I'd be very quiet.

They had sent me (me, a sporty type, see. Geddit?) to the National to appraise the sword-fencing bits of Peter Hall's new production that opens tonight. Finney is Macbeth, Dorothy Tutin is his missus into the Mogadon – and Bill Hobbs, it goes without saying, has 'arranged' all the bouts, battles and blood. In the last 18 years Hobbs has staged more famous public fights than Mickey Duff or Harry Levene have handled hot fivers.

Bill Hobbs is 39, as fit as a footballer and as keen as Colman's. He is devilish handsome in a Stoppard-like baby-faced way. He bites his nails and hates travelling by air. He has made fighting an art form. He was trained as an actor but even his best friends tell him he is not much cop without a sword in his hand. Lord Olivier made him 'Master of the Fence' when the National Company was formed 15 years ago. Sir Laurence loves labels like that. 'A splendid title,' enthuses the old Baron Knight, 'redolent of times when *le mot juste* was *le mot plus splendide*, or, to be more vaudevillian, "Those days of fame/ When a Pansy was a flower and a Fanny was a name"' (Archie Rice lives on in ermine, I'm telling you).

Hobbs's thrilling work has punctuated European theatre productions through almost two decades now, especially when the Bard is on the boards. Germany and Denmark especially relish his stuff. But in England, unless we are tourists, it is hard to get a look-in – you, me and humdrum gateposts have to rely on his cinema jobs to jog our memory about his talent.

Remember that whirling dervish, frenzied fight by those three young gentlemen of Verona in Zeffirelli's film of *Romeo*? Bill Hobbs was behind that. Or the whirligig, unending ketchup splattering in Dick Lester's *Musketeer* films – or Polanski's bloody, bold and underrated *Macbeth*? Or Ridley Scott's stunning new fencing flick, *The Duellists*? All violence by courtesy William Hobbs.

Once upon a time stage fights just sort-of-happened. Men like Patrick Crean did wonders, but for the most part directors relied on the old one-two-three rudiments of Errol Flynn's simplistic combinations: top-middle-bottom, parry, parry, parry, swipe, swipe, swipe, top-middle-bottom – all repeated *ad tedium* with some ad lib grunting. Avaunt You Cur! and the occasional jumping on to tables if the mood took you. They used to practise dying well – not killing.

As Sir Laurence puts it: 'My training in the art of fence was largely grounded on the clockwork technique of "one, two, three; two, one, four"; or "bish, bash, bosh; bash, bosh, bish; no, no, no, you should not do that bosh there, it is bash first, then bosh, now then, bosh, bash, bish, then backhand bosh." It could sound idiotic enough but could be quite good if you looked as if you really meant it, and used carefully practised variations of rhythm, also with a few escapes – purposely narrow escapes; then some surprises here and there, a frill or two, and your little fight could look quite respectable.'

Now the Society of Fight Arrangers, which Hobbs founded with William Marshall, has established a proficiency test which is on the syllabus of all the leading drama schools. He has written the definitive textbook, *Stage Fights* (1967) and this summer Barrie and Jenkins are publishing a completely reworked edition called *Action to the World*.

Hobbs gives hours to every bish and bash. Each one is planned to make an effect. It can take him weeks to block one sequence. 'I am simply a choreographer, making pictures out of movement,' he says. Actors tell you that he is devastating at getting his set-pieces to express the character of the combatants. Lay on, Macduff, and damned be he who first cries 'Enough!' He has worked for the full 90 minutes each day with Finney for the past six weeks. 'As a fighter, Finney moves very well and thinks very fast,' he says. Daniel Massey is Macduff.

Tonight's bloody barney will be light years away from the techniques of Sir Henry Irving and Co. Even though that worthy was myopic in the extreme, he very much fancied himself with the swishing blade. In *The Academy* 103 years ago this summer the Billington of the day described Irving's fight with Macduff as 'illustrating quite perfectly, in its savage and hopeless wildness, the last temper of Macbeth'.

Hobbs explains: 'Flying sparks in those days were considered an important feature of a fight. Irving was much enamoured of such effects, and would attach flints to the blade of his sword in order to achieve them. However, with the advent of electricity, Irving, in pursuit of even greater fireworks, actually had the weapons wired up to make sure they would constantly throw off sparks. Although it is not known whether he or any of his company were actually electrocuted, it wasn't long before he was using rubber insulation on the handles of the swords!'

The Fight Arranger does not like to talk about accidents – especially before a production of *Macbeth* which, traditionally, is the superstitious actor's most unfavourite play. Something terrible, they always reckon, happens behind the old cardboard battlements of Inverness. In 1896, for instance, Gordon Craig cut off Macbeth's hand while laying it on too thick as Macduff; earlier the great Macready cut off two of his Macduff's digits. The worst thing that Hobbs will admit to is arranging for Oliver Reed to be stabbed in the arm in *The Three Musketeers* – 'I told this Spanish extra to stab him in the right arm, but he goes and chooses the left, doesn't he?' Communication, in films, is very difficult, he says. In the years of Sir Laurence, one of the fine, nutty fighters, who has broken many a tib and fib, a couple of ankles and a collarbone . . . worst of all, he says, was probably his 'landing from a considerable height, scrotum first, upon an acrobat's knee'.

Hobbs was born in Hampstead in 1939. His father, who had worked in his brother's circus (speciality: a rope-spinning act under the name of Ken Larson) was shot down in a Lancaster when aged but 24. Bill can remember him – just. He and his mother went to live in Australia, where his Auntie Lesley encouraged him to fence – and act. At 14 he was a singing page in Helpmann's *As You Like It*, and at 16 he was the youngest finalist in the history of the New South Wales Foils Championships. He was in the 1956 Australian Olympic training squad – but did not budge the selectors and a year later enrolled at London's Central School of Speech and Drama. Ever he preferred the drama bit and by 1960, not long after his 21st, he was arranging the fights for Zeffirelli's stage *Romeo* at the Old Vic. The crits – 'revolutionary realism', 'naturalistic fury' and all that – have been rolling in ever since.

He does not fence as a sport any more. Nor, thank heavens, jog. As a choreographer in elegant violence he thinks Muhammad Ali's early fights were magical. He says the secret of his job now is to transmit the feel of a competitive instinct to an actor who is not competitive. He has never been a team game bod, but his eldest son now takes him to Spurs. His younger one supports Man United. His wife, Janet, as it happens, is in the middle of an Open University general course and one of her set-books is *Macbeth*. She is a distant relative of Judge Jeffreys – watch tonight's decapitation scene for further hereditary symbols.

The opening production of *Romeo* at the Redgrave Theatre, Farnham, still remains, he reckons, his best stage job ('you should never fail with *Romeo*, all young, athletic people; the whole thing so structured; no more than a Renaissance *West Side Story*, if you like'), and if he retired after reading this he'd like his laurels to be accompanied in *The Duellists*, Polanski's *Mac v Mac*, and Cardinal Christopher Lee's ring-a-ding swordfight with Captain Michael D'York at the end of Lester's *Musketeers*.

That last, if I remember right, had more revolting squirts of the old tomato than the Northampton Wimpy on a busy Saturday night. But, truth is, Bill Hobbs is wary of too much blood. In his fascinating book he writes:

'*Blood:* This should always be minimal. To use it without discretion may be realistic, but it will soon lose its shock value. Too great a use of blood can appear gimmicky, and when by repetition the audience has become used to it, the end result will be meaningless. There are three types of theatrical blood: 1, Stage Blood, which is slow running; 2, General Purpose Blood, which is normal consistency; 3, Blood Capsules, which contain a powder pigment and are for use in the mouth only. *See list of suppliers* (my italics) L. Leichmer Ltd, 436 Essex Road, London, N.1.'

I can't wait to see how his new book updates that. McFinney might give a clue tonight.

6 June, 1978   **Frank Keating**

Brecht and jam

I heard jazz at the Berliner Ensemble. I saw Hitler raging in a box at the Komische Oper. I watched a tearful Russian actress lay roses at the foot of a Brecht portrait. Those are just some of the indelible sights and sounds of an extraordinary week in East Berlin celebrating the 8oth anniversary of Brecht's birth. Directors, actors, critics, scholars came from all over the world (literally from Outer Mongolia to Peru) to take part in a Brecht Dialogue devoted to the theme of Art and Politics and to watch a ceaseless six-day flow of Brecht productions on stage, film and television. Man, a friend warned before I left, cannot live by Brecht alone; but amongst the many things the week proved was just how fertile and inexhaustible the old Marxist magpie was.

Backwoodsmen in Britain, of course, still regard Brecht as a passing intellectual fad. But the Brecht Dialogue indisputably showed that, 22 years after his death, he has already become a classic. There is hardly a country where his work is not performed. A sumptuous new pictorial biography by Ernst and Renate Schumacher (which I hope someone brings out over here) has a Brecht bibliography running to several hundred titles. And proceedings began in Berlin with the opening of a spacious new Brecht Centre (complete with study and recreation facilities) at the old home of himself and Helene Weigel at 125 Chaussee Strasse.

But canonization carries its own problems. Not long after his death a Swiss writer accused Brecht of having 'the telling inefficacy of the classical author'. And for me the test of the whole week was whether the productions would show Brecht was still a dynamic force or merely a piously-performed monument. In the end I saw five major productions at the Berliner Ensemble itself, *The Rise and Fall of the City of Mahagonny* at the Komische Oper, Moscow's Taganka Theatre doing *The Good Woman of Sezuan*, a Young People's Theatre from

Radebeul doing Brecht's version of *Antigone* and solo performances by Ekkehard Schall and Renate Richter.

Not everything was perfect. But the amount of creative energy on display was astonishing and what emerged was a confirmation of something I have argued in these columns before: that there is no standard way of doing Brecht and that every country, or company, must hack out its own individual style. Brecht may be a classic: all the more reason then to re-shape or re-define him.

The first acid test came with the Berliner Ensemble's new production of *Galileo Galilei*. For many reasons this was a crucial, nerve-tingling occasion. By all accounts the Ensemble had gone into something of a decline under Ruth Berghans's direction in the early 1970s and this production, by Manfred Wekwerth and Joachim Tenschert, marked the opening salvo of the new artistic regime. There was also the controversial casting of Ekkehard Schall as Galileo, the scientist who first of all confirms the existence of the Copernican solar system and then is forced into recantation by the Inquisition. Schall (whom Londoners will remember as Arturo Ui and Coriolanus) is unquestionably a star but his talent is for manic comedy and daemonic rage. How, it was wondered, would he cope with the role of a self-betraying rationalist?

In the event (though the production had a middling press from West Berlin critics) the fears were unjustified. For my money this is an excellent production hitting just the right note of cool clarity and emphasizing Galileo's modernity as the intellectual who sacrifices his integrity to security. It is played on a circular wooden platform backed by a long curving ramp. The costumes are lightly stylized: the Florentine courtiers play in light blue, the Roman ecclesiasts in all-white while Galileo himself is a strikingly contemporary figure in his grey cardigan and corduroys.

But what is fascinating is the way Schall approaches Galileo: not as the usual fleshy sensualist but as a small, wiry, intense man with a passionate belief in reason. When he tells us that 'He who does not know the truth is merely an idiot but he who knows it and calls it a lie is a criminal' he seizes on the damning final noun ('Verbrecher') with blazing anger. And, by an acting or directorial master-stroke, he shows Galileo ageing not after his eight years of enforced silence but only after he has been forced to recant: as he stumbles slowly up the long ramp at the back of the stage, ashen, shrunken and seemingly sightless, you realize that he is now the criminal.

As Schall plays it, the supreme irony is that, having recanted for the sake of security, Galileo ends his days a desperately insecure figure, furtively hiding his latest scientific discourse inside his workroom globe. I came out feeling I had seen a masterpiece about the betrayal of scientific responsibility; and also feeling ashamed that London had not seen this play since Bernard Miles presented it at the Mermaid in 1960.

Admittedly much of my playgoing at the Ensemble was dominated by Schall's overpowering presence. In *Puntila* he plays the Finnish farmer who is generous when drunk and selfish when sober with a blazing comic energy. When he boozes it is with such ferocity that he looks as if he is going to devour the glass along with its contents. At one point he gets into an indignant argument with a telegraph pole stretched across the bonnet of his car. And when he leaps out of his chair and takes off into space at his daughter's recalcitrance, one is reminded of Robert Hirsch in *Feydeau*. This is great comic acting but it is put to the service of the text. And it's worth recording that Peter Kupke's production, with its Bavarian-style farm houses, has been in the repertory for three years and looks as fresh as paint. Kupke himself told me afterwards that he has sat in on the production 50 to 60 times and that he and the actors are constantly changing it: the day there is nothing more to do it will be dropped from the repertory.

The ubiquitous Schall also turns up as the rogue-judge, Azdak, in Kupke's production of *The Caucasian Chalk Circle*. Once again his brilliance is not in question: he plays him as a boneless bundle of rags with a tight-cropped ginger wig and a lascivious prowl that owes something to Groucho. Schall is one of those Olivieresque beings to whom acting is as natural as breathing. But his technical bravura slightly obscures the peasant wisdom of Azdak's judgements; he also overshadows Felicitas Ritsch's somewhat mature Grusha.

But if one wanted proof that there is no one way of doing Brecht it came with Juri Ljubimow's production for Moscow's Taganka Theatre of *The Good Woman of Sezuan*. 'The Russification of Brecht' someone called it; and that neatly sums it up. After the cool clarity of the Ensemble we saw Brecht played with a jaunty fullbloodedness. The action was accompanied by a seamless flow of accordion and guitar music. Sinaida Slawina as Shen Te/Shui Ta radiated both amorous ecstasy and heartbroken despair. And Vladimir Wysozki (whom I saw playing Hamlet with the Taganka in Paris) brought to her lover, Sun, an extraordinary emotional violence. The production was not without subtleties (such as the evocation of a sweat-shop through actors beating their knees with the flat of their hands) but what was really fascinating was its high-pressure gaiety and élan.

What did astonish me was to find (in East Berlin of all places) Brecht being turned into a spendthrift bourgeois entertainment. Joachim Herz's production of *Mahagonny* at the Komische Oper (where the repertoire ranges from *Carmen* to *Fiddler on the Roof*) was extravagant in every sense of the word. It took this tuneful Brecht-Weill allegory about the collapse of capitalism and gave it the works: topless dancers, drag bands, toy steamboats, filmed inserts of the Wall Street crash and the final arrival of Hitler with police whistles and the banging of the theatre doors. It struck me as perverse, however, to spend so much money on a work that is an attack on the corrupting effect of loot.

And Herz's concept was oddly muddled: in the first act *Mahagonny* symbolized a Disneyfied American vulgarity, in the second Germany in the 1930s. This was what Brecht called culinary theatre. But I must in fairness report that the Finnish-born singer, Tamara Lund, who plays Jenny is a knockout: a looker with lung-power. I only wish Herz's production hadn't made *Mahagonny* look like *Cabaret* re-directed by Ken Russell.

I don't however, wish to end this report from Berlin on a sour note, The week of the Brecht Dialogue proved several things: that the separation of art and politics (familiar enough in Britain) is something unbelievably alien to East Europe and the Third World, that there is and never can be such a thing as a universal Brecht style and that just because he is a classic doesn't mean he is safe or aesthetically dead. Brecht himself once responded warmly to a newspaper caption of a building that had survived the Tokyo earthquake that said simply 'Steel stood'. The moral of the Berlin celebrations was unequivocally that Brecht Lives.

20 February, 1978   **Michael Billington**

Work in hand

We own, or can own, our clothes, houses, furniture and food. We can never own our words, though we use them in speech and writing throughout our waking lives. Language is as public as the water supply. It belongs to society. When we use it we have a responsibility to keep it clear – just as we keep the water supply clear. We're usually too busy to take much care over this. But when a dramatist – any writer – writes he is using public language for a public purpose. His responsibilities are clear.

Human consciousness isn't innate, it's created out of social living. One of the means of creating it is language – especially language used, with effort, to define things that were before unclear. There are several uses of language that can do this, scientific and technical for example – and one of them is art. I've heard it said that I despair over the situation of the artist in our time – that he is powerless in an age of science. The opposite is true: in an age of science he is at his most powerful.

The mistake arises because I wrote a play to show Shakespeare not as a poet *for* all time, but *of* his own time. This was to take him seriously for once. An artist has no more privilege in this respect than a scientist. Art develops as much as science develops. So I am far from despairing over the writer. There is always work for him to do.

There can be no civilization without its own art – indeed, there can be no human consciousness, no 'human nature', without it. It is certainly true that much contemporary drama is absurd or superficial – it cultivates 'the clever line' or 'the silence'. To do that in an age of science fouls the public language. Perhaps the last act of a social epoch, when it can no longer create values, is to create its own gutter – down which it will run. That is the part played by literary decadence. It may seem that our present theatrical and academic life is choked with literary debris – but, in the end, this sort of literature is seen to perform the service of revealing its own poverty.

I was lately asked to write a play commemorating the thousandth anniversary of the building of the Tower of London. The subject: prisoners of conscience in the world today. I refused – not because I'm not interested in such prisoners, but because in exporting *my* conscience I would be behaving as Wilberforce had when he fought the slave trade and, at home, exploited and crippled little children for profit.

It seems to me that the one question that will decide the future of all human beings is whether modern, technical, industrial, scientific society can create a new moral understanding which will enable all people to live together in peace. The time will soon come when we can have tools or weapons, but not both. It is a hard lesson, but we need to learn that moral behaviour depends more on social practice than individual action. In a society structurally unjust – as is ours – good deeds may in the end only support injustice.

The Bundle is set in a primitive Asian community. It will be said that this is another way of 'exporting your conscience' – just as it has been said I ignore the present when I sometimes write about the past. Reaction likes to keep its hand on the past because it throws too much light on the present. I chose the Asian setting because it enabled me to abstract certain social forces and show their effect in a direct and simple way.

Voltaire did the same. In art distance sometimes lends

clarity. The people in *The Bundle* live by a river. Directly or indirectly they all live from it. From time to time it floods and destroys them. If, as the play invites, you substitute factories and offices – all industrialism – for the river, then my purpose is plain.

The job of creative writing is to help to give rational direction to the social changes that are occurring, and to help to provoke these changes. A judge recently showed us that the racism of the gutter, and the tacitly accepted culture of our social institutions, are in a deep sense one – since they are both willing to literally speak the same language. This was not an isolated incident. So there is still work for the writer.

13 January, 1978   **Edward Bond**

Race causes an initial confusion

The man who answered 'human race' when asked to what race he belonged would get short shrift at West End Central police station, London. For there human classifications have achieved an elaborate formality, as a bemused magistrate heard yesterday.

Giving evidence in a begging case at Marlborough Street Magistrates' Court, WPC Linda Nicholls said that she saw the defendant stop an IC1 in the street. What, enquired the magistrate, Mr St John Harmsworth, was an IC1? Amid laughter the WPC explained that it was part of a code, 'An IC1 is a white man, an IC2 is an Italian, and an IC3 is a West Indian.' When WPC Nicholls reverted later in the evidence to more traditional language and said that the defendant had also stopped an Italian the magistrate, warming to the theme, translated: 'An IC2'.

Police language has long been famous for its cumbersome style, although on this occasion the WPC did not resort to the time-honoured 'proceeding in a northerly direction'. But the magistrates' court did not hear the half of it.

The Metropolitan Police are addicted to codes. Yesterday a police spokesman explained that police stations themselves are referred to in code. Thus West End Central, in copperese, is CD, Paddington Green is DD, and Kingston upon Thames is actually VD.

Coding of humans is a more sensitive matter and, although no one appears to have told West End Central – sorry, CD – about the change, Scotland Yard, which started to classify arrests in racial groups in 1975, dropped the RC (standing for race code) more than a year ago and replaced it by a system of 'Identi-Coding' on a one to six scale.

It is difficult to encompass the world with six groups but the Metropolitan Police assign 'white-skinned European types – English, Scottish, Welsh, Scandinavian and Russian' to IC1; 'dark-skinned European types – Sardinian, Spanish, Italian' to IC2; 'Negroid types – Caribbean, West Indian, African, Nigerian' to IC3; Indians and Pakistanis to IC4; 'Chinese, Japanese, Mongolians, Siamese' to IC5; and 'Arabians, Egyptians, Algerians, Moroccans and North Africans' to IC6.

A spokesman at West End Central was unable to explain why WPC Nicholls found it necessary to race-code a victim rather than a suspect but he did say that the police used their 'own internal language'. He would not give examples because they might be controversial.

The police are not alone in their difficulties. The Office of Population, Censuses and Surveys has not yet devised a question which has been accepted by everyone on how to ask people about their ethnic origins for the 1981 census.

14 June, 1978   **Lindsay Mackie**

The psychobabble enigma

Hear me. I mean, no way I'm about to lay a bad trip on you. I'm not coming down, like heavy duty on value judgements. You know the parameters and where it's at. If you've got your head

together, you'll know where I'm coming from. You into my space?
Wow! I'm really into you, you know, I mean how you went with
your initial crisis reaction. Aww-right! !

English, in a manner of speaking, in the 1970s. Here are two
other examples of this way with words.

'Harvey, I'm gonna tell you something upfront. Even if it
means the end of this relationship, like, this is going to be brutal
OK? You tell me if I'm wrong here because I'm open to it. But
I'm picking up this signal from you, you know what I mean? I
mean hostility. Now, hostility's cool, you know. It's OK. But you
wanna work through it, because you are what you do. Think
about it, Harv.' – Jerry, in Cyra McFadden's book, *The Serial.*

My experience is that if I can tell you the truth, just lay it
out there, then I have totally opened up a space for you to be who
you are and that it really opens up all the room in the world for us
to do whatever we want to do in regard to each other. If I don't
like you, I'll tell you. And that's great. – John Denver, singer.

For an explanation of my first paragraph, more in a minute.
What the other two meant is perhaps best left as vague as it
appears. The suspicion that both deeply wanted to bash someone may not be fair. They wanted to tell all, yet they said
nothing. They were speaking psychobabble, the Newspeak of
our age – puerile pap, specious speech, yet a dangerously
pretentious nonsense talk which one day could engulf us all.

Here's a rough translation of my opening paragraph: I
don't want to disturb you with grave intellectual opinions. But
I'm sure, with your understanding, you will grasp my point of
view. Good. I'm delighted you can accept this without any
upset. Splendid!

Nobody quite knows when psychobabble began. It was
named only recently in a book called Psychobabble by R. D.
Rosen, an author from Boston. The most likely origins were on
the opposite side of America and a likely source is Marin. Here
lives another opponent of psychobabble, Cyra McFadden,
whose succinctly satirical book, *The Serial*, which topped a best-
seller list and is now published in Britain. She cleverly mocked
the manners and morals and especially the 'mindless prattle'
of the psychobabblers, among whom she lives. This article

owes much to these two books.*

Marin is a county in California facing San Francisco across the Golden Gate Bridge. It stretches across the north bay enclosing a series of enchanting inlets and curious coves – the latter not all geographical. Sometimes Marin's coast resembles parts of Cornwall, if the Cornish all owned a car, a £72,000-plus house with patio and pool, and a sailing boat, two big dogs, and at least one cat.

It is no coincidence that psychobabble is spoken most monotonously by an affluent middle-class taking selfconscious pride in that their luxurious life should never mean vulgarity. The Marinites have taste. They would dearly like to remind us of this, except of course, taste is not mentioned by those who know they have it.

For them, Los Angeles and 'that whole southern California bit' is sun-baked territory with half-baked people in white patent leather shoes and matching pastel leisure (pronounced leezher) suits whose conversational preoccupation is money, demonstrated by driving Bentley Continentals while wearing shorts.

In Marin they are 'heavily into' modesty. One drives a Volvo while wearing tailored blue overalls, never washed but dry-cleaned in case the Esso sign on the back runs red.

Marin is where many beautiful human beings live, they would like you to know. Ascetic and aesthetes all, they are also heavily into lentil soup and grande cuisine, second-hand clothes and tennis parties, herbal tea and large Tequila Sunrises, getting rid of body toxins and taking cocaine, puffing pot, and a no-smoking zone from Monterey to Cape Cod.

This is where, on a bright Saturday morning, you clip your ten-speed Tour de France Special on the MGB's grid and roar up the hills where, after some brisk pedalling, you roar back and enthuse about the 'total physical body experience' and the importance of not 'destabilizing the environment'.

* *The Serial, A Year in the Life of Marin County, by Cyra McFadden is published by Alfred A. Knopf, New York, 1977. Psychobabble, Fast Talk and Quick Cure in the Era of Feeling, by R. D. Rosen is published by Athenaeum, New York, 1977.*

Marin, divided from San Francisco by the bay, is absolutely not, you understand, a suburb. That is why it is so far out. It provides an 'ultra high psychic energy dynamic' but is also very 'laid back'. It is where you can buy dope on a credit card from a pedlar who keeps the stash in a briefcase, but agonizes about whether or not the case should be leather (animal product) or plastic (non bio-degradable.)

Marin is where all the bar interiors are of stone, wood, and hanging plants. 'Real neat' (nice) but, as Cyra McFadden points out, it's the new Formica.

Apart from gang rape, about the worst sin for a male here is to be fat and to smoke a cigar in a book shop. The Marinite must have been in Gloria Vanderbilt's mind when she said that it is impossible to be too thin or too rich.

Conspicuous consumption in Marin is a very, very cool trip. Cool trippers, those who 'go with the flow while experiencing the whole eclectic Gestalt in the cosmic overview process' tend to be, as reported, middle-aged (they hate that), middle-class and moneyed: rejecting the hedonism of the bourgeoisie while directing the inner self to simplicity can be expensive.

One week's abnegation of opulence at the mind farms – as opposed to health farms – which dot California can cost a rich recluse over £500. But it is from these merchants of spirituality, the 'human potential movement', that much of the tiresome cant which is psychobabble emanates.

As a language it is not as sinister as the planned creation of Newspeak in *1984*. However, as Orwell explained in an appendix, Newspeak was to supersede traditional English only by 2050. Psychobabble may beat his deadline.

Orwell's description of Newspeak remains prophetic: 'The purpose of Newspeak was not only to provide a medium of expression for the world-view and mental habits proper to the devotee but to make all other modes of thought impossible.' Cyra McFadden has written: 'While elsewhere in the country one hears psychobabble spoken by members of the "counter-culture" here, the counterculture has come from under the counter and become the dominant culture itself, its dialect the language of polite society that one must speak in order to belong.'

It spreads from a cult to an elite, and perhaps finally to becoming the language of the middle-to-upper classes.

Neither elitist nor cult languages are new. Sir Ernest Gowers, who called it gobbledygook, failed in his various books to persuade the British Civil Service to exchange, say, 'accommodation units' for 'homes'. Claude Cockburn at the old *Daily Worker* finally gave up on Communist jargon translated from Comintern pronouncements such as 'the advanced parts of the working class must make every effort to penetrate the backward parts of the bourgeoisie'.

And in the forties and fifties, as Rosen points out, Freudian phraseology became modish among middle-class liberals as a form of intellectual one-upmanship.

As with slang, new styles of speech survive only after a natural birth. As most people do not or cannot speak like bureaucrats, Communist Party theoreticians, or trained Freudians, these have a brief life in the spoken form and continue as a genre only in the written (for which praise the Lord).

The danger of psychobabble is precisely that nobody deliberately invented it. It is spoken all over California, in bars and on buses, on television and in boardrooms, in drawing-rooms and in vegetarian communes. It is established on the East Coast and is beginning to catch on in south-east England.

Youth, with its babble language disseminated by the international pop music network, is psychobabble's leading export vehicle. But teenage psychobabble is almost pidgin, confined – at least in the presence of adults – to monosyllabics mixed with ghetto drug slang and four letter words, such as 'far out', 'gross', 'freaky', and 'shit'.

In Marin the most verbose psychobabblers are the prosperous parasites – or 'service industry professionals' if you like – of the super-rich. Plastic surgeons, landscape architects, dentists, urban planners, sociologists, corporate lawyers, bankers, advertising executives, or child psychologists.

Leonard, the child psychologist in The Serial, was into

corporal punishment. He said he'd had amazing results just 'acting out' his anger with his patients.

Such Marinites live at a level undreamed of by their British equivalents. They float, in McFadden's phrase, in a 'sybaritic miasma'. They have reached for and grasped an apparent paradise which many in Britain believe could be theirs if only they could slam the pearly gates on the Inland Revenue. But the Marinite sybarites, in their lavish, post-industrial limbo, are apparently not fulfilled.

Having passed by the struggle which afflicts most of us, the plastic surgeons and landscape architects who have done so much to beautify us and our surroundings, seem to feel they have missed 'the fundamental human experience' – a phrase which is one of the foundation stones of psychobabble.

R. D. Rosen quotes the social historian Russell Jacoby: 'The more the development of late capitalism renders obsolete, or at least suspect, the real possibilities of self or self-fulfilment, the more they are emphasized as if they could spring to life through an act of will alone.'

Rosen comments: 'If Jacoby is right, and I think he is, then psychobabble must be seen as the expression not of a victory over dehumanization, but as its latest and very subtle victory over us. What the casual use of psychobabble accomplishes is this: it transforms self-understanding, which each must gain gradually through experience and analysis, into tokens of self-understanding that can be exchanged between people, but without any clear psychological value.'

The sterility of the lush life, the paradoxical experience of those who had arrived at it by their late thirties or early forties, appears even emptier by comparison with their early twenties. Many middle-class Americans of the Marinite-type are a product of the heady student days of the early sixties: the clashes at Berkeley and other universities which stimulated campus protests all over the world.

Like Cyra McFadden, who is 40, these Americans prided themselves on resisting the Vietnam war before it became fashionable to do so. They are veterans not of Khe San but of the American Civil Liberties Union. Cyra McFadden herself is a feminist of nearly 20 years' standing.

Yet many, deprived of such obvious targets of radicalism as the war and the worst injustices of racism, and passing the age of 30 – at one time the upper limit for anyone worthy of trust – quickly turned inwards. With America technically at peace in the world, they sought interior peace for themselves. Not that this is discreditable, but concerned so much with themselves and the vanished glorious days, they developed a language to describe their new position. For lack of a dialectic, they gave us a dialect: psychobabble.

Rosen says: 'The roots of psychobabble are also firmly planted in the language of the "human potential movement" . . . its insistence on interpreting an individual's history, and history in general, as the result of conscious choices; in this, psychobabble has fed both on the tendency towards shallow political analysis and sloganeering that was certainly one feature of the sixties counterculture, as well as on the human potential movement with its emphasis on ego psychology.'

This movement, or industry as I prefer to call it, put down its roots in the rich soil of California and grew faster than crab grass.

Here we have actualism, analytical tracking, *est*, Feldenkrais functional integration, Fischer-Hoffman Process, Gurdjieff, Human Life Styling, integral massage, manipulation, Neo-Reichian bodywork, orgonomy, polarity balancing, postural integration, Primal Therapy and screaming, Scientology, Silva Mind Control, Synanon, Tai Chi, Theta, Yoga (hatha and raja), and Zen. Outside the Top Twenty are oldies but goldies such as orthodox Buddhism or becoming a Born Again Christian. Then there are the Maharaj Ji and the Rev Sun Myung Moon. After that there's not much except Scouting or punk rock.

The benefits are described by a McFadden character: '*Est* just changed my whole life. I never knew before what a total shit I was'. The choice of words should not offend the founder of *est*, Jack Rosenberg, a former car salesman who changed his name legally to Werner Erhard after reading an article about the creators of post-war West Germany, and who addresses his audiences as 'You arseholes'.

I have offered some examples of psychobabble and tried to show its origins and history. Now let us take a closer look at the monster itself. This is Rosen's description:

It is a jargon which 'seems to free-float in an all-purpose linguistic atmosphere, a set of repetitive verbal formalities that kills off the very spontaneity, candour, and understanding it pretends to promote. It's an idiom that reduces psychological insight to a collection of standardized observations, that provides a frozen lexicon to deal with an infinite variety of problems.

'"Uptight", for instance is a word used to describe anything from mild uneasiness to clinical depression. To ask why someone refers to another as being "hung-up" elicits a reply that reveals neither understanding nor curiosity: "Well, you know, he's just, well, hung-up". And interestingly, those few psychiatric terms borrowed by psychobabble are used recklessly. One is no longer fearful; one is paranoid. Increasingly, people describe their moody acquaintances as manic-depressives, and almost anyone you don't like is psychotic or at the very least, schizzed-out.'

Psychobabble and its speakers are also maddeningly smug. Trying a rational argument is like trying to chew on candy floss; it disintegrates into a sticky sweetness without offering a trace of nutrition. Opinions are dismissed as 'value judgements' as if they were unspeakable oaths. Or one is told with a beatific smile: 'I don't relate to that. It's not in the space where I'm at. It's just not in my conceptualization of personal meaningfulness'.

The almost mesmeric response of the psychobabbler's 'I hear you, I hear you' when one is offering something important, is an example both of complacency and selfishness. The intrusion of 'I' as in 'I know, I mean, I grab' is to direct the emphasis to the person who is supposed to be listening. 'It means,' as Cyra McFadden points out, 'that the focus is on me the listener; pay attention to me; see how sensitive I am.' Except, of course, the listener is not listening.

This current preoccupation with self was spotted in America years ago by Tom Wolfe's label of the 'Me' generation. Rosen demurs here by suggesting: 'Their words don't belong to them so much as to the current guru of choice or best-selling self-help book. It's as if they've rented their insights for the occasion.'

Psychobabble, a language born or rented, is nevertheless pervasive and frighteningly contagious. To converse or 'rap' with the cognoscenti is to risk a fall into the same abyss of mental laziness which makes psychobabble such a fiendish 'trip' wire.

Cyra McFadden seems to have come out the other side unscathed, retaining her considerable talents for observation. Here are some of her characters 'dialoguing' on their constant game of marital musical chairs in Marin, the county with the highest divorce rate in America. (Translation is impossible as psychobabble means anything.)

Marriage: 'This whole dynamic process. You have to really stay in touch with yourself if you are going to relate to the other person's feelings instead of just ego-tripping.'

Marital bliss: 'Getting inside each other's head, a high-energy trip that doesn't leave a lotta space for outside interaction.'

Reconciliation: 'Having a good rap about re-defining the parameters of our interface.'

Deep into the interior of this wonderland there is no reality, only the 'reality principle'. One does not receive advice from friends, but 'counselling from a positive-reinforcement support group.'

Psychobabble has intruded on worthy social movements and nowhere more so than Women's Liberation, perhaps because it lacked traditional language of its own. Cyra McFadden, whose feminist credentials are, as she says, impeccable, is sadly at odds with her psychobabbling-dabbling sisters. They are neatly satirized in the book. There is Debbie Ann Sulzberger who gives demonstrations in gynaecological self-examination and legally changed her name to Woman. Then there is the female Marinite (no, not Marinette) sybarites' consciousness-raising group, little more than gossip about partner-swapping, made legitimate in the name of the cause.

In one hilarious chapter they gang up to ambush the anti-hero Harvey in his living-room. He has been exploiting the conceptualization of open marriage with more enthusiasm, though less pleasure, than anticipated. He is denounced as 'a microcosm of the whole male power base', a broadside which leaves him reeling. Perhaps because of this, Harvey is quite unable to 'relate' to the group when it admits males but begins the proceedings with two minutes of silence to 'privately celebrate womanhood'.

Although psychobabble cannot be blamed for the ludicrous semantics of 'herstory' for history, those feminists seduced by its bland pseudo-psychology have made it too obvious a target for mockery. Some feminists' more thoughtful pronouncements have been lost amidst attacks on 'the male ego syndrome', 'macho power tripping', or 'pulling the head-honcho number' – all of which phrases are meaningless.

Psychobabble's intrinsic lack of humour might be its weakest point. We can defeat it. All we need is plain English and good jokes.

14 January, 1978   **Christopher Reed**

The void around, within

'Who is really in charge of things?', asks someone on a Parisian bus halfway through Robert Bresson's *The Devil Probably* (Camden Plaza, AA). 'Obscure forces,' mutters his companion. 'The Devil, probably,' a third person opines. At that moment the driver slams on his brakes, throwing his passengers off-balance. The sequence, one of the most eloquent the veteran director has given us, holds more than that brief exchange. But the words not only explain the title of his remarkable new film but usefully encapsulate its meaning.

Here is one of the world's great directors (Bresson is now 70) tapping out what could just possibly be his final 'state of the union' message and using characters, two young men and two girls, who could be his grandchildren, in a parable that illustrates both his profound pessimism and his continuing need for something to transcend it. It will not be a film for everyone, as I know from experience as a juror at Berlin last year when a substantial section of the jury looked at it with either overt hostility or incomprehension. Hostility because its story about a rather charmless young man who, after trying to find some meaning for life, asks a friend to shoot him, seemed to several a void and dangerous manifesto of despair. Incomprehension because Bresson has by now so refined his style that the film's superficial lack of emotion, its almost abstract feel, the way its characters speak their lines with deliberate lack of emphasis, make it totally different from conventional didactic drama.

Some of us, however, believed we had seen a masterpiece with undeniable claims to attention, both as a work of art and as an argument. Which is not to say that one has to regard it as a correct analysis. Old men grow sad, and seldom completely understand the young. These students are not necessarily realistic representatives of their generation. Yet the arguments presented by the film are not easy to refute, nor is its story an impossible one to imagine.

The student (Charles) finds no source of inspiration in either science or religion, politics or love. The ecological horrors he sees on film are plainly irrefutable. And who would easily deny that political revolution generally substitutes one kind of tyranny for another, or that the 'progressive Church' isn't just the same old reactionary wolf in sheep's clothing? As for love, it too can be corrupted by the emphasis on love-making. The girls who take Charles, the incipient suicide, into their beds can only send him on to a psychiatrist who tries to force him to accept evils he cannot cure.

The final death scene does legitimately seem the student's only possible way out, a martyrdom through which he can achieve a kind of nihilistic grace. Bresson's vision of a society so ruled by indifference and greed that it has even robbed nature of its former purity is all too terrifyingly understandable. And it is made the more so by his insistence that life is still not a thing to give up easily.

When Charles pauses, on the way to his death, he hears a few bars of Mozart from an open window. It is a moment that seems to express exactly what he is losing, and perhaps what the world has lost. Yet Bresson still hasn't finished with us. The student's last words to his junkie friend before the shot are: 'You know, I was sure I'd have some sublime thought at a moment like this but what I'm actually thinking about is . . .' He never completes the sentence. The void around you makes the void within you. It is a final extraordinary moment in a film that, right or wrong, is impossible to forget.

16 February, 1978 **Derek Malcolm**

A country diary: Keswick – 2

There is a barn, not a long one by Cumbrian standards, on a high shelf of land facing its farmhouse across their shared track, and in about ten days' time the sun will set behind one end of the barn and rise at the other and, in between, there will be no real darkness, only a long dusk. This evening too the light seemed reluctant to leave the fell-side, the last sunlight laid long fingers into the oakwood above the farm, showing how clean and strong the new oak leaves are, quite free of caterpillars, unlike many of the valley oaks. It lay warmly on the grey, fissured tree trunks, on the scarlet lichen fruits on dead stumps and made the yellow cow-wheat in the short turf shine with reflected light. The sheep and lambs, which have grazed the nearby fields to a dull and uniform green, have been kept out of here lately, only getting in by mistake, so small blaeberry shoots are appearing in the grass. There is yellow tormentil, many-coloured spring vetch and even blue milkwort with oak seedlings at the wood's edge. There will be orchids soon if no more sheep get in. A young brown owl called monotonously, waiting for a parent with food, a willow warbler scattered its descending scale of notes and a party of swifts screamed round the low roofs. A woodcock roded sedately down the green lane. A cool breath rose as the light died but it was not cool enough to subdue the smell of hawthorn blossom, of growing spruce across the beck from the farm, and a tall clump of bluebottles,

Centaurea, by the house wall loosed its warm apricot scent on the evening air. A star brightened over the ridge. An ordinary place you might say, any Cumbrian fell farm, but where else could you look along a lake and its river valley running to the west with a prehistoric fort in view, a megalithic circle on its hill beyond, and an ancient signal station to the north. In very few places is there such peace or such solace.

12 June, 1978   **Enid J. Wilson**

Great chair theft shakes Government

It happened last February, it seems. There was a great push of scantily-clad Rajasthan womanhood trying to get into the village cinema at Khetri, near Jaipur, one hot night and, as often happens outside cinemas, there was a riot. Within moments, the police were called, supposedly to break up the fight. Only, so the story went, they did no such thing. They laid out the women on the burning sand and, helmets put aside, ravished the lot. *The Arabian Nights*, it seems, had nothing on this.

We all got to hear about it because an upstanding public citizen wrote a letter to the papers. Then a local reporter picked up the tale, added a few colourful embellishments, and wrote it for the front page. A day later a Hindi paper in Delhi had it, splashed columns wide. Typical Janata mismanagement, everyone said. Governments had fallen for less.

There was the most fearful row about it in Parliament. People shouted and bellowed at each other, papers got tossed around, books got hurled, and the Speaker, who surely has the most arduous task of any Speaker anywhere, was hard pushed to prevent another mass assault erupting around his feet. But the Minister responsible, an ancient farmer called Mr Charan Singh, could just be heard responding to the various charges. In fact, he was heard denying them. There had been no rape, he said. Not even a lascivious glint in a copper's eye.

That started the editors hopping around – a Minister telling

233

them they had got it all wrong. So they set up a committee of three top reporters and dispatched them to Khetri to interview alleged rapers, rapees, and witnesses, to find out who was right. For two weeks the capital held its breath.

The truth has now emerged. No, there had been no rape. But what there had been was one of those deliciously Indian happenings, far more colourful than anything the imagination could conjure up. There had been a film down at the Khetri Odeon with some of India's female stars on hand for the show. A big marquee had been put up outside the picture theatre, and about 2,500 people, mainly women, had crammed themselves into it. About 500 more were left outside, somewhat upset that they had failed to make it, as it were.

One testy individual took the most direct action he could: he picked up a piece of wire (of which there is sure to be plenty on any Indian street), and hurled it up across the power cables. There was a massive short circuit, all the lights went out, and things began to get out of hand.

Someone then went and ripped the blouse off the shoulders of one of the film stars. Fingers reached out to grab at jewellery, earrings, or other dangling items. A few more blouses got ripped, plus a few of those little shirts known as cholis that North Indian women wear under their saris. So lots of ripping and grabbing, it appears, but, say the reporters in their official conclusions, 'with more than 2,000 people in the compound, it is difficult to imagine that a rape could have taken place'.

Things didn't stop there. The people in the tent were cross that they never saw the film, so they took the natural next step. They picked up a chair each as compensation, and marched out of the tent. The cinema manager saw what was happening, and let down the tent, catching a lot of people, who then dropped their chairs and got in some more grabbing and ripping for good measure.

But 400 chairs went missing that evening, and the Khetri cinema would like them back, please.

So the reporter who wrote the original tale missed the story. The great chair theft of Khetri makes much better reading. Especially as it turns out that the man who first wrote a letter

about the mass rape didn't exist. It was all a big joke. Except
for the Janata Government, and for the women of Jaipur, who
weren't the least bit amused.

10 April, 1978   **Simon Winchester**

The old girl network

There is a youngish man who lives on my street and he is
always around. I see him in the mornings, ambling down the
High Road, I see him in the afternoons pottering in his front
garden, I see him any time of day playing with his three small
children, stuffing local postboxes with local bumf, chatting
with neighbours on his doorstep or theirs. Last week I mentioned
him to a friend. I said, 'There's this man down our road, he
doesn't seem to *do* anything.'

A second later, skies darkening, thunder rumbling, lightning
sizzling, alarm bells screaming in my head, I grovelled on the
kitchen floor, tearing my hair, wringing my hands, begging
forgiveness from the Great Goddess. Years of feminism
cracked across like the mirror of the Lady of Shalott. What was
I, after all, but a Pavlov dog or, better, a Pavlov pig, conditioned
beyond redemption into making the piggiest remark of them
all. That man was doing what women do, he did not vanish
from my ken at 9 a.m., and return at six. *Ergo*, he was doing
nothing.

My sisters of the hearth and home, forgive me. My only
excuse is that I, too, have fallen victim to the brainwashing
of a male world. Far below the level of consciousness I have
absorbed by osmosis the male belief. Men are paid for what
they do and therefore what they do is work. Women are not
paid for what they do in the home and therefore what they do
in the home is nothing.

Shocked by this involuntary treachery, this male face beneath
the feminist front, I did penance. Meticulously I listed what
women do, that frequently evoked half-joking list often quoted
when the question of women's monetary value comes up and

235

some assessment is attempted of what they might be paid were their services offered on the open market. Nanny, charwoman, chauffeuse, cook, hostess, sex object, gardener, handywoman, decorator and so on and on. For which the payments usually mount up to a weekly three figures that we can all have a good giggle about and promptly forget.

But this time I dredged up from the bottom of my mind a whole lot of other things women do, and I had to dredge them up because most are undertaken so automatically, and are so much a part of simply being a woman, that they are invisible, taken for granted even by women themselves. And these things worried me because already almost all single women and well over half of all married women are working in paid jobs outside the home, as they have every right to do, and yet if women disappear from the home, who then will do these endless invisible tasks?

For example, a quick survey of the past two weeks taken from the experience of my women friends and myself. A son had to be taken to hospital and, once there, sat with for four hours so that he would feel easy in uneasy circumstances. A mother had to be visited in hospital so that she did not feel lonely and unloved. A father had to have meals cooked and house cleaned while the mother was in hospital – can't cook scrambled eggs for himself, poor old boy, and too late to learn now. One aunt and one step-daughter needed birthday presents and cards to be bought and sent off. A daughter needed a birthday party to mark a coming-of-age.

A mother-in-law had to be written to with news of family doings and enquiries as to aching feet and general well-being. Two letters had to be written to distant friends for how should they stay friends without occasional letters? A child's school had to be visited for talks with teachers, a child's school had to be provided with jumble to raise money for the child's eventual benefit. A sister had to be given hours of time to support her through impending divorce, a brother had to be listened to through the woes of impending redundancy, a neighbour eased in her loneliness with a chat about greenfly on the roses. A house-bound relative had ill-fitting shoes returned to a shop. A friend's child had to be baby-sat while the mother took herself to the doctor. Another friend wanted comfort about an erring child.

The list is, of course, as long as life itself and the things it lists encompass life itself, a part of that intangible network which keeps the human community afloat and into which, at one time or another, all of us will fall. When zoologists study animals, they study a particular species' network, the social pattern and behaviour that define them as a species and enable them to survive. When anthropologists study primitive people, what they care about, what they write about, is the tribal network, the particular tribal ways of coping with grief, happiness, reproduction, bonding, aggression and the rituals that mark them, assuage them and preserve them.

In other words, when we look at the fox, the bee, the Eskimo or the Kikuyu, we see quite clearly the social relationships and we recognize their over-riding importance in the scheme of things. But when we look at our own society, we appear to be exclusively concerned with the hardware of living – monetary policies, foreign policies, legislation, mergers, gold standards, earnings and outgoings – and blind to that network which is just below the surface of every outside activity; so essential to human happiness and even to human existence that it is counted as a reflex happening, like breathing. And yet that whole network is most carefully and lovingly woven, erected, repaired, serviced and staffed by the unpaid women at home.

If it were not for them (and women who have paid jobs and still service the net because they are women) I verily believe that civilized life as we know it would simply collapse. All across the country, community festivals and jamborees would cease for lack of organization, jumble sales and fêtes and sales of work would be no more. No flowers would brighten churches, no gold or silver glitter on the altars. No children would have costumes for school plays or dancing classes. No errands would be run for the old or handicapped, no doors opened to the gas or electricity men, no coffee trolleys wheeled for those in hospital, no gossip exchanged between neighbours, no love exchanged between friends. If women did not do it, who would celebrate a single milestone, arrange a single party, make memorable a day in a child's life? Who would maintain and nurture our tribal life?

Thank heavens there's a man in my road who has taken up one strand of that net before the last woman drops it.

15 June, 1978   **Jill Tweedie**

Love bugs

Human Motivation is quite interesting, isn't it? I once stayed up until five o'clock in the morning debating with Cedric why he was so peculiar; after hours of Freud, Jung, Adler, and the rest we got nowhere until, as dawn broke and the sparrows started to cough, Cedric mentioned that, when a baby, his mother had dropped him downstairs on his head. 'You might have mentioned it earlier,' I said. The yen for the simple explanation, like your poor, is always with us.

That's why I like the imprinting theory and that Tom and Jerry cartoon where Tom is about to eat an egg when out pops a chick and says 'You're my mommy.' The c. follows Tom about the place: a plot heavily indebted to Konrad 'Baggy Trousers' Lorenz and his performing goslings. In early summer, those imprinting mechanisms start whirring away at the behest of Mother Nature, Trouble Maker, and people do the craziest things, in spite of themselves.

Psychology owes a lot to ethology and, in fact, if people were decent enough to act in the same way as the Norwegian White Rat then psychology could be a real science and its practitioners paid more. I learned early not to mess about with people: most unreliable. My first piece of research was on the three-spined stickleback (Gasterosteus Aculeatus to us in the know) and found out that lady sticklebacks really dug the male's red waistcoat; indeed, given a fair facsimile of a male's and a round bit of metal with a red blob on, she went for the red blob. That was the *specific releaser* and she was crazy for it.

238

The same thing happens with human beings. They think they love somebody. In reality, they're hooked on to one tiny part of the dream-boat's physiognomy; in my case, it's eyes. I am imprinted on X-coloured eyes (in order not to cause offence I'll refrain from mentioning the particular hue) and have *never* fallen in love with a Y-eyed girl. I have been in love with a woman who picked her nose, had thighs like a Roman soldier, never stopped talking, towered above me, wore a bra fashioned by Wimpey Construction (these are not the same woman) but all had one thing in common: X-coloured eyes.

One more example. Last year, elsewhere, I wrote that the child in all of us responded to Mrs Thatcher's voice: the echo of infant school headmistresses stirred in all our breasts. Lo, this year, Mrs T. has changed her voice: it's better, it's sexier and, no doubt, all over GB men (and some women) are working themselves into sexual frenzy every time Margaret opens her mouth. To avoid accusations of bias, let me say that I remain calm, and see the behaviour of those who are imprinted on the new timbre as no worse than a chap I know who bifurcates himself every time he sees a pair of leather boots (he rarely goes out). Does anybody know the colour of Mrs T's eyes? It's important to me.

Some women are imprinted, for life, on their father's moustaches; a clean shaven man will leave them cold. Some children are imprinted upon their grandmother's wrinkled faces: the clear, unblemished, peaches-and-cream visage elicits no response from them at all. You find that social workers, and some psychologists, attempt 'therapy' with clients without taking into account these imprinting mechanisms. It is, if you happen to be the wrong sex, or the wrong shape, a complete waste of time. Mother Nature has fixed who, or what, the clients can love long before they, or we, arrive on the scene.

Early in my professional career I met a man who used to have a violent erection every time he saw somebody open a safety pin. 'How terribly inexpensive,' I told him (I used to talk posh in those days). He, poor man, could never wear jeans. I've seen, besides Konrad's goslings, humans and animals imprinted upon the most curious things: birds upon the human hand, kittens upon a monkey, a duck upon hens (the duck was terrified of water).

Cedric, as I was going out of the door, asked: 'What colour are your mother's eyes?' (He knows my little foibles). 'X,' I say. 'One for Freud,' says he. Not so: one for Konrad, Nikko Tinbergen and the ethologists. Give me any old shape, but make sure it has the coloured blob.

The ugly girl playing the piano: the handsome, blind ex-RAF officer falls in love with the music, her hands. In these matters, we're all blind. I knew a beautiful girl once who married a policeman. Her father looked the spitting image of Oliver Hardy. When I first met her fiancé I couldn't help noticing that he had a round, frying-pan face and a moustache, but his moustache was a Viva Zapata, not a square-ended. Odd, I thought: not much resemblance there. Then I remembered the three-spined s., Mother N., and those imprinting mechanisms whirring away: especially in the summer.

28 June, 1978   **Tom Crabtree**

Wrong again

A South London factory owner, Mr Philip Bowen, is at the John Ruskin Infant School near the Elephant and Castle to give a talk on a modern miracle or moral morass. With him he takes a black executive case with a large letter Z on the side; myself as his scientific adviser and Miss Moody as my secretary.

Mr Bowen, a tall young man in black pinstriped three-piece and intense spectacles, faces a combination of two classes, fifty young children between five and seven years old, mostly sons and daughters of Bermondsey biscuit packers, manual workers or clerks in the nondescript businesses of the neighbourhood. There is a sprinkling of eager black faces.

The school, built at the turn of the century, backs on to a decrepit terrace. Its catchment area includes the notorious Aylesbury Estate where mugging is routine, and the Brandon

Estate, where broken-down lifts in high-rise blocks are a standard explanation for lateness to school.

Mr Bowen, looking suitably entrepreneurial, produces from his executive case an orange. I, looking suitably scientific, and Miss Moody, looking suitably eye-catching, watch it with rapt attention. What is the first thing you have to do with an orange, demands Mr Bowen? Peel it, says a little boy in a stylish white sweater. Quite, says Mr Bowen; peel is nature's way of wrapping it up. Probably the cave men wrapped up the nuts they were going to eat later in a banana skin. He produces a banana skin from his executive case. Now what was the main thing against banana skins as wrappings?

'Too dirty,' says a little girl with very clean blonde hair. 'Yes,' says Mr Bowen, and in the way of entrepreneurs is in a very few minutes discussing his very own product, Zotowrap. This is so good that you cannot tear it like you tear paper. It will not fall apart in the rain, like cardboard. It will not burn, or rust and will not smash like glass. In short, it's indestructible. He produces two sheets of it, bright silver on one side and bright red on the other – and says these are the only two sheets at present in the world. When produced commercially, it will be as cheap as ten sheets a penny.

Fifty admiring little faces stare up at him but in fact the businessman and his acolytes are just as fictional as his 'scientific adviser'. They are all connected with the newly-launched Young Vic Education Service, taking one of its first week's play schemes to London schools on the theme of pollution.

Mr Bowen is unwrapping a tomato he says he wrapped in Zotowrap a month ago. He is claiming that it is as fresh as it was four weeks ago when he wrapped it, when he is interrupted by the appearance in the classroom of a Miss Cox. Her duffel coat and assertive manner proclaim her to be a reporter from 'City Radio.' Mr Bowen huffily refuses to give his talk again for her benefit so she asks the children to tell her about Zotowrap. They tell her enthusiastically that it won't burn, won't tear, and won't wear out.

But, says Miss Cox, the radio station has been having a lot of mysterious telephone calls from a Miss Clara Cleanup, saying she doesn't like the new product. Ah, says Mr Bowen, she must be the one who has been writing him letters threatening that unless he stops making his 'horrible' product 'something is going to happen to you, so watch out!'

What has already happened to him is soon revealed over City Radio – the secret formula for Zotowrap has been stolen. The reporter produces a photograph of Clara Cleanup, and asks if the children have seen her. The children file out to the playground to see if they can find her. They do find her, with a bag of waste paper. She says paper is nice because the sun and rain can rot it and get rid of it. The secret formula for Zotowrap, on a large silver card, sticks out of the top of her overalls.

Mr Bowen, verbalizing like a member of the Monday Club in good standing, demands his formula back, while Clara Cleanup brandishes her broom, talks about her rights and solicits the opinions of the children. There is enough rubbish in the world already, she says. She wants Mr Bowen to change his formula so that Zotowrap can be destroyed.

Well, says the reporter to the children, should Mr Bowen change his formula or should Clara Cleanup give him his formula back? 'Give it back!' cry the law-abiding younger citizens of SE5 – which may not be quite the answer that was hoped for.

Mr Bowen's visit is certainly ingenious in that it makes the children think about the problems of pollution. But his first week's visit to the John Ruskin School seems to prove chiefly that when it comes to questions of long-term social morality, children will instinctively be on the side of anything that is a bright red on one side and bright silver on the other.

10 July, 1978   **Dennis Barker**

Wrangling over the genes

There is good news on page 4 today for all those who have experienced slips between cups and lips and would like in future to keep them to a minimum. The institute of biochemistry at Strasbourg University has discovered, or thinks it may have discovered, or at least concludes that there is sufficient evidence to allow it to advance the tentative hypothesis, that genetic engineering is not as simple as some people would have us believe. Now this finding will be represented as a set-back. Chemists will complain that the prospect of persuading bacteria to manufacture human insulin is now more remote. That may be. Let it not be gainsaid. It is a sacrifice we shall have to make. But on the other side it will be slightly harder for viruses to be turned into even nastier creatures than many of them are already, and those amiable bacteria which ruminate in our stomachs will not suddenly find themselves genetically programmed to give us all chronic indigestion. There is a law of science (in the sense that no exceptions to it have ever come to light) which says that if a thing can be done it will be done. It is refreshing to learn, therefore, that Labrador retrievers are not to be given the tongues of rattlesnakes; or not just yet.

What went wrong, or turned out right as it happens, is that the genetic code for egg white (the benign sort of substance which is always tackled first, to reassure the public that nothing horrid is afoot, like giving cucumbers the properties of deadly nightshade) is in four places on the chain instead of one. Instead of playing a huge game of Master Mind, hundreds of pegs wide, the technicians find themselves playing not even four such games but possibly hundreds simultaneously because of the mysterious peg-holes in between. The Almighty Code-maker knew what he was about, and some Jovian chuckling may be heard on Olympus, shaking a Nobel prize or two on its mantelpiece.

28 November, 1977   **Leader**

A country diary: Skiddaw

Nine years ago old Pearson Dalton locked up Skiddaw House, 'the loneliest house in England', for the last time and walked over the fells, with his five dogs, into retirement. For nearly half a century he had lived there alone, with his dogs, cats and goats – 1600 feet up and four rough mountain miles from the nearest habitation – looking after 1000 sheep roaming the northern slopes of Skiddaw. But every Saturday he walked seven trackless miles over the fells to his sister's home at Fellside for a weekend in 'civilization', and every Monday, no matter what the weather, he walked back to the bleak house on the moors and his workaday week. When he retired at 75 – he had gone to Skiddaw House at 28, on a month's trial, and stayed on for 47 years – they thought the place would be closed down and become a ghost house, but for some time now, the building, once a shooting lodge, has been used by young people as a base for outdoor activities. And one room is kept open, as a mountain bothy, for travellers spending a night in the wilds. The other day the old man's room, now in use for courses, was locked. Here, for recreation on wild, lonely nights, he had his old sofa covered with sacking, a few tattered books, and an old battery radio. Lighting was by oil lamp but he always kept a good fire. I heard he was still alive last year. His little vegetable garden is now overgrown and the shelter trees, the only ones left in Skiddaw Forest, looked more windswept than ever. But the view of soaring fells, grass, heather and sheep, and nothing else except the sky, was just the same.

19 June, 1978   **A. Harry Griffin**

Primrose pate to paradise

Yesterday, as if you didn't know, was Primrose Day, the anniversary of the funeral of Disraeli to which his lumpen little queen sent a posy of primroses. By chance yesterday marked too my own particular and annual Primrose Day – the start of the cricket season, the day on which, whistling a private *Trumpet Voluntary* between my teeth, I always buy the newly minted primrose bible that has been handed down to us by John Wisden's heirs for 115 years now. Incidentally, I can never understand those who go for the more expensive mud-dull hardback.

All the way up from Baker Street you could tell by their gait those of similar expectations. The same grey gateman in his same grey mac is the same grey governor of the Grace Gates as he ever was. None shall pass remains his orders. You fancy he was prodded awake by Donald Carr only yesterday morning after a cuddly curled-up hibernation in his hut. Two Americans, flourishing a wad of notes, tried to enter the Warner Stand, only five of whose 2000 seats were being occupied. 'Members only,' the doorman growled. The Yanks, understandably, could not understand.

The Tavern patio filled up only slowly. But through the morning familiar faces started to emerge. I missed the beery, bearded man with the booming voice, and although he is a bore I do hope nothing has happened to him. Nor to that over-made-up old duck who promenades round and round the ground with a sad desperation as if she is looking for a war-lost lover or perhaps an elder brother. Then again, she might have found him in the winter.

At 10.56 in the umpires' room Arthur had looked at Sam: 'Got ball and bails, lad? Rightyho, let's get another season started.' And the two sprightly cronies from another age eased their way to the wicket, examining in detail the gleaming milk-white sky with a nip in the air but also very much the promise of summer. The sun was to come out on the stroke of *The World At One*.

Because of all the furtive Packer chat around the old place it was touchingly nice that Jepson and Cook were first to centre-stage in their white coats. Men like them italicize the lovely continuity of our game: between them they played over 30 first-class seasons and took nearly 3000 wickets (Sam took 1782 with lefty cunning, Arthur 1051 off, if memory really remembers, a far longer run than his nippiness warranted). Sam turned down the seasons's first appeal when England's bouncy new puppy, Botham, shrieked for caught behind.

Over in the nursery the new Pakistanis practise. Their timing is still to pot on England's holding turf. They all look fiercely handsome until they smile. I could not put a name to any of them. We wondered, though, which unknown would carve bold his name this summer. Somebody usually does.

Brearley hit a glorious square-drive with mellow clunk to Father Time and at once it seemed warmer. Noon, and old school friends turned up. A laughing drink to summers past and then one more for the primrose path which started yesterday. And then yet another, in celebration for just deserts, when you see that Alan Jones of Glamorgan has at last been honoured as one of *Wisden*'s famous five.

20 April, 1978   **Frank Keating**

The Campiello Band

oh for the good old days the good old days old days when all us friends and folk we'd get together in the good old days and we'd play together on all and everything and sundry pieces piano harmonium mandolin clarinets saxophone rebecs violin curtals all mixed up together no fixed form

and we'd play together repeating and repeating over and over and over again just some bits and pieces of old old favourites just the rhythms just the chords and happy memories oh happy memories of rumbas and ravel and mozart's madamia oh what a catalogue oh the sound of music floating in from nowhere and no need to end let the music repeat and repeat over and over and over again until it tails off into

oh magical minimal magical minimal magical minimal music of the campaniello ring out the bells for michael inimical michael nyman and the institute of contemporary arts oh happy emporium of sunday evening bliss and delights unending oh guardian readers

22 May, 1978   **Meirion Bowen**

Index

Adam, Corinna	Gentlemanly mask of the iron manner *page*	93
Adamson, Lesley	The battle of Warwick Castle	32
	Cutting the cloth	52
Aitken, Ian	The political football	119
Armstrong, George	Diva takes dive, brings house down	42
Banks-Smith, Nancy	Public enemy no. 1	28
	Durrel's Egypt	103
	Americans	144
Barker, Dennis	Jerry's way	129
	Up the Blue Creek with the GBP	132
	Sole of honour	187
	Wrong again	240
Billington, Michael	Brecht and jam	214
Blandford, Linda	Mood indigo	10
	Live and let die	183
Bond, Edward	Work in hand	218
Bowen, Merion	The Campiello Band	246
Cameron, James	Broken fences	68
Carter, Angela	Max Ernst's novel without words	100
Christmas, Linda	Beginning	163
Condry, William	A country diary: Machynlleth	204
Cooke, Alistair	Across the fairway and into the booth	23
Crabtree, Tom	Love bugs	238
Cunningham, John	Mother and daughter	200
De'Ath, Wilfred	Problem people	125

Dodsworth, Martin	Images of history	208
Ezard, John	Frank Raymond Leavis	153
Fenton, James	The watch on Germany	81
	Ups and downers in Cologne	155
Gott, Richard	Demo diary	34
	At the aerodrome	43
Griffin, Harry A.	A country diary: Skiddaw	244
Hamilton, Alex	Greek bearing gifts	39
Harris, Alan	Difficulties in getting the bird	68
Hartley, Alex	How we run them in	96
Herbert, Hugh	A hospital made for two	47
Hillmore, Peter	Queen's messenger	36
	Flying high	99
	Power play	147
	Ranier check	177
Hirst, David	Warm welcome in Hadatha	71
Hoggart, Simon	A dog's life	29
	Hair apparent	122
Hope-Wallace, Philip	Healing Comedy	48
	Otello	143
Jenkins, Peter	The flip-flop President	62
	On not being terrorized	77
Keating, Frank	Rubbing shoulders with the mighty	108
	Sorry Brian	111
	Master of the Fence	209
	Primrose path to Paradise	245
Leader	Mr Justan Larstinpeece	9
	The Series 3 Nativity	51
	On the 'now' switchback	59
	Trading blow for blow	98
	Bank Holidays while you wait	172
	Wrangling over the genes	243

McNay, Michael	Roman courage	204
McRae, Hamish	That's torn it	50
Mackie, Lindsay	Transcendental reconstruction	45
	Race causes an initial confusion	220
Malcolm, Derek	The blue Elizabethans	38
	The void around within	230
Parkin, Michael	Theresa finds a gap in the FA's defence	117
Pick, Hella	Aches en Provence	56
Reed, Christopher	The psychobabble enigma	221
Rosen, Jane	Androids for the chores	186
Samuel, John	Diary of a skier	174
Schwartz, Walter	On the beach	145
	The journeyman's return	149
Shrapnel, Norman	The English religion	92
Sigal, Clancy	Jus' folk	135
Steele, Jonathan	A welcome for the Shah	61
	News from the pulpit	140
Summers, John Aeron	Letters from Kazakhstan	105
Tisdall, Caroline	The inland sea of pleasure	101
Toynbee, Polly	One was not amused	13
	Trying for Millwall	88
	Gone dancing	159
	Dog tired	192
Tucker, Anthony	Good work of Cobden, Bright and Co.	180
Tweedie, Jill	Loving neighbours	189
	The old girl network	235
Wainwright, Martin	Boyson's law gets lordly rebuke	124
	Body politic	131
	The case of the disappearing fritillary	198
Ward-Thomas, Pat	Home from the sea	27

Webb, W. L.	Solzhenitsyn's Testament	84
Webster, Paul	France foots the Imperial bill	167
White, John T.	A country diary: Kent	67
	Kew	166
Williams, Peter Meredith	Pressure waves	110
Wilson, Enid J.	A country diary: Keswick 1	197
	Keswick 2	232
Winchester, Simon	Still glad to see an Englishman	20
	Calcutta Christmas	54
	Great chair theft shakes government	233
Woollacott, Martin	The boat people	169